## Reviewing the GED Tests

The GED tests are of different lengths and have different numbers of questions. The table gives you a brief overview of each test. For more detailed information, see Chapter 1 and the chapters in Part II.

| Test | Structure of the Test | Time Allowed (In Minutes) |
|---|---|---|
| Language Arts, Writing, Part I | 50 multiple-choice questions | 75 |
| Language Arts, Writing, Part II | 1 essay | 45 |
| Social Studies | 50 multiple-choice questions | 70 |
| Science | 50 multiple-choice questions | 80 |
| Language Arts, Reading | 40 multiple-choice questions | 65 |
| Mathematics, Part I (with calculator) | 25 multiple-choice and fill-in-the-blank questions | 45 |
| Mathematics Part II (without calculator) | 25 multiple-choice and fill-in-the-blank questions | 45 |

## Knowing What to Bring to the Tests (And What to Leave at Home)

### Do bring the following with you to the test site:

- Identification with your picture, birth date, and address on it
- Pens and pencils: Make sure pencils are sharpened (or if mechanical, that you bring refill leads) and pens have new refills
- A watch with a new battery and, if possible, a stopwatch feature
- The test fee (if not prepaid)

### Don't take the following into the test room:

- Pager, cellphone, or other communication devices
- A portable music device
- Electronic device, games, or calculator (a calculator is provided)
- Food or drink
- Textbooks, notebooks, reference books
- Purse, backpack, briefcase, or duffel bag
- Jacket, coat, hat, gloves

# The GED For Dummies®

Cheat Sheet

## Doing Your Best on the Tests

During each GED test, keep the following tips in mind:

- ✔ Listen to all directions given before the test.
- ✔ Read and follow all the directions given.
- ✔ Carefully read each question and the answers offered.
- ✔ Always choose the best answer based on the material presented.
- ✔ Answer all the questions. Practice guessing logically if you aren't sure of an answer.
- ✔ Trust your instinct. Your first answer is usually right. Don't spend a lot of time changing questions.
- ✔ Mark the answer sheets carefully: You get points only for answers marked correctly on the answer sheets.
- ✔ If you're absolutely positive that an answer is wrong, make sure your first mark is completely erased.
- ✔ Watch the time. You have a strict time limit.

## Keeping Panic at Bay

Keep from panicking by doing the following:

- ✔ Double-check the time and place of each test.
- ✔ Plan a route to get there in plenty of time and plan an alternate route in case of problems in the road.
- ✔ Arrive early and prepared.
- ✔ Arrive well rested.
- ✔ Remind yourself of all the preparation you've done.

Wiley, the Wiley Publishing logo, For Dummies, the Dummies Man logo, the For Dummies Bestselling Book Series logo and all related trade dress are trademarks or registered trademarks of Wiley Publishing, Inc. All other trademarks are property of their respective owners.

**For Dummies: Bestselling Book Series for Beginners**

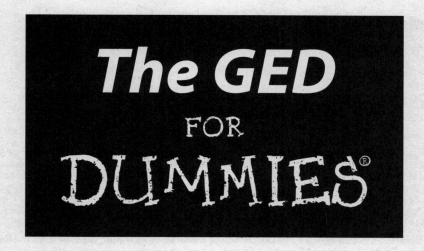

# The GED
## FOR
# DUMMIES®

**by Murray Shukyn and Dale E. Shuttleworth, Ph.D.**

WILEY

Wiley Publishing, Inc.

***The GED* For Dummies**®

Published by
**Wiley Publishing, Inc.**
909 Third Avenue
New York, NY 10022
www.wiley.com

Copyright © 2003 by Wiley Publishing, Inc., Indianapolis, Indiana

Published by Wiley Publishing, Inc., Indianapolis, Indiana

Published simultaneously in Canada

For general information on our other products and services or to obtain technical support, please contact our Customer Care Department within the U.S. at 800-762-2974, outside the U.S. at 317-572-3993, or fax 317-572-4002.

Wiley also publishes its books in a variety of electronic formats. Some content that appears in print may not be available in electronic books.

Library of Congress Control Number: 2002114774

ISBN: 0-7645-5470-0

Manufactured in the United States of America

10  9  8  7  6  5

1B/RX/QS/QT/IN

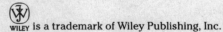 is a trademark of Wiley Publishing, Inc.

# About the Authors

**Murray Shukyn,** Associate Director of The Training Renewal Foundation, is a graduate of the University of Toronto, with professional qualifications as a teacher at the elementary and secondary levels, including Special Education. During an extensive career spanning more than thirty years, he has taught at the elementary, secondary, and university levels. Murray has also taught professional development programs for teachers and training courses for adult learners. He is acknowledged as a Canadian leader in the field of alternative education through his work in the creation of such innovative programs for the Toronto Board of Education as SEED, LEARNXS, Subway Academy, SOLE, and ACE. In 1995, he became Associate Director at The Training Renewal Foundation, which introduced the GED to the province of Ontario. Over the years, he has been a consultant to government, media, and public relations companies, as well as an author of textbooks and numerous articles in magazines and periodicals. He is a co-author of the Third and Fourth Canadian editions of *How to Prepare for the GED,* published by Barron's Educational Series in the United States.

**Dale E. Shuttleworth, Ph.D.,** is the Executive Director of The Training Renewal Foundation. Dale's career as a community educator has included experience as a teacher, school-community worker, consultant, principal, coordinator, superintendent, and university lecturer. In the fields of education and community economic development, he is a founder of the Learnxs Foundation Inc., Youth Ventures Developments of Metropolitan Toronto, the Learning Enrichment Foundation, the York Business Opportunities Centre, the Centre for Community and Economic Renewal, and The Training Renewal Foundation. He has been the recipient of the prestigious Dag Hammarskjold Gold Medal for Excellence in Education and the author of *Enterprise Learning in Action,* published by Routledge in London and New York.

In 1995, Dale created the GED Preparation Centre pilot project, which brought the High School Equivalency Certificate to the Province of Ontario. In 1998, he was co-author of *How to Prepare for the GED,* Third Canadian Edition, published by Barron's Educational Series in the United States. In 2000, he was named lead author/consultant for a study on "Innovations in School Management," conducted by the Organization for Economic Co-operation and Development (OECD) in Paris, France, resulting in the publishing of the book, *New School Management Approaches* in 2001. That same year he co-authored *How to Prepare for the GED,* Fourth Canadian Edition. His latest book, *School Management in Transition,* is scheduled for publication by Routledge in 2003.

# Authors' Acknowledgments

We wish to express our appreciation to Marilyn Shuttleworth, who assisted us in the preparation of this manuscript; The Training Renewal Foundation for the opportunity to work in the world of the GED; and the late Peter Kilburn, former Canadian GED Administrator, for his inspiration, friendship, and encouragement in introducing us to the potential of the GED to be a source of fulfillment and liberation in the lives and careers of so many adult learners who have dropped out of traditional schooling accreditation systems.

**Publisher's Acknowledgments**

We're proud of this book; please send us your comments through our Dummies online registration form located at www.dummies.com/register/.

Some of the people who helped bring this book to market include the following:

*Acquisitions, Editorial, and Media Development*

**Project Editor:** Tere Drenth

**Acquisitions Editor:** Kathy Cox

**Technical Reviewer:** Marjorie M. Mastie

**Acquisitions Coordinator:** Elizabeth Rea

**Editorial Manager:** Michelle Hacker

**Cartoons:** Rich Tennant, www.the5thwave.com

*Production*

**Project Coordinator:** Kristie Rees

**Layout and Graphics:** Carrie Foster, Joyce Haughey, Jacque Schneider, Erin Zeltner

**Proofreaders:** David Faust, Andy Hollandbeck, Arielle Carole Menelle, Carl Pierce, Dwight Ramsey, Charles Spencer

**Indexer:** Sherry Massey

**Publishing and Editorial for Consumer Dummies**

> **Diane Graves Steele,** Vice President and Publisher, Consumer Dummies

> **Joyce Pepple,** Acquisitions Director, Consumer Dummies

> **Kristin A. Cocks,** Product Development Director, Consumer Dummies

> **Michael Spring,** Vice President and Publisher, Travel

> **Brice Gosnell,** Publishing Director, Travel

> **Suzanne Jannetta,** Editorial Director, Travel

**Publishing for Technology Dummies**

> **Andy Cummings,** Vice President and Publisher, Dummies Technology/General User

**Composition Services**

> **Gerry Fahey,** Vice President of Production Services

> **Debbie Stailey,** Director of Composition Services

# Contents at a Glance

# Table of Contents

# Introduction

● ● ● ● ● ● ● ● ● ● ● ● ● ● ● ● ● ● ● ● ● ● ● ● ● ● ● ● ● ● ● ● ● ● ● ● ● ● ● ● ● ● ● ● ● ● ● ●

**P**erhaps you've applied for a job and have been refused an application because you don't have a high-school diploma. Or maybe you were up for a promotion at work, but when your boss found out you didn't finish high school, he said you weren't eligible for the new job. Maybe you've always wanted to go to college, but couldn't even apply because the college of your choice requires a high-school diploma. Or perhaps your kids are just about to graduate from high school, and you're motivated to finish, too.

If you fit into any of these scenarios or have other reasons for wanting a high-school diploma, this book is for you.

## About This Book

If you want a high-school diploma, you can always go back and finish high school the old-fashioned way. Of course, it may take you a few years, and you may have to quit your job to do it. You'd have to sit in a class with teenagers (and probably be treated like one).

This solution is usually not the ideal one for most people. This book presents a different solution: to get a high-school diploma in the shortest time possible. If you don't mind preparing yourself for challenging tests that determine whether you've mastered key skills, you can get a General Educational Development (GED) diploma that's the equivalent of a high-school education.

If you fit this group, this book is a necessity, because it's a fun and friendly instruction manual for succeeding on the GED tests. It is not a subject-matter preparation book — that is, it doesn't take you through the basics of math, and then progress into algebra, geometry, and so on. It does, however, prepare you for the GED by giving you detailed information about each test, two sets of full-length practice tests, and plenty of easy-to-understand answers and explanations for those tests.

Use this book as your first stop. After taking the first set of practice tests, you know which subject areas you need to work on. Chapter 28 recommends additional books (or a GED course) that can help you brush up on those areas.

## Foolish Assumptions

Here's who we think you are:

- ✔ You meet state requirements regarding age, residency, and the length of time since leaving school. (Check with your local GED Administrator listed in the Appendix.)

- ✔ You're serious about getting a high-school diploma as quickly as you can.

- ✔ You're willing to put in the time to prepare, keeping in mind that you have a lot of other responsibilities, too.

- ✔ Your getting a high-school diploma is a priority in your life.

✔ You want a fun and friendly guide that helps you toward your goal.

✔ You want to gain from the experience of others.

If this sounds like you, welcome aboard. We have prepared an enjoyable tour of the GED.

# How This Book Is Organized

This book has five parts, each of which prepares you for the GED.

## Part I: Putting the GED into Perspective

If you have never heard of the GED tests, this part explains them to you. If you have heard of them, this part gives you extra information and some handy tips for succeeding on all of the five GED tests. You find out how to register for the tests and how to figure out your scores after you receive them.

## Part II: Reviewing the Five GED Tests

This part is the heart of the book, telling you everything you need to know about each of the five GED tests. You find tips, hints, and a whole lot of information about what is in each of the tests.

Each of the chapters in this part talks about one specific GED test. For each, you find out what's tested and how you can brush up on your skills so you can ace the test.

## Part III: A Set of Full-Length Practice Tests

This part gives you (horror!) full-length practice tests, along with answers and explanations. We recommend that you take a set of these tests under the same conditions as you would on the GED, using a quiet room and utilizing a stopwatch to tell you when time is up. Grade these tests and see in which areas you need to study. You can then focus your preparation on those areas by reading additional books (including several in the Dummies, CliffsNotes, and CliffsQuickReview series) or taking a preparation course.

## Part IV: Once More, with Feeling: Another Set of Full-Length Practice Tests

This part gives you one more complete set of full-length practice tests. We recommend that you take this set after you've studied and prepared yourself in your weak areas. Take these as a final practice just before heading off to ace the real tests.

## Part V: The Part of Tens

This part is a treat to read — and you can review it in no time at all. You discover some key ways to prepare for the tests, what not to do, how to put to rest some false rumors about the tests, and how passing the GED tests can help you in life.

# Icons Used in This Book

Icons — little pictures that you see in the margins of this book — highlight bits of text that you want to pay special attention to. Here's what they mean:

Whenever we want to tell you a special trick or technique that helps you succeed on the GED tests, we mark it with this icon. Keep an eye out for them.

This icon tells you what sort of stuff you want to burn into your brain. Think of the text with this icon as the sort of stuff you'd tear out and put on a bulletin board or your refrigerator.

Take this icon seriously! While the world won't end if you don't heed the advice next to these icons, the warnings are important to your success in preparing to take the GED tests.

This icon is used sparingly, and when it is, feel free to skip the material next to it. It usually provides additional technical information that you don't need to lose sleep over.

# Where to Go from Here

Some people like to read books from beginning to end. Others prefer to read only the chapters or sections that interest them. Still others look in the index or Table of Contents for specific information they need. However you want to approach this book is fine with us — just don't peek at the practice tests until the moment you're ready to take them.

# Part I
# Putting the GED into Perspective

# In this part . . .

This part introduces you to the GED and gives you a brief look at each of the five tests. You get a chance to see what the GED expects you to know to receive your high-school equivalency diploma

In this part, you also find out how to succeed on the GED tests. You find out when and how to schedule your tests, what to take with you and what to leave at home, and what to do if you have special needs.

# Chapter 1

# Taking a Quick Glance at the GED

• • • • • • • • • • • • • • • • • • • • • • • • • • • • • • • • • • • • • • • • • • • • • • • • • •

### In This Chapter
▶ Reviewing the different GED tests and the questions on them
▶ Registering for the exam
▶ Determining your scores

• • • • • • • • • • • • • • • • • • • • • • • • • • • • • • • • • • • • • • • • • • • • • • • • • •

The GED tests measure whether you understand what high school seniors across the country are supposed to have learned before they graduate. When you pass these tests, you earn a high school equivalency diploma, which can open many doors for you.

Ready to get going? This chapter gives you the basics: what the tests look like, how you answer the questions, how to schedule the tests, and what to do after you get your scores back.

## Reviewing the Test Sections

The GED tests include the five following tests, each of which can be taken separately:

✔ Language Arts, Writing, Parts I and II

✔ Social Studies

✔ Science

✔ Language Arts, Reading

✔ Mathematics, Parts I and II

Note that while you can take each of the five tests separately, you must take both parts of the Language Arts, Writing or Mathematics tests at the same time.

## Language Arts, Writing

The Language Arts, Writing test is split into two parts:

✔ Part I asks you to rewrite and revise passages. This is a test of your grammar, punctuation, and spelling skills.

✔ Part II asks you to write an essay on a given topic. This part examines your skills in organizing your thoughts and writing.

You have to pass both parts to get a mark in this test. If you pass one part of the test but not the other, you must retake both parts the next time.

### Language Arts, Writing, Part 1

Language Arts, Writing, Part I has 50 multiple-choice questions and a time limit of 75 minutes. In this test, you're asked to edit and revise material that's given to you. This material comes from the following sources:

- **Workplace materials** include work-related letters, memos, and instructions that you may see on the job.

- **How-to books** are samples of all general reference books that are supposed to make you richer, stronger, and lighter or a better cook, driver, investor, or student. Now you get a chance to revise and edit them as well as read them.

- **Informational works** are documents that present you with information (often dry and boring information), such as the instructional manual that tells you how to set the clock on your VCR.

You find three types of question in this test:

- **Correction:** In these questions, you're asked to correct sentences presented to you.

- **Revision:** In these questions, you're presented with a sentence that has a word or phrase underlined. If a correction is needed, one of the answers will be better than the words or phrase underlined. If no correction is needed, one of the answers will be the same as the underlined portion or one of the choices will be "No correction needed."

- **Construction shift:** In these questions, you have to correct a sentence by altering the sentence structure. The original sentence may not be wrong but can be improved by editing.

See Chapter 3 for the lowdown on this test. See Chapters 8 and 18 for sample Language Arts, Writing tests.

Consider the following examples:

The following two questions are based on the following business letter.

Dear Mr. Snyder:

I have received your letter of February 3 and offer my apologi for the mistake in your account. The charge for your checks should have been $16.20, not $1,620.00. I have credited the entire amount, making your checks free. I hope this settles the matter.

1. Sentence 1: **I have received your letter of February 3 and offer my apologi for the mistake in your account.**

    (1) insert a semi-colon after <u>February 3</u>

    (2) change <u>February</u> to <u>Feb.</u>

    (3) insert a period after <u>February 3</u> and capitalize <u>and</u>

    (4) change <u>apologi</u> to <u>apology</u>

    (5) no correction needed

*Correct answer:* **4.** The correct spelling is "apology."

2. Sentence 3: I have credited the entire amount, making your checks free.

   (1) change <u>credited</u> to <u>credit</u>

   (2) change the comma after <u>amount</u> to a semi-colon

   (3) change <u>free</u> to <u>freely</u>

   (4) change the comma after <u>amount</u> to a colon

   (5) no correction needed

*Correct answer:* **5.** The sentence is correct in its current form.

## Language Arts, Writing, Part II

In this part of the test, you write an essay in 45 minutes. Because the two parts of the test are given together, however, you can share time between the two parts. If you finish Part I in less than 75 minutes, you can use the extra time on Part II.

The topic you're given may sound like the questions in a Miss America Pageant, such as the following:

- ✔ What is the most important invention discovered in your lifetime?

- ✔ How have computers allowed you to accomplish everyday tasks more efficiently?

See Chapter 3 for more examples of topics and take a stab at the sample Language Arts, Writing tests in Chapters 8 and 18. Time the tests so that you're taking them under the same conditions as the real GED tests.

In your essay, you give your opinion or explain your view, backing up that opinion or viewpoint with your own experiences and facts you may know from your life. This isn't a research paper. The information for these topics is in your head and not in a research library.

When you write this essay, make sure it's a series of interconnected paragraphs on a single topic. Not only should the entire essay begin with an introduction and end with a conclusion, but each paragraph needs an introductory sentence and a concluding sentence.

Write only on the assigned topic. Read it several times to make sure you understand what the topic is about. Essays written on topics that weren't assigned aren't graded.

Real people grade your essay. In fact, two different people grade it, and they're looking for the following:

- ✔ Material that's clearly organized

- ✔ Main points that are well focused

- ✔ Ideas that are well developed

- ✔ Words that are used properly

- ✔ Sentences that are well structured

- ✔ Sentences that are well punctuated and use proper grammar and spelling

Neat writing or printing makes grading easier for these real-life graders.

Read the newspapers and watch television news for a few months before the tests. This practice gives you some material to back up your opinion or viewpoint.

# Social Studies

For the Social Studies test, you answer 50 multiple-choice questions in 70 minutes. These questions deal with the following areas:

- American history (25 percent)
- World history (15 percent)
- Geography (15 percent)
- Civics and government (25 percent)
- Economics (20 percent)

The questions in this test are based on written texts or pictures, charts, tables, graphs, photographs, political cartoons, diagrams, or maps. These come from a variety of sources, such as government documents, academic texts, material from work-related documents, and atlases. See Chapter 4 for more information about the Social Studies tests and be sure to take the sample tests in Chapters 10 and 20.

You may see the following types of problems on the Social Studies test.

Question 1 is based on the following table.

| Type of Religion | Date Started (Approximate) | Sacred Texts |
| --- | --- | --- |
| Buddhism | 500 B.C. | None |
| Christianity | 33 A.D. | Bible (Old Testament and New Testament) |
| Hinduism | 4000 B.C. | Vedas; Upanishads |
| Islam | 600 A.D. | Qur'an; the hadith |
| Judaism | 2000 B.C. | Hebrew Bible; Talmud |

1. According to the table, Hinduism:

    (1) started in 600 A.D.

    (2) uses the Qur'an as one of its sacred texts

    (3) is the oldest religion

    (4) has no known sacred texts

    (5) has one known sacred text

*Correct answer:* **3.** The table shows that, because it was started in 4000 B.C., Hinduism is the oldest of the five religions listed.

Question 2 is based on the following excerpt from the diary of Christopher Columbus.

Monday, 6 August. The rudder of the caravel Pinta became loose, being broken or unshipped. It was believed that this happened by the contrivance of Gomez Rascon and Christopher Quintero, who were on board the caravel, because they disliked the voyage. The Admiral says he had found them in an unfavorable disposition before setting out. He was in much anxiety at not being able to afford any assistance in this case, but says that it somewhat quieted his apprehensions to know that Martin Alonzo Pinzon, Captain of the Pinta, was a man of courage and capacity. Made progress, day and night, of twenty-nine leagues.

2. Why would Rascon and Quintero have loosened the rudder?

    (1) they were trying to repair the rudder

    (2) the Admiral found them in an unfavorable disposition

    (3) the captain was very competent

    (4) they wanted to stop to fish

    (5) they did not want to be on the voyage

*Correct answer:* **5.** This answer is the only one supported by the text. The others may be related to statements in the passage, but they do not have anything to do with the question.

## Science

When you take the Science test, you answer 50 multiple-choice science questions in 80 minutes. The questions deal with the following topics:

- Earth and space science (20 percent)
- Life science (45 percent)
- Physical science (chemistry and physics) (35 percent)

 Some of the information is written in passages that you read before answering the questions. Other information is presented in charts, figures, graphs, maps, or tables. Chapter 5 discusses these types of formats in detail. Chapters 12 and 22 give you sample Science tests that are similar to the real ones.

 Most of the information you need to answer the questions is given in the passages and other material given, although in order to get a perfect score, you're expected to have picked up a bit of science information throughout your life. However, if you answer the questions only from the information presented, you should get a high enough score to pass.

Here are some sample problems that may be on the Science test; they're based on an excerpt from a press release:

A key feature of the Delta 4's operation is the use of a common booster core, or CBC, a rocket stage that measures some 150 feet long and 16 feet wide. By combining one or more CBCs with various upper stages or strap-on solid rocket boosters, the Delta 4 can handle an extreme range of satellite applications for military, civilian, and commercial customers.

1. The CBC in this context is a

    (1) Canadian broadcasting corporation

    (2) common booster core

    (3) cooperative boosters corp

    (4) civilian barbers cooperative

    (5) common ballistic cavalier

*Correct answer:* **2.** The only answer that is mentioned in the passage is (2).

2. How can the Delta 4 handle a wide range of applications?

   (1) using the Delta 4 with different names

   (2) developing a Delta 5

   (3) continuing research

   (4) using the CBC as the base of a rocket ship

   (5) creating a common core booster

*Correct answer:* **4.** The passage says that "By combining one or more CBCs with various upper stages or strap-on solid rocket boosters . . . ," and this answer comes closest to answering the question.

# Language Arts, Reading

The Language Arts, Reading test includes 40 multiple-choice questions that you must answer in 65 minutes. Chapter 6 gives you more information about the test, while Chapters 14 and 24 test your knowledge with full-length sample tests.

Seventy-five percent of the questions are based on passages from literature and include at least one piece from each of the following:

- Drama
- Poetry
- *Prose fiction* (that's novels and short stories) before 1920
- Prose fiction between 1920 and 1960
- Prose fiction after 1960

Twenty-five percent of the questions are based on non-fiction texts. You find two passages from any two of the following:

- **Critical reviews of visual and performing arts:** Most people go to the theater, movies, and concerts for entertainment. If, after you leave, you tell other people your impression of what you saw, you're *reviewing* the presentation. If you make recommendations about the performance, you're *critically reviewing* it. In this test, you may see critical reviews.

- **Nonfiction prose:** *Prose* is defined as written words not written as poetry. Prose can be divided into two main categories. If the story is made up by the author, it is usually referred to as *prose fiction.* If the words are based on facts, the work is considered *nonfiction prose.* A biography, an instruction manual, or a history text (even this book!) are examples of nonfiction prose.

- **Workplace and community documents:** These are the types of materials you see on the job or living in a community, such as workplace rules, employment contracts, wills, deeds, mortgage documents, instructions on how to use a voting machine, and income tax forms.

You may see questions like the following in the Language Arts, Reading test. Both questions are based on the following excerpt from a play.

Irvin and Mervin enter from stage left. Irvin is dressed sloppily in torn jeans, he wears a flannel shirt over a dirty T-shirt, and he has unkempt hair. Mervin is dressed more neatly in khakis, a blue buttondown shirt open at the neck, and loafers.

Irvin: What you want to do, man?
Mervin (laughing): With you or *to* you?
Irvin (looking up): What do you mean by that?
Mervin: What are you wearing?
Irvin: What's wrong with it?
Mervin: What's *not* wrong with it?
Irvin: So what? You don't want to go to the mall now?
Mervin: Why would I want to go to the mall with you, looking like that?
Irvin: Aren't I your best friend?
Mervin: Can't you dress a little better?
Irvin: Would I be a better friend if I dressed more like you?
Irvin and Mervin look at each other and shuffle off toward the mall.

1. What form of sentence does the author use to create this conversation?

    (1) all of the dialogue is boring

    (2) all of the dialogue is in questions

    (3) every sentence is in a different form

    (4) this is the way I talk to my friends

    (5) all of the dialogue is in exclamatory sentences

*Correct answer:* **2.** Each line of dialogue is a question.

2. According to the dialogue, why do Irvin and Mervin want to go to the mall?

    (1) the latest *Harry Potter* movie is playing there

    (2) they are going to meet friends

    (3) Irvin wants to shop for clothes

    (4) Mervin works there

    (5) they are looking for something to do

*Correct answer:* **5.** According to the first line of dialogue, they are looking for something to do. In another scene, you may find out that they're going to see a movie, meeting friends, shopping for clothes, or going to work, but GED questions are based only on the dialogue presented.

# Mathematics, Parts 1 and 11

The Mathematics test has two parts: One allows you to use a calculator, the other doesn't. Each part has 25 questions. You're given 45 minutes per part, for a total of 50 questions in 90 minutes.

The Mathematics Test covers four major areas:

- ✔ Algebra, equations, and patterns (20 to 30 percent)
- ✔ Data analysis, statistics, and probability (20 to 30 percent)
- ✔ Measurement and geometry (20 to 30 percent)
- ✔ Number operations (20 to 30 percent)

Here are examples of questions you may see on the Mathematics test:

1. A right-angle triangle has a hypotenuse of 5 feet and one side that's 36 inches. What is the length of the other side in feet?

   (1) 3

   (2) 48

   (3) 243

   (4) 6

   (5) 4

*Correct answer:* **5.** Using the Pythagorean Relationship (a formula that's given to you on the Formula page of the test), you know that $a^2 + b^2 = c^2$, where $c$ is the hypotenuse and $a$ and $b$ are either of the other two sides. Because you know the hypotenuse and one side, turn the equation around so that it reads $a^2 = c^2 - b^2$.

To get $c^2$, you square the hypotenuse: $5 \times 5 = 25$.

The other side is given in inches — to convert inches to feet, divide by 12: $36 \div 12 = 3$. To get $b^2$, square this side: $3 \times 3 = 9$.

Now solve the equation for $a$: $a^2 = 25 - 9$ or $a^2 = 16$. Take the square root of both sides, and you get: $a = 4$

The Mathematics Test presents real-life situations in the questions. So, if you find yourself answering 37 feet to a question about the height of a room or $3.00 for an annual salary, recheck your answer.

Each part of the test contains 25 questions — for a total of 50 — that you must complete in 90 minutes. Eighty percent of the questions are multiple-choice, but 20 percent require you to answer the question yourself in what is called an alternate format grid.

An *alternative-format grid* is either a standard grid or a coordinate-plane grid. Instead of getting a set of multiple-choice answers, you come with an answer and enter it on whichever of these two grids you're given on the answer sheet. (Note that the coordinate-plane grid may require some practice — if you need help, contact a tutor to walk you through it.) The sample questions that follow show you what these grids look like. Chapter 7 gives you additional information, while Chapters 16 and 26 show you sample tests that include some of these types of answers.

Consider the following alternate format grid problems that are similar to what you may see on the Mathematics test:

2. Barb is counting the number of boxes in a warehouse. In the first storage area, she finds 24 boxes. The second area contains 30 boxes. The third area contains 28 boxes. If the warehouse has 6 storage areas where it stores boxes, and the areas have an average of 28 boxes, what is the total number of boxes in the last three areas? Record your answer on the standard grid.

*Correct answer:* **86** (on the standard grid). If the warehouse has 6 storage areas and they have an average of 28 boxes in each, they have 6 × 28 = 168 boxes in the warehouse. The first three areas have 24 + 30 + 28 = 82 boxes in them. The last three areas must have 168 − 82 = 86 boxes in them.

3. A rectangle has one corner on the origin. The base goes from the origin to the point (3,0). The right side goes from (3,0) to (3,4). Draw the missing point on the coordinate plane grid.

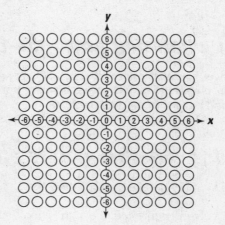

If you shade the three points given on the coordinate-plane grid, you see that a fourth point at (0,4) creates the rectangle. Just be sure, however, that you don't draw on the GED test book as you're taking the test! Instead, draw the point as shown on the following page.

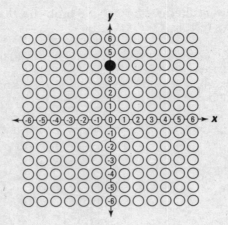

# It's a Date: Scheduling the Test

Each state or local testing center sets its own schedule for the five GED tests, which means that your state decides how and when you take the five tests.

All of the GED tests together take seven hours and five minutes, with breaks in between the tests. Depending on your local testing center, you may have to take all the tests in one sitting (this is rare), or you may be able to break the tests up into two or more sittings. Some states allow you to take one test each time you go to the testing center, and some offer the tests in the evenings or on weekends. Your local GED Examiner can give you all the information you need. Locate the GED Examiner in your area by logging on to www.gedtest.org or by calling 800-62-MY-GED. In addition, local school districts and community colleges can provide information about local test centers in your area.

Schedules for the tests vary by state or local testing center and may be offered as often as once every week or as seldom as once every couple of months.

## Knowing when you can take the tests

The simple answer is this: If you're eligible and prepared, you can apply to take the GED tests. You can also apply to take the tests if you're not prepared, but if you do that, you don't stand a very good chance of passing the tests.

## Discovering whether you're eligible

You are eligible to apply to take the GED tests if:

- ✔ You're not currently enrolled in a high school.
- ✔ You're not a graduate of high school.
- ✔ You meet state requirements regarding age, residency, and the length of time since leaving high school.

# Signing up

To sign up for the test, you do the following:

- ✔ Contact your local GED administrator to make sure you are eligible.
- ✔ Ask the office for an application (if needed) or an appointment.
- ✔ Complete the application (if needed).
- ✔ Return the application to the proper office, with payment, if necessary. Check with your local administrator, listed in the Appendix, to make sure of the rules. In some states, if you fall into a low-income bracket, you can have the fees paid for you.

# Working with unusual circumstances

If you feel that you may have a special circumstance that prevents you from taking the GED tests, contact the GED administrator in your area. If, for example, the tests are going to be held on your Sabbath, the testing center may make special arrangements for you.

When applying for special circumstances, keep the following in mind:

- ✔ Document everything in your appeal for special consideration.
- ✔ Contact the GED administrator in your area as early as you can.
- ✔ Be patient. Special arrangements can't be made overnight. Often, the administrator must wait for a group with similar issues to gather, and then make arrangements for the entire group.

## Are accommodations available?

The GED testing centers make every effort to ensure that all qualified people have access to the tests. If you have a disability, you may not be able to register for the tests on Monday and take them on Friday, but with some advance planning, you can probably take the tests. Here's what you do:

- ✔ Contact the GED Testing Service or your local GED center and explain your disability.
- ✔ Request any forms that must be filled out for your special circumstances.
- ✔ Ensure that you have a recent diagnosis by a physician or other qualified professional.
- ✔ Complete all the proper forms and submit them with medical or professional diagnosis.
- ✔ Leave yourself plenty of time to be able to take the tests.

Please note that, regardless of your disability, you still have to be able to handle the mental demands of the test.

The GED Testing Service in Washington, D.C. defines specific disabilities for which they make special accommodations as the following, provided the disability severely limits your ability to perform essential skills required to pass the GED:

- ✔ Medical disabilities, such as cerebral palsy, epilepsy, or blindness
- ✔ Emotional disabilities, such as schizophrenia, major depression, attention deficit disorder, or Tourette's Syndrome
- ✔ Specific learning disabilities, including perceptual handicaps, brain injury, minimal brain dysfunction, dyslexia, and developmental aphasia

### Taking the test when English is your second language

The GED tests are offered in English, Spanish, and French.

If none of these is your first language, you must decide whether you read and write English as well as or better than 40 percent of high school graduates. If you do, prepare for and take the tests. If not, take additional classes to prepare yourself in English until you think that you're ready.

In many ways, the GED tests are like the TOEFL (the Test of English as a Foreign Language) comprehension tests. If you've completed the TOEFL tests with good grades, you're likely ready for the GED. If you haven't taken the TOEFL tests, enroll in a GED preparation course to see whether you have difficulty. GED courses provide you not only with some insight into your comprehension ability, but also with a teacher to discuss this with.

## Knowing How Scores Are Determined

Except for the essay, each correct answer is worth one point. No matter how hard or easy the question, if you get it right, you get one point. In each test, the points you get are totaled. The total converts to a standard score, ranging from 200 to 800 on each test.

### Scoring well

To pass the tests, you have to score at least 410 on each test and have an average score of 450 on the five tests. If you achieve this, congratulate yourself: You've scored better than at least 40 percent of today's high school graduates. You become a graduate of the largest virtual school in the country.

### Knowing what to do if you score poorly on one or more tests

If you discover that your average score is less than 450, start planning to retake the tests after additional studying.

As soon as possible after seeing your results, contact your local GED administrator to find out the rules for retaking tests. Some states may ask that you wait for a time. Some may ask that you attend a preparation course and show that you have completed it. Some may charge you an additional fee.

---

## A virtual graduation ceremony

Can you imagine what your graduation ceremony could look like? The line up for diplomas would stretch for miles and miles. If you could gather all the one million GED graduates each year into a stadium and spend two minutes reading each name and giving each diploma, it would take over three years to read the names.

If every graduate took three seconds to say "Thank you," the graduation ceremony would become more than a month longer. If the graduates stood with their arms outstretched, they would form a line about 1,000 miles long.

You are entering a very large group.

# Chapter 2

# Succeeding on the GED

. . . . . . . . . . . . . . . . . . . . . . . . . . . . . . . . . . . . . . . . . . . . . . . . . . . . . .

### In This Chapter

▶ Discovering what to take to the tests

▶ Revealing the secrets of the test room

▶ Becoming a test-taking expert

. . . . . . . . . . . . . . . . . . . . . . . . . . . . . . . . . . . . . . . . . . . . . . . . . . . . . .

Not everyone has taken standardized tests. Not everyone has experienced the joys and sorrows of multiple-choice tests. But to succeed in the GED, you have to do well on a standardized test that consists mostly of multiple-choice answers. What to do?

Reviewing this chapter is a good beginning. Here, we let you in on some of the secrets of passing the GED.

## Finding Out What to Take to the GED Tests

The first most important thing to bring to the GED tests is you. Make sure you know where the tests are held and what time your tests begin. Examiners don't have a lot of sympathy for you if you show up late because you didn't check the starting time. They have even less sympathy if you show up on the wrong date.

Besides yourself, other items you want to bring or wear include the following:

- ✔ Comfortable clothes
- ✔ Comfortable shoes
- ✔ Watch
- ✔ Two #2 pencils or HB mechanical pencils; a pen for the essay (all of these may be provided for you at the testing center)
- ✔ Photo ID
- ✔ Any fees you may still owe
- ✔ The registration confirmation, if one was sent to you

These are possibly the most important exams you'll ever take. Treat them seriously and come prepared.

Be sure *not* to bring the following:

- ✔ Books
- ✔ Calculator (one is provided for you — see Chapter 7)
- ✔ Notes or scratch paper
- ✔ Anything valuable, like a laptop computer or radio, that you don't feel comfortable leaving outside the room while you take the exams

# Knowing What to Expect When You Get There

You usually take the GED tests in a large examination room with at least one official (sometimes called a *proctor* or *examiner*) who is in charge of the test. The test booklet and an answer sheet are given out, and then the proctor or someone chosen to conduct the test reads the instructions to all the students. Listen carefully to the instructions so that you know when and if you can take bathroom breaks, how much time is available to take the test, and so on.

As soon as you're allowed to open the test booklet, skim the questions. Don't spend a lot of time skimming, just enough to spot the questions you absolutely know and the ones you're going to leave until the end. After you're finished skimming, you can then answer all the questions you know first, leaving you much more time per question for those you're less sure of.

Because taking tests is probably not a usual situation for you, you may feel nervous. This is perfectly normal. Just try to focus on answering each question and push any other thoughts to the back of your mind.

For each question — except for a few on the Mathematics test (see Chapter 7) and the essay in Part II of the Language Arts, Writing test (see Chapter 3) — you're given five answers to choose from. Read each question carefully, keeping in mind that only one is correct. Choose the answer that's closest to the correct answer as you know it.

You don't have to answer questions in order. Nobody except you will ever know in which order you answered the questions.

Throughout the test, keep your eyes on your paper. If your eyes glance around the room, the GED examiner may become suspicious.

During the test, the examiner will tell you how much time has elapsed or how much time is left. Listen to these instructions. When time is up, immediately stop writing, put down your pencil, and breathe a sigh of relief.

When the test is over, you hand in your answer sheet and test book. Listen for instructions on what to do or where to go next.

# Discovering General Test-Taking Strategies

You can increase your score by practicing smart exam-taking. This section gives you some tips for planning your time, guessing intelligently, and reviewing your work.

## Watching the clock

When the test begins, check your watch and write down the time you start *and* the time that you'll finish. (Write this near the top of your answer sheet in very light pencil marks that you erase before handing it in.) This way, you don't have to waste time figuring out how much time you have left partway through the test. Don't try to remember the time; instead, write it down.

During the test, you'll probably be warned — perhaps more than once — about how much time remains. Check what you're told against the time you write down.

Table 2-1 shows you how much time you have, on average, for each question.

| Table 2-1 | Time Per Question for Each GED Test | | |
|---|---|---|---|
| *Test* | *Questions* | *Time Limit (in Minutes)* | *Time per Question (in Minutes)* |
| Language Arts, Writing, Part I | 50 | 75 | 1.5 |
| Language Arts, Writing, Part II | 1 essay | 45 | 45 |
| Social Studies | 50 | 70 | 1.4 |
| Science | 50 | 80 | 1.6 |
| Language Arts, Reading | 40 | 65 | 1.6 |
| Mathematics, Parts I and II | 50 | 90 | 1.8 |

Keep in mind that if you take two minutes for each question, you won't complete all the answers on the test.

Time a bunch of questions as a group, for example, spending 15 minutes on each group of 10 questions.

## Guess for success: Using intelligent guessing strategies

The multiple-choice questions provide you with five possible answers: You get one point for a correct answer, and nothing is subtracted for an incorrect answer. Because you aren't penalized for guessing, you want to guess logically by eliminating as many wrong choices as possible and choosing from just one or two.

When the question gives you five possible answers and you randomly choose one, you have a 20 percent chance of guessing the correct answer without even reading the question. We don't recommend doing this, of course.

However, if you know that one of the answers is definitely wrong, you now have just four answers to chose from and have a 25 percent chance (1 in 4) of choosing the correct answer. If you know that two of the answers are wrong, that leaves 3 possible answers to chose from, giving you a 33 percent (1 in 3) chance — much better than 20 percent! You now have a 1 in 3 or 33% chance of getting the right answer by guessing. And finally, if you know that three of the answers are wrong, your chances of choosing the correct answer move up to 50 percent. That's as good as a random choice gets!

So, if you don't know the answer, you need to know how to spot wrong choices:

- Wrong choices usually don't answer the question; that is, they may sound good, but they're answering a different question.

- Sometimes, two answers are very close. Consider both of these for future consideration, because they both can't be right, but both can be wrong. Answers that are very close are sometimes given to see if you really know the answer.

- Look for opposite answers in the hopes that you can eliminate one. Both answers can't be right, but both can be wrong.

- Some wrong choices may just strike you as wrong when you first read them. Trust your instincts. If you spent time preparing for these exams, you have probably learned more than you think.

## Practice makes perfect

The important tool on the GED tests is your brain, which is filled with useful information. You can make all the stored data in your brain more useful by using it regularly, that is, by practicing.

Practice on sample tests, including the ones in Parts III and IV of this test. If you've gone through those and want more challenges, look for other GED preparation books that offer sample tests or get an Official GED Practice Test from your local test center.

## Leaving time for review

Try to finish a few minutes early in order to review questions, especially those that you're unsure about. Allowing extra time at the end also keeps you from scrambling at the very end.

In answering multiple-choice questions, the answer you think is correct usually is. Don't change an answer unless you're sure that it's wrong. If you're positive, make sure you completely erase your original answer.

GED tests are scored by machines (except the essay in the Language Arts, Writing, Part II test). If the machine believes you've marked two answers, neither one counts. If you ever change an answer, be sure to *completely* erase the original answer before you turn in your test.

In order to leave time for review at the end of the test, you have to spend less time on each question than Table 2-1 suggested. Table 2-2 suggests a way to allow time for review.

| Table 2-2 | Time Per Question Plus Time for Review | | | |
|-----------|-----------|-----------|-----------|-----------|
| Test | Questions | Time Limit (in Minutes) | Time per Question (in Minutes) | Time for Review (in Minutes) |
| Language Arts, Writing, Part I | 50 | 75 | 1.2 | 10 |
| Language Arts, Writing, Part II | 1 essay | 45 | 30 | 15 |
| Social Studies | 50 | 70 | 1.2 | 10 |
| Science | 50 | 80 | 1.4 | 10 |
| Language Arts, Reading | 40 | 65 | 1.4 | 10 |
| Mathematics, Parts I and II | 50 | 90 | 1.5 | 15 |

If you use your review time wisely, you may be able to improve your score. But you can't panic: The worst thing you can do is to panic and change answers with no reason.

## Reviewing a Few Rules of the Road

Consider the following rules for taking any of the GED tests. Note that Chapters 3 through 7 contain additional rules of the road for each specific test.

- **Take the time to relax.** Passing the GED tests is an important milestone in your life. Make sure you leave a bit of time to relax, both while preparing for the tests and just before taking them.

- **Get enough sleep.** We're sorry if this sounds like your parents talking, but it is true. When you're approaching exhaustion, you shouldn't be taking tests. Plan your time so that you can get a good night's sleep for several days before the tests.

- **If you need something, take it.** In the instructions you receive for the tests, you're told what you need to bring with you. The only additional item is a watch, and you want to make sure it has a fresh battery. If you can't remember when you last changed the battery, you may want to change it before the tests.

- **If you don't need it, leave it at home.** The rules about what enters the room are strict. Don't take chances. If an item isn't on the list of acceptable items and isn't clothing, leave it at home. The last place on earth to discuss whether or not something should enter the test room is at the door of the test room. If you have questions, ask them in advance. In the Appendix is a list of state officials who may be able to answer your questions. You can also call 1-800-62-MYGED and ask questions of real people.

- **Be on time.** Most examination centers don't let you enter if you're late. Don't take a chance — arrive early. If necessary, take a practice run to make sure you have enough time to get from your house or workplace to the testing center. You don't need the added pressure of worrying about whether you can make the test on time. This can create industrial-strength panic in the calmest of people.

  Traffic happens. No one can plan for it, but you can leave extra time to make sure that it doesn't ruin your day. Plan your route and practice it. Then leave extra time in case a meteor crashes into the street and the crowd that gathers around it stalls your progress.

- **Bring the correct identification.** Before you're let into the room to take the test, test officials want to make sure that you're you. Bring the proper approved picture ID. Your state GED office (see the Appendix) can tell you what's an approved form of photo ID. Have it in a place where you can reach it easily. When asked to identify yourself, don't pull out a mirror and say, "Yep, that's me."

- **Make sure you know the rules of the room before you begin.** If you have questions about using the bathroom during the test or what to do if you finish early, ask before you begin. If you don't want to ask your question in public, telephone the GED office in your area and ask your question over the telephone. You can always e-mail the question if you get caught in the jungle of unanswered voice mail. GED maintains a special number, 1-800-62-MYGED for all your questions and a web site at www.gedtest.org. Check the Appendix for a list of state-specific phone numbers.

- **Keep your eyes on your paper.** Everybody knows you're not going to look at other people's papers during the test. To be on the safe side, though, don't stretch, roll your eyes, or do anything else that may be mistaken for looking at another test.

- **Leave time to check your work.** Having a few minutes at the end of a test to check your work is a great way to set your mind at ease. These few minutes give you a chance to look at any questions you may have had trouble with. If everything is complete, enjoy the few minutes, without any panic. Do anything to keep yourself from trying to change a lot of answers at the last minute.

# Part II
# Reviewing the Five GED Tests

The 5th Wave     By Rich Tennant

SHERLOCK HOLMES TAKES A GED TEST

Hmm... ELEMENTARY!
Ah, yes...ummm...A HA!
ELEMENTARY! ELEMENTARY!
Now, let's see. Ahhhhh HA!
ELEMENTARY INDEED!!

Gimme a break.

# In this part . . .

This part takes you inside the tests, giving you the low-down on each of the five GED subject areas.

Each chapter in this part describes one of the five GED tests in detail, telling you how many and what types of questions are on the test. You also find out what skills and information you're expected to know before taking the tests. From here, you determine whether you need to brush up on your skills with further reading, a GED-preparation class, or one-on-one tutoring.

# Chapter 3

# The Write Stuff: The Language Arts, Writing Test, Parts I and II

- - - - - - - - - - - - - - - - - - - - - - - - - - - - - - - - - - - - - -

*In This Chapter*

▶ Preparing for the writing tests of the GED

▶ Reviewing the required writing skills

▶ Understanding some tips and tricks for succeeding

- - - - - - - - - - - - - - - - - - - - - - - - - - - - - - - - - - - - - -

**M**uch of Part I of the Language Arts, Writing test determines how well you know grammar. Grammar is the basic structure of language, and you have a chance to answer 50 questions on it in 75 minutes. Most of what you're tested on is stuff you've picked up over the years, either in school or just by living and speaking and reading, but this chapter also gives you skill-building tips.

Part II of this test is different from all the other GED tests, because you have to write an essay. Instead of coloring in circles, you write real words that are connected to each other and make sense to a reader. You have 45 minutes to produce a readable, coherent piece of work.

## Passing Part 1

Part I of the Language Arts, Writing Test asks you to read and then revise and edit documents that may include how-to information and workplace material. This test isn't evil. Just because you haven't taken grammar for years doesn't mean you don't know it. You probably know more than you think.

The questions are all multiple choice, which means that, along with four incorrect answers, you're given the correct answer.

You begin by carefully reading the assigned passage. Always read the entire document before answering the questions, because those questions make more sense if you have an idea of what the whole passage is about. As you're reading, however, if you think you see an error, read it over again and ask yourself, "How can I correct this?"

If you find sentences that sound out of place or in the wrong order, note them mentally. If you think you see spelling errors, make note of them, too. (Don't write in your test booklet, though!)

### Preparing for Part 1

To succeed on Part I of the Language Arts, Writing Test, you can prepare in advance by reviewing rules of grammar, punctuation, and spelling. Here are some ways you can do that:

✔ **Master the rules of basic grammar.** On this test, you're not asked to define a gerund and give an example of its use, but you need to know about verb tenses, subject/verb agreement, pronoun/antecedent agreement, possessives, and so on. One great way to brush up on these skills is to get a copy of *English Grammar For Dummies* by Geraldine Woods (Wiley Publishing, Inc.).

✔ **Practice grammar in everyday speaking.** As you review the rules of grammar, practice them in everyday speaking. Although correct grammar usually "sounds" right to your ears, sometimes it doesn't, because you and your friends, co-workers, or family have become used to using incorrect grammar. If you see a rule that seems different from the way you talk, put it on a flashcard and practice it as you go through your day. Before long, you'll train your ear so that correct grammar sounds right.

Correcting other people's grammar out loud doesn't make you popular. However, correcting it in your head helps you succeed on this test.

✔ **Understand punctuation.** Know how to use capitals, commas, semicolons, colons, and other forms of punctuation. *English Grammar For Dummies,* in addition to giving you the lowdown on grammar, tells you the details of punctuation rules.

✔ **Practice writing and reading.** Write as much and as often as you can, and then review it for errors. Look for and correct mistakes in punctuation, grammar, and spelling. If you're not able to find any, ask someone who knows grammar and punctuation for help.

✔ **Read as often as you can, too.** Read the newspaper, magazines, novels, textbooks, or whatever else you can get your hands on. As your knowledge of grammar and punctuation improves, have a bit of fun by correcting what you read in small-town newspapers and in trashy novels — both tend to have poor editing.

✔ **Improve your spelling.** As you practice writing, keep a good dictionary at hand. If you're not sure of the spelling of any word, look it up. Add it to a spelling list that you keep and practice from. In addition, get a list of common *homonyms* (words that sound the same but are spelled differently and have different definitions) and review those every day. (You need to know, for example, the difference between "their," "there," and "they're.") Many dictionaries contain a listing of homonyms.

✔ **Keep in mind that these questions are multiple choice.** Multiple-choice questions always give you the correct answer. Of course, they also tell you four other answers that are incorrect. All you have to do is find the correct one! As you practice speaking and writing, you tune your ears so that the correct answer sounds right. This makes finding the correct answer easier.

✔ **Take practice tests.** Take as many as you can. Be strict about time and check your answers when you're finished. Don't move on until you know and understand the correct answer. The time you spend is worth it.

## Understanding the Part 1 test format

This 75-minute test has 50 multiple-choice questions in it. The test covers the following subjects, each of which is described in detail in the "Testing your skills for Part I" section:

✔ Mechanics (25 percent; 12 or 13 questions)

✔ Organization (15 percent; 7 or 8 questions)

✔ Sentence structure (30 percent; 15 questions)

✔ Usage (30 percent; 15 questions)

You aren't penalized for guessing, so if you don't know the answer, guess. While you can't get any points for omitting a question, you may get a point if you can eliminate all but one answer. The more incorrect answers you eliminate, the better the chance that you'll guess the correct one.

For each question, the answer is scored by a pesky machine. Always follow instructions and fill in each circle fully.

## Testing your skills for Part 1

The questions in this test expect you to know the following:

✔ **Mechanics:** The mechanics of writing include:

- **Capitalization:** You have to recognize which words should start with a capital letter and which words don't. All sentences start with a capital letter, but so do titles, like "Miss," "President," and "Senator," when followed by a person's last name. Names of cities, states, and countries are also capitalized. *English Grammar For Dummies* reviews these rules.

- **Punctuation:** This includes everyone's personal favorite, commas. (Actually, most people hate commas because they aren't sure how to use them, but the rules are simple to apply after you know them.) The more you read, the better you get at punctuation. If you're reading and don't understand why punctuation is or isn't used, check with your guidebook (such as *English Grammar For Dummies*).

- **Spelling:** You don't have to spot a lot of misspelled words, but you do have to know how to spell contractions and possessives and understand the different spellings of homonyms.

- **Contractions:** This has nothing to do with those painful moments before childbirth! Instead, *contractions* are formed when the English language shortens a word by leaving out a letter or a sound. When you say or write, "can't," you're using a shortened form of "can*not.*"

The important thing to remember about contractions is that the *apostrophe* (that's a single quotation mark) takes the place of a letter or letters that are left out.

- **Possessives:** Do you know people who are possessive? They're all about ownership, right? So is the grammar form of possessives. *Possessives* are words that show ownership or possession, usually by adding an apostrophe to a person or object's name. If Marcia owns a car, we say that it is Marcia's car. The word, "Marcia's" is a possessive.

✔ **Organization:** On the test, you're asked to correct passages by changing the order of sentences or leaving them out when they don't fit. You have to work with passages to turn them into logical, organized paragraphs.

✔ **Sentence structure:** Every language has rules about the order in which words should go in a sentence. English is no different, but if you're not comfortable with this, check out *English Grammar For Dummies.*

✔ **Usage:** Grammar has rules. Subjects and verbs must agree. Verbs have tenses that must be consistent. Pronouns must refer back to nouns properly. If the last three sentences sound like Greek to you, get a copy of *English Grammar For Dummies.* It gives you the whole kit and caboodle about grammar rules.

## What's not being tested in Part I

You aren't expected to be a grammarian. You are expected to be able to recognize correct and incorrect sentences and paragraphs. The questions are multiple choice. You have to know enough to mark the best answer.

## Reviewing a few rules of the road for Part 1

The following rules will serve you well:

- ✔ **Read the entire passage.** Before you start to answer the questions, read the passage. The questions make more sense after you read the passage.

- ✔ **Read carefully.** As you read the passage, look for errors and hard-to-read sentences. The more carefully you read, the better chance you have of getting the right answers.

## Passing Part 11

We've tried to figure out a way to sugar-coat this and can't: For Part II of the Language Arts, Writing Test, you have to write an essay that's graded by real people. Thankfully, it's not a full-blown research paper with footnotes and a bibliography like the ones your teachers made you write. Instead, this essay is a series of connected paragraphs written from your own experiences and observations.

One of the advantages of growing older is that your head fills with more information and opinions, which form the basis of your essay. You can't leave the room to go to the library to find extra material; instead, you bring it in your head.

Be kind to the people reviewing your essay: Write neatly. You may have to practice your penmanship in addition to your writing skills. The best essay in the world has to be understood by the graders to get a passing grade.

## Preparing for Part 11

The following tasks help you prepare for the Language Arts, Writing, Part II test:

- ✔ **Practice writing neatly.** You were taught how to write neatly in grade school, right? Then it became cool to have your own style of handwriting, and the fewer people who could read your style, the better. Well, now is the time to become very uncool. Graders have to read your essay. They don't have time to figure out if something is a word or just a doodle.

- ✔ **Practice editing your own work.** After the test starts, the only person available to edit your essay is you. If that thought scares you, practice editing your own work now. Take a writing workshop or get help from someone who knows how to edit. And practice writing a lot of essays and then reviewing them shortly after.

✔ **Review how to plan an essay.** Few people can sit down, write a final draft of an essay, and receive a satisfactory grade on it. Instead, you have to plan what you're going to write. The best way to start is to jot down everything you know about a topic without worrying about the order: This is called *brainstorming*. From there, you can organize your thoughts into groups. The "Watching the clock" section, later in this chapter, helps you plan your essay.

✔ **Practice writing on a topic (and not going off topic!).** Your essay must relate to the topic as closely as possible. If they ask you to write about your personal goals, and you write about a hockey game, it's game-over for your essay.

✔ **Think about and use related examples.** If you're writing about how machines make our lives easier or harder, your problem getting your toaster fixed under warranty makes a good example. A story about painting your bike fluorescent pink doesn't. Examples must relate to the topic.

✔ **Practice general writing.** If writing connected paragraphs isn't part of your life at the moment, practice it! Write long e-mails. Write long letters. Write to your Member of Congress. Write to your friends. Write articles for community newspapers. Write stories. Just keep writing.

✔ **Write practice essays.** See Chapters 8 and 18 of this book for practice essays. Ask a knowledgeable friend or former teacher to grade them for you. And consider taking a preparation class in which you're assigned practice topics to write about. When you're finished practicing, practice some more.

## Understanding the Part II test format

This 45-minute test has only one question on it, and it's an essay. Any time that you have left after completing Part I of the Language Arts, Writing Test is added to your time for Part II. Let the GED examiner know when you're ready to begin the essay.

You're given one topic and a few instructions. Your task is to write approximately 250 words on that topic. You can't write about another topic or a similar topic.

---

### Ten practice topics for essays

✔ What steps can you, as an individual, take to help save the environment?

✔ Inner beauty is far more important than outer beauty. Do you agree or disagree?

✔ If you were talking to your mentor, what would you tell him or her about how that mentoring has affected your life?

✔ Cars are wonderful toys but they may be destroying our cities and our environment. How can you convince people to get out of their cars and into mass transit?

✔ If you think about your most valued friend, what qualities does he or she possess that are important to you?

✔ Road rage kills. How could you convince your friends that road relaxation is a better way to live?

✔ Children take after their parents. Explain how you or someone you may know may set a good example for children every day.

✔ Computers are now a part of everyone's lives. Describe a day without computers and the effects that this day would have on you.

✔ Everyone has events that shape their lives. Choose four of these events and explain their effect on your life.

✔ Everyone talks about the good-old days. In what ways is today better?

When writing about the topic given, you're asked to use your personal observations, knowledge, and experience in your writing.

# Watching the clock

You have 45 minutes to finish your essay, and in that time, you have four main tasks:

- ✔ Plan
- ✔ Draft
- ✔ Edit and revise
- ✔ Rewrite

If you take ten minutes to plan, twenty minutes to draft, five minutes to edit and revise, and ten minutes to rewrite, you will do fine. This is a tight schedule, though. If it makes your writing too sloppy to read, consider allowing more time for rewriting. No one but you will see anything but the final version.

### Planning

Read the topic carefully several times and ask yourself what the topic means to you. Then brainstorm on the scratch paper given to you at the test. *Brainstorming* is like dumping the contents of a portion of your brain. Write down everything you can think of that relates to the topic, no matter how silly it seems and without worrying about the order you're writing it in.

Don't censor your thoughts. When you brainstorm, write down everything you can think of. You can sort all the information out in the next phase.

For example, if the question asks you to discuss a major milestone in your life, your topic may center around the following: "Passing the GED will be a major milestone in my life." In your essay, explain why this is the major milestone for you at this moment and how you plan to use the GED for the betterment of your life. Use your personal observations, experience, and knowledge to support your essay.

After you have these points written down, sit back for a moment to reflect. (Don't reflect too long, because you still have an essay to write, but do take a few minutes.) Look over your points and find an introduction, such as, "I have accomplished many things in my life, but my major milestone will be passing the GED tests." Write this down as a sentence. Beneath this sentence, write down all the points that back up your introduction. These should be your strongest points.

Now, write down a concluding sentence, such as, "Of all my accomplishments, passing the GED tests will be the most important because it will open doors that are closed to me now." Glancing at your introduction and the topic, you can select points that strengthen your conclusion. These may be some of the same points used in your introduction.

Plan a path from your introduction to your conclusion. The path may be several points long, for example:

Introduction: "I have accomplished many things in my life, but my major milestone will be passing the GED tests."

✔ List my accomplishments

✔ Discuss my goals

✔ Discuss what's stopping me from reaching my goals

✔ Tie in which of the things stopping me will be helped by my having a GED

✔ Discuss which goals are attainable with the GED diploma

✔ Envision how my life will change as I accomplish those goals

Conclusion: "Of all my accomplishments, passing the GED tests will be the most important because it will open doors that are closed to me now."

Now, reflect again. Would any additional points improve the essay? Don't just add points to have more points, though. This isn't a contest in which the one with the most points wins. This is an essay in which the one with the best points, logically written, gets the passing grade.

Look over your path and your points. Can you combine any parts of the path to make it tighter? Here's an example:

Introduction: "I have accomplished many things in my life, but my major milestone will be passing the GED tests."

✔ List my accomplishments

✔ Discuss my goals and what's stopping me from reaching them

✔ Tie in which of the things stopping me will be helped by my having a GED and discuss which goals are attainable with the GED diploma

✔ Envision how my life will change as I accomplish those goals

Conclusion: "Of all my accomplishments, passing the GED tests will be the most important because it will open doors that are closed to me now."

Now that you have the outline, you're ready to go on to the next step.

### Drafting

As you add subpoints under each main point, you begin to see your essay taking shape.

Introduction: "I have accomplished many things in my life, but my major milestone will be passing the GED tests."

✔ List my accomplishments

- Coaching youth hockey

- Keeping a job for 4 years

- Getting a small promotion

- Getting married

✔ Discuss my goals and what's stopping me from reaching them

- People expect more education from hockey coaches in the minor leagues.

- Many promotions are blocked to me because of my education.

- My children may be embarrassed to have an uneducated parent.

- My boss likes people with diplomas and certificates.

✔ Tie in which of the things stopping me will be helped by my having a GED and discuss which goals are attainable with the GED diploma

- I may be able to coach in the minors.

- I can apply for more promotions.

- My boss may like me more.

- My children will be impressed by my accomplishment.

- I will have graduated from high school.

✔ Envision how my life will change as I accomplish those goals

- As a minor-league coach, my picture will be in the papers.

- I could become a manager at my company.

- I may be invited to lunch by my boss to discuss ideas.

- I could be invited to my children's class to talk about the importance of education.

- I will have a diploma to hang on the wall.

Conclusion: "Of all my accomplishments, passing the GED tests will be the most important because it will open doors that are closed to me now. The doors are open — promotion, dreams, recognition — and that creates so many more possibilities."

Notice how each point becomes a paragraph. Now, you can come up with subpoints that form the sentences in each paragraph.

 Each paragraph starts with an introductory sentence, which hints at what is to come, and ends with a transition sentence that leads from the paragraph you're on to the next one. Your subpoints are your sentences within the paragraphs. If you put your sentences in a logical order from introduction to transition, you start to see paragraphs emerging.

### Editing and revising

Now comes the hard part. You have to be your own editor. Turn off your ego and remember that every word is written on scratch paper, not carved in stone. Make your work better by editing and revising. Make this the best piece of writing you've ever done.

### Rewriting

Neatly rewrite your edited work — in pen — in the proper place in the answer book. Two graders have to read this essay, so write neatly and clearly. Write large enough to be read. Leave some room between lines. Your essay has to be well written, but it also has to be readable. If you make a mistake, neatly cross it out and move on. It will not count against you.

## Testing your writing skills

Graders will be looking for a good essay. A good essay has:

✔ Main points that focus on the topic

✔ Points that are clear and organized both in the paragraphs and throughout the entire essay

✔ Ideas that are developed logically and clearly

✔ Transitions throughout for a smooth flow between ideas

✔ A good vocabulary

✔ Proper punctuation

✔ Correct spelling

Your essay is graded by real, live people. Always follow instructions and write neatly and clearly.

If you don't pass this part of the Language Arts, Writing test, you have to take both parts over again. That should be an incentive to practice writing.

## Reviewing a few rules of the road for Part II

Here are a few rules that will serve you well in this test:

✔ **Use the scratch paper provided.** You're given scratch paper at the test site. Use it to make notes and write down your rough work. The graders don't look at it, so what you write on the scratch paper is just for you.

✔ **Write about the topic and only about the topic.** You are graded for writing an essay *on the topic.* Make sure you really do this. One of the greatest failings on this test is to write about something that's within driving distance of the topic, but not on it.

✔ **Use stuff from your life to make points.** You're writing an essay about you, your life, and your experiences.

See Chapters 9 and 19 for more tips on writing a great essay.

# Chapter 4

# A Graph, a Map, and You: The Social Studies Test

*In This Chapter*

▶ Reviewing the types of questions on the Social Studies Test

▶ Getting yourself ready for this test

▶ Exploring some sample problems

**D**o you enjoy knowing about how events in the past may help you to foretell the future? Do the lives of people in far away places interest you? Are politics something you care about?

If so, you like social studies! You discover how humans relate to their environment and to other people through social studies, which includes subjects like history, government, geography, and economics.

The information in this chapter helps you prepare for the Social Studies Test.

## Understanding the Test Format

The Social Studies Tests contains 50 multiple-choice questions that you must answer in 70 minutes. The questions check your knowledge in the following areas:

✔ **American history (25 percent; 12 or 13 questions):** You may be asked to read passages about the American Revolution, the Civil War, colonization, reconstruction, settlement, industrial development, or the Great Depression — and answer questions about them. If you didn't have to answer questions, this would be a dream assignment, because American history can be a lot of fun.

To practice, read articles and books about historical events and trends (see Chapter 28). Remember that 60 percent of these questions will be based on visual passages, including illustrations, maps, and charts, so take a look at those, too.

✔ **World history (15 percent; 7 or 8 questions):** These types of questions and potential sources of information are identical to the American history questions, except that they deal with history from around the world, which means it dates much further back than does U.S. history.

✔ **Civics and government (25 percent; 12 or 13 questions):** These passages are about civic life, government, politics (especially the American political system), how Americans relate to other countries, and America's role in the world. Your job, if you wish to accept it, is to read and understand the passages and questions about those passages. Material about civics and government is usually found in newspapers and news magazines. If you don't read these regularly and want to look at old issues, visit your public library (or go to your doctor's waiting room). Try to get a sense of what's going on by pretending you want to explain the issue to a friend. (Don't actually do this, though, because you'll probably run out of friends before you run out of issues).

✔ **Economics (20 percent; 10 questions):** Economics is the study of how the earth's resources are used to create wealth, which is then distributed and used to satisfy the needs of mankind. It involves the worlds of banking and finance in both small businesses and large corporations. It includes workers and owners importing and exporting manufactured goods and natural resources and services. You can find sources of economic articles on the Internet and in newspapers, magazines, textbooks, and software programs.

✔ **Geography (15 percent; 7 or 8 questions):** Geography passages usually read like a list of places you want to go. Geography deals with the world and what's going on in it, including the impact of weather and environmental conditions, along with the political divisions of land and its use by living creatures. You have to read maps and answer questions about them. This is a different kind of reading, but with a little practice, it can be fun.

You can find several good geographic magazines with fascinating articles and beautiful photographs. In addition, your public library has books about any and every place on earth. The important thing is to read, read, and read some more just to become comfortable with the language of geography.

# Sources of passages

To see more examples of passages than you may find in this or other test-preparation books, check out the Web sites in this sidebar. If you don't have Internet access at home, try your local library or community center. This information gives you some practice reading the types of materials that will be used on the Social Studies Test. You're not expected to memorize this information, just understand it enough to answer questions about it.

An interesting Web site is http://personal.pit net.net/primarysources. The links provide many interesting primary sources relating to American history, including many originals, sometimes in translation.

www.archives.gov include archives for the U.S. government. This site is chockfull of information and images of every important historical document you can think of — and maybe some you have never thought of. You can even find photographs of some of the original documents to show you how neat handwriting used to be.

www.loc.gov is the Web site of the Library of Congress, an important source for government documents. While you're there, visit http://thomas.loc.gov, a source for bills that go through Congress.

http://supct.law.cornell.edu/supct has recent Supreme Court decisions and includes a glossary of terms. Unfortunately, historical decisions are available only on a CD for a small fee.

www.law.uiuc.edu/fac/rrotunda/www/const.htm has an interesting selection of historical documents for downloading. Try to ignore the first page: The sparkles and flames can become annoying.

www.pueblo.gsa.gov is the home page for the Federal Consumer Information Center, which is just full of links to interesting consumer information.

www.fec.gov is the home page of the Federal Election Commission, with links to the type of material you may be asked to read for civics and government questions.

www.irs.gov/formspubs has forms and material from the Internal Revenue Service. There is enough material here to give you nightmares for weeks.

www.ustreas.gov/budget/ref.htm has a lot of budget material; more than enough to make your head spin.

A good collection of almanacs is at www.infoplease.com/states.html. Follow the links to almanacs. This is a commercial site, so you may see banners and small ads, but the site does have a good collection of almanacs, which is more than we can say about many small libraries.

All the statistical material you can want is available at www.census.gov/main/www/cen2000.html, provided that the material you want concerns the 2000 census. The site provides links to statistical abstracts that you may not have seen before, but may see on the Social Studies Test.

You can find speeches by presidents and comments on speeches by presidents by entering "speeches (name of president)" into any search engine.

The passages in this test are taken from the two following types of sources:

- **Academic material:** The type of material you find in a school — textbooks, maps, newspapers, magazines, software, and Internet material.
- **Workplace material:** The type of material found on the job — manuals, documents, business plans, advertising and marketing materials, correspondence, and so on.

The material may be from *primary* or *secondary* sources, which means the following:

- **Primary sources:** The original documents, such as the Declaration of Independence.
- **Secondary sources:** Material written about an event or person, sometimes long after the event takes place or the person dies.

# Preparing for This Test

To prepare for the Social Studies Test, you want to read as much as possible and also spend time reviewing visual materials (charts, diagrams, graphs, maps, photographs, political cartoons, and artistic works) to figure out what they mean.

## Working with text passages

The more you read, the more you discuss, the more you ask yourself questions about what you have read and reviewed, the better prepared you will be.

Read between the lines, looking at implications and assumptions. An *implication* can be understood from what's written but isn't directly stated. An *assumption* is accepted as the truth, although proof isn't presented in the text.

When you're taking the test, be sure to read each question carefully to know what it's asking for. If you're being asked for facts, they are presented to you. If you're asked for opinions, they may be stated or implied in the passages (and they may disagree with your opinions). Keep in mind that you usually find opinions in text, political cartoons, and works of art.

If you're asked a question that doesn't specifically tell you to use additional information that's not in the passage, use only the information presented. In your opinion, an answer may be incorrect, but according to the information presented, it is correct (or vice versa). Go with the information presented unless told otherwise.

The best way to prepare is to answer all the social studies sample test questions you can get your hands on. Do practice tests (see Chapters 10 and 20), practice questions (see the "Looking at Sample Problems" section later in this chapter), and examples. After each question, check your answer. Make sure you know why your answer is right or wrong. Also, get used to being in a test situation. If you take a full sample test, stick to the time limits exactly.

## Working with visual materials

To make sure that you don't get bored taking this test, only 40 percent of the questions are based on reading material. Another 40 percent is based on maps, graphs, tables, political cartoons, diagrams, photographs, and artistic works. The remaining 20 percent of the questions are based on a combination of visual material and text.

While the 40 percent of visual material may seem overwhelming, consider the following:

- **You're probably familiar with maps.** Travel maps (see Figure 4-1) help you get from place to place. Weather maps help you see what the weather has in store for your area. When you see maps on TV or in a newspaper or magazine, study them carefully.

- **Every time you turn around, someone in the media is trying to make a point with a graph.** The real reason they do this is because a graph can clearly show trends and relationships between sets of information. The next time you see a graph, such as the one in Figure 4-2, study it carefully to see whether you understand what the information is telling you. (Graphs are often also called *charts*.)

- **Tables are everywhere.** If you've ever looked at the nutrition label on a food product, you've read a table. Study any table you can find, whether in a newspaper or on the back of a can of tuna. See Figure 4-3. (Note that tables are also sometimes called *charts*, which can be a little confusing.)

- **Political cartoons appear every day in the newspapers.** If you don't read political cartoons (usually on the Editorial or Op-Ed pages), give them a try. Some days, they're the best entertainment in the paper. Political cartoons are usually based on an event in the last day or week. If you want to get the most out of political cartoons, look for small details, facial expressions, and background clues.

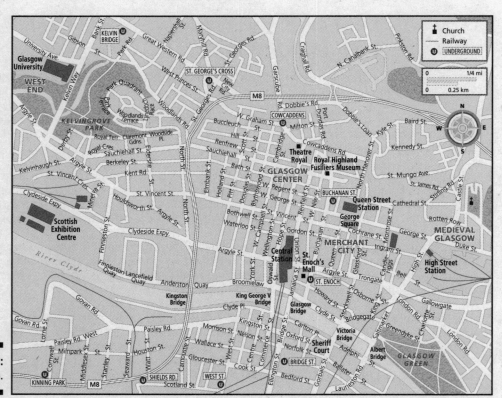

**Figure 4-1:**
Map.

✔ **You've seen photographs.** Photos are all around you. All you need to do is begin getting information from photographs. Start with the newspapers or magazines, where photos are chosen to provide information that connects with a story.

✔ **You probably like to look at works of art.** On the Social Studies Test, you have a chance to "read" works of art. You look at a work of art and gather information you can use in order to answer the question. Aside from art galleries, you can find magazines and books that contain photos of works of art. Some books even give some background or other explanation for these works.

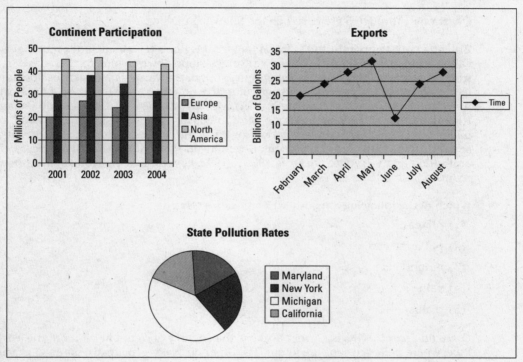

**Figure 4-2:**
Graphs.

**Impact on the Environment**

| Type of Vehicle | MPG | Cost of Resources |
|---|---|---|
| SUV | 12.8 | $3,900 |
| Sedan | 19.6 | $2,400 |
| 2-door | 19.5 | $2,700 |
| All-wheel drive | 17.2 | $3,100 |
| Sports car | 18.6 | $3,300 |

**Figure 4-3:**
Table.

All of the items you're given to review on this test are familiar. Now all you have to do is practice until your skill level increases. Then you, too, can be boring at parties, discussing the latest political cartoon or pontificating about a work of art.

# Looking at Sample Problems

The sample problems in this section give you a taste of what to expect in the practice tests in Parts III and IV of this book.

Remember that the Social Studies Test doesn't measure your ability to recall information, such as dates, facts, or events. It requires you to read a passage, analyze the information, evaluate its accuracy, and draw conclusions according to the printed word or graphics contained in the passage. You then choose the one best answer to each question.

Questions 1 through 5 are based on the following passage.

Bridging both temperate and tropical regions, Mexico's terrain includes mountains, plains, valleys, and plateaus. Snow-capped volcanoes slope down to pine forests, deserts, and balmy tropical beaches. This diverse topography supports a variety of industries, including manufacturing, mining, petroleum, and agricultural production. As a member of the North American Free Trade Agreement (NAFTA), Mexico has the United States and Canada as main trading partners. In economic terms, Mexico boasts a GDP (gross domestic product) of $370 billion ($8,100 per person), which ranks it thirteenth in the world. Mexico currently enjoys an annual growth rate of over 6 percent. Beginning in 1985, Mexico began a process of trade liberalization and privatization. From 1982 to 1992, government-controlled enterprises were reduced from 1,155 to 217.

1. Which of the following are not part of Mexico's terrain?

   (1) plateaus

   (2) polar ice cap

   (3) mountains

   (4) valleys

   (5) plains

*Correct answer:* **2.** This is correct because the country does not lie either at the North or South Pole, where polar ice caps are found. The other answers — plateaus, mountains, valleys, and plains — are mentioned in the passage, but this question asks what's *not* mentioned.

2. Which adjectives demonstrate that the Mexican climate represents extremes in temperature?

   (1) sunny and rainy

   (2) dark and misty

   (3) plains and valleys

   (4) snow-capped and balmy

   (5) forests and deserts

*Correct answer:* **4.** Snow-capped volcanoes represent an extremely low temperature, while balmy beaches refer to the higher temperatures found in a tropical climate. Other adjectives — such as sunny and rainy or dark and misty — don't refer to changes in temperature. Plains and valleys and forests and deserts are nouns that refer to terrain, not temperature.

3. What does diverse topography refer to?

    (1) differences in terrain

    (2) uniqueness in manufacturing

    (3) differences in agriculture

    (4) diversity of tropical beaches

    (5) abundance of petroleum production

*Correct answer:* **1.** *Topography* is another word for terrain. *Diverse* means different. Manufacturing, agriculture, and petroleum production are types of industries. Tropical beaches are just one type of terrain.

4. Which countries are Mexico's trading partners in NAFTA?

    (1) United States and United Kingdom

    (2) France and Germany

    (3) North America

    (4) Canada and the U.K.

    (5) United States and Canada

*Correct answer:* **5.** The United States and Canada joined with Mexico to form the North American Free Trade Agreement, and the text states this. The U.K., France, and Germany are not partners in NAFTA.

5. What happened in Mexico between 1982 and 1992?

    (1) government control of enterprises increased

    (2) the government controlled fewer enterprises

    (3) they achieved the highest GDP in the world

    (4) their growth rate was less than 6 percent

    (5) they won the World Cup

*Correct answer:* **2.** According to the passage, during the decade from 1982 to 1992, Mexico reduced its control of enterprises from 1155 to 217. They did not increase enterprise control, nor did they achieve the highest GDP in the world — 12 countries are higher. Their growth rate was more than 6 percent. Although Mexico would love to win the World Cup in soccer, the passage does not say that happened during the decade.

# Reviewing a Few Rules of the Road

The following rules can serve you well in this test. See Chapter 1 for general rules that apply to all the GED tests.

    ✔ **What's it all about?** When reading passages of text, ask yourself what the passage is all about. The answer is usually in the first or last sentence. If you don't see the answer there, you may have to look carefully through the rest of the passage.

    ✔ **What's it all about (part II)?** When reading maps, charts, graphs, political cartoons, diagrams, photographs, and artistic works, ask yourself what the visual material is all about. Look for the answer in the title, labels, captions, and any other information that's included.

✔ **Now that I have the main idea, what do I do with it?** Some questions ask you to use information from one situation in another. If you know the main idea of the passage, you have an easier time applying it to another situation.

✔ **Know the cause and effect.** A *cause* refers to something that produces a certain outcome or effect. An *effect* is a change or result caused by someone or something. In answering a question about cause and effect, you may find more than one cause for an effect or one cause that results in many effects. Read carefully and try to ensure that there is a cause and effect relationship before you choose to imply one.

✔ **Don't assume.** Don't assume something is true just because it looks that way in a diagram, chart, or a map. Visual materials can be precise drawings, with legends and scales, or can be drawn in such a way that at first glance, the information appears to be different than it is. Verify what you think you see.

# Chapter 5

# From Aardvarks to Atoms: The Science Test

This chapter makes the Science Test format clear. We lift the fog on the different types of questions that may appear on your test. We also help you stay awake for some of the driest material on any of the GED tests.

The Science Test is the same as the other tests and different from the other tests. Although the questions are multiple choice, they are based on text passages or visual images, including charts, diagrams, graphs, maps, and tables.

The Science Test covers material from biology, earth sciences, chemistry, ecology, and space science. You don't need to memorize material from those subjects. Instead, you need to be able to read and understand the material and correctly answer questions about it.

## Understanding the Test Format

This 80-minute test contains 50 multiple-choice questions. The questions are grouped as sets. All the questions in a particular set refer to a given passage, chart, diagram, graph, map, or table. You read or review the material and decide on the best answer for each question.

Remember that answers are scored by a machine. Always follow instructions and fill in the circles fully.

## Types of questions

The test questions are broadly based on the following:

▶ **Physical science (35 percent; 17 or 18 questions):** Physical science is a study of atoms, chemical reactions, forces, and what happens when energy and matter get together. As a basic review, keep the following in mind:

  • Everything is composed of atoms. The paper this book is printed on is composed of atoms.

- When chemicals get together, they have a reaction, unless they are inert.

- You're surrounded by forces and their effects. If the floor didn't exert a force up on you when you stepped down, you would go through the floor.

For more information about physical science (which includes basic chemistry and basic physics), read and review a basic science textbook, which you can borrow from your local library (or from your local high school, if you call the office in advance and ask whether the school has any extras).

- ✔ **Life science (45 percent; 22 or 23 questions):** Life sciences are concerned with cells, heredity, evolution, and other processes that occur in living systems. A biology textbook can help you review.

- ✔ **Earth and space science (20 percent; 10 questions):** This part of science looks at the earth and the universe: weather, astronomy, geology, rocks, erosion, and water.

Because you're answering questions about science materials from information provided in the passages, any science reading you do prior to the test helps you improve your vocabulary.

The Science test uses the NSES (National Science Education Standards) content standards, based on content developed by science educators from across the country. For more specific (and sometimes interesting) information, check out the Web site at www.nap.edu/html/nses/html/.

## Questions about passages

On the test, you're presented with passages that you need to read and understand. Everything you need in order to answer the questions is presented to you in the passages — *but* you have to understand all of the words used (which is why we recommend that you read as much science information as you can prior to the test). In fact, the only difference in the passages in the Science and Language Arts, Reading, and Social Studies Tests is the words used.

Keep the following tips and tricks in mind:

- ✔ Read each passage and question carefully.

  - Try to understand the passage and think about what you already know about the subject.

  - If a passage has only one question, read that question extra carefully.

  - If the passage or question contains words you don't understand, try to figure those words out from the rest of the sentence or the entire passage.

- ✔ Read each answer carefully.

  - If one answer is right from your reading and experience, mark it.

  - If you aren't sure, exclude wrong answers and then exclude possible wrong answers.

  - If you can exclude all but one answer, it is probably correct.

## Questions about tables

A table is a graphical way of organizing information, as shown in Figure 5-1. It allows for easy comparison between two or more sets of data. Some tables use symbols to represent information; others use words to present the data.

**Science Subjects and Learning Time**

| Subject | Time to Prepare (Hours) | Average Grade |
|---------|------------------------|---------------|
| Earth science | 10.8 | A- |
| Biology | 17.6 | B+ |
| Chemistry | 17.5 | B |
| Physics | 25.2 | B- |

**Figure 5-1:** Table.

Each table almost always has a title that tells what it's about. Always read the title first, so that you know what information is presented. If the table gives you an explanation of the symbols, read the explanation carefully, too.

## Questions about graphs

A graph is a picture that shows how sets of numbers are related. You can find three main types of graphs, as shown in Figure 5-2:

- **Bar or column graphs:** Use bars (horizontal) or columns (vertical) to present information. Bar graphs are often used as a comparison.

- **Line graphs:** Use one or more lines to connect points drawn on the grid from information.

- **Pie graphs (also called pie charts or circle graphs):** Use arcs of circles (pieces of a pie) to show how data relates to a whole.

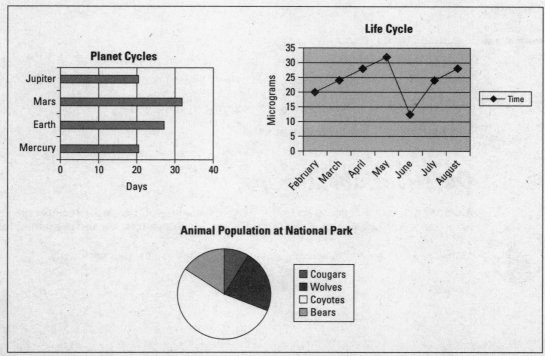

**Figure 5-2:** Graphs.

All three of these types of graphs usually share some common characteristics:

- ✔ **Title:** Tells you what the graph is about. Always read the title before reviewing the graph.

- ✔ **Horizontal axis and vertical axis:** Bar, column, and line graphs have a horizontal and a vertical axis. (Pie graphs do not.) Each *axis* is a vertical or horizontal reference line that's labeled to give you additional information.

- ✔ **Label:** The label on the axis of a graph usually contains units, such as feet or dollars. Be very careful with an axis label. They can help you with the answer or lead you astray.

- ✔ **Legend:** Pie graphs usually give you a *legend* or printed material that tells you what each section of the graph is about. They may also label the pieces of the pie so that you know what each piece represents.

Graphs and tables are often also called *charts,* and these naming inconsistencies can be rather confusing.

## Questions about diagrams

A diagram, such as the one shown in Figure 5-3, is a drawing that helps you understand how something works. If you want to fix your coffee maker, a diagram helps you figure out what has to be done. (It may also convince you that the job is too complex.)

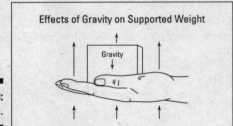

Effects of Gravity on Supported Weight

Gravity

**Figure 5-3:**
Diagram.

Diagrams on the Scinece Test often have the following common components:

- ✔ **Title:** Tells you what the diagram is trying to show you
- ✔ **Labels:** Indicate the names of parts

## Questions about maps

A map is a drawing of some section — large or small — of the earth. Because the entire world is too large to show you on a test, a section of it is drawn to scale and presented to you.

Maps are seldom used in science passages, but they are used occasionally.

Most maps give you the following information:

- **Title:** Tells you what area of the world the map focuses on.
- **Legend:** Gives you general information about the colors, symbols, compass directions, or other graphics used on the map.
- **Labels:** Indicate what the various points on the map represent.
- **Scale:** Tells you what the distance on the chart represents in real life. For example, a map with a scale of 1 inch = 100 miles shows a distance of 500 miles on the real earth as a distance of 5 inches on the map.

# Testing Your Ability to Synthesize Science Information

You're not being tested on your knowledge of science, nor are you expected to memorize information. Instead, you're tested on your skills at ferreting out information presented to you in passages or visual materials, and you answer questions by selecting the correct answer from among five.

If you're totally unfamiliar with science and its vocabulary, you will likely have trouble with the questions. You're expected to have some basic knowledge about how the physical world works, how plants and animals live, and how the universe operates. You're tested on ideas that you observe and develop throughout your life, both in and out of school. You probably know a little about traction, for example, from driving and walking in slippery weather. On the other hand, you may not know a lot about equilibrium except for what you read.

You're expected to understand that science is about inquiry. A good scientist follows these steps when faced with an unknown:

- Ask questions.
- Gather information.
- Do experiments.
- Think objectively about what is found.
- Look at other possible explanations.
- Draw one or more possible conclusions.
- Test the conclusion(s).
- Tell others what you found.

This process is called the *scientific method*.

Look upon your study for the Science Test as a scientific problem. The question is, "How can you increase your scientific knowledge?" Follow the scientific method to come up with a procedure to fix the problem.

The likely answer is read, read, read! A high-school science book will help, as will a preparation book or course that teaches the basics of high-school science.

# Preparing for This Test

To prepare yourself for the Science Test, use the following tips:

✔ **Review science material.** The written passages on this test are very much like a reading comprehension test: You're given material and have to answer questions about it. The difference between this test and other reading comprehension tests is that the terminology and examples are about science. The more you read about science (Chapter 28 gives you some ideas), the more science words you will know, understand, and be comfortable seeing on the test.

✔ **Practice reading graphs, diagrams, maps, and tables.** About half the questions require you to answer questions based on these visual materials, so you need to practice. Always read the titles, scales, keys, labels, and any other information.

✔ **Create your own dictionary.** Get a notebook and keep track of all the new words (and their definitions) that you discover as you study.

Make sure you understand science terminology. Of course, you can't do this overnight. Take time and make sure that they have become part of your brain.

✔ **Take practice tests.** Chapters 12 and 22 give you full-length Science Tests. If you need more, consider purchasing additional preparation manuals that offer sample tests. Take as many of these practice tests as you can. Be strict about time and check your answers when you're finished. If you are unsure about answers, ask a tutor, take a preparation class, or look up the information in a book or on the Internet. Be sure you know why every answer was right or wrong.

# Looking at Sample Problems

Because most of this chapter has been pretty heavy, we're lightening up a bit with these sample problems. In any case, read each question carefully and find the best answer from the passages.

---

## Science on the Internet

Internet sites can increase your scientific knowledge or simply introduce you to a new area of interest. If you don't have an Internet connection at home, try your local library or community center. Check out some of these sites for additional practice in reading science material.

You can find information about life sciences at www.els.net and www.sciencegems.com/life.html, two sites that have links organized by grade level and topic.

NASA has an interesting Web site at www.earth.nasa.gov.

If you're interested in learning about chemistry, try http://chemistry.about.com. This is a commercial site, which means you'll see pesky banners and commercial links, but the information is interesting.

If you don't know much about physics, check out http://physics.webplasma.com/physicstoc.html. It has definitions, formulas, and stuff that physicists like to play with. Also try www.colorado.edu/physics/2000/index.pl. This site contains some interesting physics lessons that are presented in an entertaining and informative manner.

To explore on your own, use science key words (like biology, earth science, and so on) in any search engine.

---

Questions 1 and 2 refer to the following passage.

One of the great discoveries in earth sciences is rocks. Rocks have many useful purposes in science. They can be used as paperweights to keep academic papers from flying away in the wind. Rocks can be used to prop laboratory doors open when the experiments go wrong and horrible smells are produced. Smooth rocks can be rubbed when pressure builds and you just need a mindless activity to get through the day.

1. According to the passage, one of the great discoveries in science was

   (1) atomic energy

   (2) static electricity

   (3) rocks

   (4) nectarines

   (5) DNA

*Correct answer:* **3.** The important words in the question are "According to the passage." When you see this phrase, you know to look in the passage for the answer. Because none of the answers except rocks is even remotely mentioned, it must be the best answer.

2. How do rocks help scientists when experiments go horribly wrong and produce terrible odors?

   (1) they can be used to smash the windows

   (2) they can prop open the doors

   (3) they can be thrown in anger

   (4) they can be rubbed

   (5) only scientists know the answer to this

*Correct answer:* **2.** According to the passage, the rocks can be used to hold open the door of the lab. Rocks can also be used to smash windows and can be thrown in anger, but that's not mentioned in the passage. Rubbing rocks is mentioned in the passage, but in another context.

Questions 3 through 5 refer to the following passage.

Dr. Y. Kritch was a world-famous botanist. He spent his life in search of an early-blooming, colorful spring flower. He first developed the onelip flower, which bloomed so early that it immediately froze in the winter weather. After many years of research, he developed a new strain of flowers called the threelip, which bloomed in the late fall, just after the first frost. Frustrated, he decided to cross-pollinate the two blooms to develop a plant that would bloom in the spring. Using a special cross-averaging-pollination process, he managed to develop a plant that would bloom in the early spring and came in many colors. In honor of the averaging process, he called it a twolip, which was later changed to tulip.

3. Why did Dr. Kritch want to develop a new flower?

   (1) he was bored

   (2) he wanted something named after him

   (3) he wanted to sell the flowers to stores

   (4) he needed a gift for his wife

   (5) not enough information is given

*Correct answer:* **5.** The first four answers are all possible, but not one of them is mentioned in the passage. The only correct answer can be 5, because not very much information is given about the doctor himself.

4. What was wrong with the onelip flower?

   (1) it bloomed so late that everyone was tired of flowers

   (2) it never bloomed at all

   (3) it was an ugly color

   (4) it bloomed too early

   (5) not enough information is given

   *Correct answer:* **4.** The passage states that the onelip bloomed so early that it immediately froze in the winter weather.

5. Based on the information in the passage, what can you assume a botanist does?

   (1) studies the averaging process

   (2) studies plants

   (3) freezes to death

   (4) sells flowers

   (5) not enough information given

   *Correct answer:* **2.** The passage describes how Dr. Kritch studies and develops tulip plants. Although he uses the average process to develop the tulip, the passage doesn't mention that he studies that process. No mention is made of Dr. Kritch selling flowers or freezing to death.

# Reviewing a Few Rules of the Road

Here are a few rules that will serve you well when taking the Science Test. See Chapter 1 for general rules that apply to all GED tests.

- ✔ **Read each question carefully.** Some of the questions on the science test assume that you know a little bit from past experience. The test doesn't expect you to know something like an explanation for nuclear fission, but it may expect you to know that a rocket is propelled forward by an engine firing backward. If you come across a question that assumes knowledge, spend a little extra time making sure that the knowledge you have is the knowledge that's needed.

- ✔ **Read everything.** Read every word and symbol printed on each chart, diagram, graph, map or table. Information — both relevant and irrelevant — is everywhere, and you may need it to answer the question. Don't skip something because it doesn't immediately look important.

- ✔ **Understand graphs and maps.** The *scale* on a graph or map is an important piece of information. Many graphs show relationships. If the scale of the horizontal axis is in millions of dollars and you think it's in dollars, your interpretation of the graph is incorrect.

# Chapter 6

# Reading Between the Lines: The Language Arts, Reading Test

. . . . . . . . . . . . . . . . . . . . . . . . . . . . . . . . . . . . . . . . . . . . .

### In This Chapter

▶ Finding out what the Language Arts, Reading Test is all about

▶ Reviewing the types of passage you may see

▶ Exploring some sample problems

. . . . . . . . . . . . . . . . . . . . . . . . . . . . . . . . . . . . . . . . . . . . .

The Language Arts, Reading Test determines how well you read and understand what you've read. That's pretty much this test in a nutshell, although this chapter gives you more detail about the types of passage that appear on the test.

If you're not a big fan of reading, start with something simple, like a daily newspaper or a weekly news magazine. Every day, switch off the TV for an hour and read something, instead. Gradually advance to how-to books (like this one) and short stories from an *anthology* (a fancy name for a collection of short stories or poems). Eventually, begin reading novels, longer poems, and plays. In order to do well on this test, you have to be in the practice of reading different types of material and comprehending what you read.

## Understanding the Test Format

This 65-minute test has 40 multiple-choice questions in it, ten fewer than the other tests. The questions test whether you can understand and interpret passages presented to you.

Before each passage is a question in bold. This is called a *purpose question* and doesn't have to be answered but is included to help you focus on what's important in the passage. You may also see explanatory notes set off in square brackets [like this].

Passages may come from workplace (on-the-job) materials or from academic reading materials. Thirty of the questions are based on literary texts (plays, poetry, short stories, novels, and so on), and ten are based on non-fiction texts (biographies, reviews, memos, directions, and so on).

Passages are 200 to 400 words long. Poetry passages are from 8 to 25 lines long. After each passage, you're given four to eight multiple-choice questions to answer.

Passages are passages. Although the two following sections describe where they come from so that you can prepare yourself, when taking the test, don't worry so much about what type of passage you're reading. Instead, spend your time reading and understanding what's presented to you.

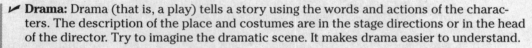

## Reading is reading, right?

Actually, no. You read in different ways and have to choose the best one for each situation:

- You can read the passage as you would a love letter, reading carefully and looking for meaning in each word.

- You can read the passage as you would a newspaper when you're passing time. You skim over the words and stories quickly until you find a word or phrase that interests you.

- You can read the passage as you would the phone book. You have a name in mind and you quickly look for that name before you begin reading carefully.

Whichever way you read the passages, always read the questions first. That way, you have an idea of what you're looking for.

The test material includes literary and non-fiction texts. Practice reading these types of materials and asking yourself questions. The more you practice, the better your skills become.

## Literary passages

Literary text questions include at least one passage from each of the following:

- **Drama:** Drama (that is, a play) tells a story using the words and actions of the characters. The description of the place and costumes are in the stage directions or in the head of the director. Try to imagine the dramatic scene. It makes drama easier to understand.

  Stage directions are usually printed in italics, *like this*. Even though you're not an actor in the play, pay attention to the stage directions. They may provide you with valuable information.

- **Poetry:** Poetry is the concentrated juice of literature. The ideas and emotions are closely packed. Read poetry slowly and carefully. If you do this, poetry does make sense and may be quite beautiful! Enjoy it as much as you can on a test.

- **Prose fiction before 1920:** *Prose fiction* refers to novels and short stories.

- **Prose fiction between 1920 and 1960**

- **Prose fiction after 1960**

The differences between the time periods is usually in the words used and the situations described. Spend your time reading and understanding and don't worry too much about which time period the test passages come from, but do recognize that some passages are newer, and some are older.

## Non-fiction passages

Non-fiction text questions include passages from any two of the following:

- **Critical review of visual and performing arts:** You can find plenty of critical reviews in the newspapers. Read them regularly. The next time you go to a movie, watch television, or go to a play, write your own critical review (what you thought of the piece of work). Put some factual material into your review and make suggestions for improvement. Compare what the critics have to say with your own feelings about the book, movie, or television show. Do you agree with their opinions?

- **Non-fiction prose:** The next time you read the newspaper or a magazine, tell yourself, "I am reading non-fiction prose." Just don't say it out loud in a coffee shop or your break room at work, or people may start to look at you in strange ways.

✔ **Workplace and community documents,** such as the following:

- **Mission statements:** Organizations and companies often write mission statements. These are short statements, telling the world what the company's role is in this world. "I live to party" or "I hate reading" may be your mission statement. Of course, you may have to change that if you want to pass this test.

- **Goal (or vision) statements:** Companies and organizations may also have goal statements. These tell the world what they intend to accomplish. The goal statement for your study group could be as follows: "We're all going to pass the GED tests on our first attempt."

- **Rules for employee behavior:** Every company, school, or organized group has rules of behavior. Some are written down, while others are unspoken but understood. Some of the passages on the Language Arts, Reading test come from real or imaginary rules of behavior. You probably already know how to read these.

- **Legal documents:** Legal documents are drafted by lawyers and may include leases, purchase contracts, and bank statements.

    If you're not familiar with legal documents, collect some from banks or libraries and review them. If you can explain these types of documents to a friend, you understand them.

- **Letters:** It is not very often that you get to read other people's letters without getting into trouble. Here's your chance.

- **Manuals:** Every time you invest in a major purchase, you usually get a manual that tells you how to use the item. Some of them are short and straightforward; others are long and complicated. It took me so long to read the manual that came with my new camera that I thought my hobby was reading manuals, not photography.

# Preparing for This Test

To prepare for the Language Arts, Reading Test, keep the following tips in mind:

✔ **Read.** Read whatever you have available, but also look for the specific types of texts that are discussed in the preceding section. Become a reading addict. Read labels, cereal boxes, novels, magazines, poems, plays, short stories, and newspapers. Read everything and anything. And don't just stop with reading — also digest and think about everything you read, just as you're asked to do on this test. Ask yourself questions about what you've read. Do you understand it well enough to explain it to a stranger?

Ask for help if you don't understand something. You may want to form a study group and work with other people. If you're taking a test-preparation course, ask the instructor. If you have family, friends, or co-workers who can help, ask them.

✔ **Use a dictionary.** Not many people understand every word they read, so use a dictionary whenever you can. Looking up unfamiliar words increases your vocabulary, which makes passages on the Language Arts, Reading Test easier to understand. Plus, it improves your Scrabble game.

✔ **Use new words.** A new word doesn't usually become part of your vocabulary until you put it to use in your everyday language.

✔ **Practice.** Practice taking the Language Arts, Reading Tests in Chapters 14 and 24. Do the questions and check your answers. Look for explanations of the answers. Don't leave an answer until you understand it. If you want more sample tests, look for additional test-prep books at your bookstore or local library.

Take as many practice tests as you can. Stick to the time limits and keep the situation as realistic as possible. When you go to the test center for the official test, you will have done it before. Familiarity breeds ease.

You're not being tested on anything but reading. There are no tricks. The information you need in order to answer the question is given in the passage. You're not expected to recognize the passage and answer questions about what came before or what comes after. The passages are complete in themselves.

Many people get hung up on the poetry and drama. These are just different ways of telling a story and conveying feelings. If you're not familiar with these types of literary texts, read poems and plays before taking this test. Discuss what you have read with others; in fact, consider joining (or starting) a book club that discusses poems and/or plays.

# Looking at Sample Problems

The following passage and sample problems give you some idea of what the Language Arts, Reading Test questions look like.

Choose the one best answer to each question. Questions 1 through 5 refer to the following passage.

### Does Employment Need a New FACE?

Facilities for Access to Creative Enterprise (FACE)

Originally founded in 1982 to train unemployed youth in small "handskill" craft workshops, this project provides occupational and entrepreneurial skills as an alternative to traditional manufacturing jobs. Beginning with glass engraving and signwriting, FACE now offers training in more than 200 handskill occupations, including antique restoration, clothing manufacture, graphic design, masonry, sail-making, specialist joinery, weaving, and wood turning. Funded through the Youth Training Scheme, FACE provides 800 training places in the west and northeast of England under the premise that even if the young people can't secure employment, they at least will have the skills to create their own businesses.

Based on its experience, FACE has developed, with the Royal Society of Arts, a Certificate in Small Business and Enterprise Skills. The aim of the certificate is "to develop the basic skills of enterprise across a range of occupational sectors, within small business and in general employment and which are applicable in a wide range of personal and social contexts outside work." Competencies include self-evaluation, decision-making, initiative-taking, resource and time management, opportunism and self-motivation, problem-solving, and learning-to-learn skills, as well as communication and number skills vital to personal effectiveness.

1. What is the overall purpose of the FACE project?

   (1) to provide manufacturing jobs

   (2) to engrave glass

   (3) to train unemployed youth

   (4) to write signs

   (5) to restore antiques

*Correct answer:* **3.** The overall purpose of the FACE project is to train unemployed youth. Glass engraving, sign writing, and antique restoring are just some of the skills they may learn. Manufacturing jobs are in short supply, resulting in the need for entrepreneurial skills.

2. What answer is not an example of a handskill craft occupation?

    (1) weaving

    (2) wood-turning

    (3) sail-making

    (4) specialist joiner

    (5) robotic assembly

*Correct answer:* **5.** Robotic assembly is a high-tech computer-assisted approach to manufacturing that seeks to replace workers with robots. The other answers — weaving, wood-turning, sail-making and joining (carpentry) — are all examples of handskill craft occupations.

3. How can young people best secure employment in the northeast of England?

    (1) engaging in traditional manufacturing

    (2) creating new enterprises

    (3) joining the Royal Society of Arts

    (4) obtaining a Certificate in Small Business

    (5) 800 training places

*Correct answer:* **2.** The best way for youth to secure employment is "create new enterprises." Jobs are being lost in traditional manufacturing. The Royal Society, Business Certificate, and training places don't refer directly to securing employment.

4. Who helped FACE develop the Certificate in Small Business and Enterprise Skills?

    (1) Youth Training Scheme

    (2) west and northeast England

    (3) handskill workshops

    (4) Royal Society of the Arts

    (5) occupational sectors

*Correct answer:* **4.** The Royal Society of the Arts assisted FACE in developing the Certificate. The Youth Training Scheme, while providing funding for FACE, was not directly involved with the Certificate. Handskill workshops and occupational sectors have no direct relation to the Certificate. West and northeast England refers only to locations.

5. Which competency is not included in training for the Certificate?

    (1) self-evaluation

    (2) anger management

    (3) decision-making

    (4) problem-solving

    (5) number skills

*Correct answer:* **2.** Anger management was not mentioned as one of the competencies, while the other skills were included.

# Reviewing a Few Rules of the Road

Here are a few rules that will serve you well on this test. See Chapter 1 for additional rules that apply to all the tests.

- **Look at the purpose question.** Before every passage is a purpose question. Read it. This question doesn't have to be answered, but it gives you a direction for reading the passage. Take any clues that you can get.

- **Read carefully.** If reading poetry and drama are unfamiliar, read them even more carefully. The more carefully you read any material, the easier it will be for you to get the right answers.

- **Ferret out the meaning of new words from the surrounding text.** Even the best readers sometimes come to a word that they don't recognize or understand. Luckily, the sentence around a new word can give you clues to the meaning of the word. Ask yourself, "What word would make sense in place of the one I don't know?"

- **Recognize that everything's important.** In this test, information may be hiding in many places. It may be in explanatory notes set off in square brackets [like this]. It may be hiding in stage directions, usually printed in italics, *like this*. It may be hidden in the speaker's name before the dialogue. Read everything and skip nothing.

# Chapter 7

# Safety in Numbers:
# The Mathematics Test, Parts I and II

................................................................

................................................................

**W**elcome to the dreaded Mathematics Tests. Although you may have done everything to avoid math in high school, you can't escape this test. This is the one test that test-takers have nightmares about, but this chapter helps you prepare.

Most of the questions in the other GED tests are about reading comprehension: You're given a passage and are expected to understand it well enough to correctly answer the questions that follow. Although you can prepare for the other tests by doing a lot of reading and taking sample tests, you don't have to come in with a lot of knowledge or great skill in the test area.

The Mathematics Tests, however, test your math abilities, so you have to spend time solving as many problems and improving your math skills as much as possible. This chapter gives you some tips and tricks for studying for the GED Mathematics Tests.

## Understanding the Test Format

This 90-minute test has two parts, each with 25 questions. Part I allows you to use a calculator. Part II bans the calculator in favor of your brain. (You're given scratch paper to use for rough calculations.) You have to pass both parts to pass this test.

The Mathematics Tests are different from all the other tests in the GED. Why? Because you have different ways of answering the questions. We run through them all in the sections that follow.

A formula sheet is provided for you to use during the test. You may not need all the formulas provided, and you may not need a formula for every question. Part of the fun of the mathematics test is knowing when you really need a formula and which formula to use.

## Multiple-choice questions

Multiple choice is the old standby for questions. Most of the questions in the GED tests are multiple choice. You're given five possible answers, and you choose one. Most of the multiple-choice questions on the Mathematics Tests give you some information or show you a figure and ask you to solve the problem. In addition, you may also see a few special types of questions:

✔ **Set-up questions:** These questions don't expect you to calculate a specific answer but ask you what steps you *would* take to solve them. Before you declare this to be your favorite type of question, keep in mind that you still have to choose the correct way to solve the problem. You just get to skip the final step.

✔ **Not sufficient information questions:** These questions don't give you enough information to calculate a specific answer. The only right answer is "not enough information given." Only four percent of the answers are of this type, so if you answer more than two questions this way, you may not be looking at the questions carefully enough.

If you're given more information than you need, ignore the extra. However, double check that the information you think is extra is really extra before you ignore it.

Because you're assessed no penalty for guessing, if you don't know the answer, guess. While you can't get a point for a blank answer, you can get a point for eliminating all but the most possible answer and marking it.

# Alternate-format questions

Alternate-format questions ask you to calculate the answer without choosing from five possible answers. You write down real numbers or fill in actual graphs. Because the Mathematics Tests are machine marked, you can't just write down numbers. Instead, you use an *alternate-format grid,* which comes in one of two flavors (see the two following sections).

Ten questions, seven in Part I and three in Part II, require recording your answer on an alternate-format grid. Don't panic: These are just ways of recording your answers, not part of a torture test. Read and follow the instructions, and you should do well.

### Standard grid

Questions that give you a standard grid are very similar to multiple-choice questions except that you aren't given five answers to choose from. When you come up with your answer, you write it on the standard grid, as shown in Figure 7-1, both writing in the number and filling in the corresponding circles below the numbers. (If you don't fill in the circles, you can't get a point for your answer.)

Before

After

**Figure 7-1:** Standard grid.

If you're asked to enter an answer on a standard grid that contains a *mixed number* (a whole number and a fraction), convert your answer to a decimal before entering it on a grid. You convert to a decimal by dividing the top number of the fraction by the bottom number and adding that decimal to the whole number; for example, 1¾ becomes 1.75. If, on the other hand, your answer is an *improper fraction* (one in which the top number is larger than the bottom number), you have the choice of entering the number this way on the grid or converting it to a decimal and entering that number.

No answer entered on a standard grid can be negative. If you come up with an answer that's a negative number that has to be entered on a standard grid, check your calculations: It's wrong.

### Coordinate-plane grid

Coordinate-plane grid questions are mostly geometry problems. Take a look at the coordinate-plane grid in Figure 7-2.

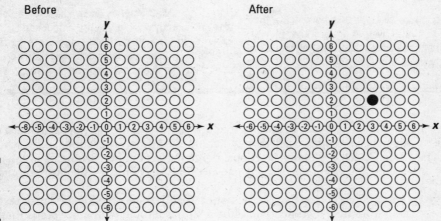

Before      After

**Figure 7-2:**
Coordinate-plane grid.

The coordinate-plane grid is a two-dimensional graph with circles placed at regular points. You indicate your answer by filling in a circle to indicate a point.

The best way to prepare for questions that ask you to fill in a coordinate-plane grid is to practice geometry questions (see the "Geometry" section, later in this chapter). If you can borrow a high-school geometry textbook, you'll have your fill of sample questions. Just be sure you understand the answers, too.

Answering on a coordinate-plane grid is tricky in only one respect. You must fill in the circles completely. Around your GED test-taking day(s), consider it national *be kind to machines day*.

## Questions with a calculator

Part I of the mathematics test lets you use a calculator — not just any calculator, but a very special one supplied to you for the test. This calculator may seem like a real bonus, but you have to return it. The Mathematics Tests use the Casio FX-260 solar calculator. If you're calculator-phobic or worried about using a scientific calculator, try to get one to practice with before the test. The GED Testing Service, which produces the GED, claims that the Casio FX-260 solar calculator is not an expensive calculator, so shop around.

## Help for the calculator-deprived

The Casio FX-260 is a scientific calculator. This doesn't mean it wears a white lab coat. Instead, it's capable of performing advanced scientific and mathematical calculations.

The display has ten large numbers and two small numbers. The large numbers are the numbers you're used to seeing on any regular calculator. The two small numbers to the right represent the exponent of a number written in scientific notation. For example, in the number $5.5 \times 10^3$, the $^3$ is an *exponent* and represents the number of times that 10 is multiplied by itself.

This calculator is accurate to 11 digits, which means that if you multiply 10 numbers by 10 numbers, the answer will be too large to appear on the display. The calculator rounds off the answer to 11 digits.

The Casio calculator performs operations in a specific order: First numbers within brackets, and then exponents. After that, it multiplies, then divides, then adds, and then subtracts.

You can remember this order by remembering the mnemonic, "**B**etty **e**ats **m**ore **d**uck **a**t **s**upper."

Remember that the FX-260 is a solar calculator. Don't cover the four dark rectangles at the top of the calculator. They need to catch the light to provide the energy to run the calculator.

During the Mathematics Test, the test administrator explains exactly how to use the calculator. Listen to this explanation. If you do not understand, that's the time to ask questions. The sample tests in Chapters 16 and 26 of this book also give explanations of how to use the calculator.

You're probably familiar with calculators that add, subtract, multiply, and divide. The Casio FX-260, however, is a *scientific calculator,* which does all those operations and a whole lot more. The Casio FX-260 calculates fractions, percents, exponents, problems involving parentheses, and so on. You won't necessarily use all of the keys on the calculator, though.

Being given a calculator to use in a Mathematics Test has a down side. Because test takers can use a calculator, the questions tend to be a bit harder and with more steps than in the non-calculator part. However, in general, if you know how to set up the problems, the calculator makes them easier for you.

The most important things you can do for the Mathematics Tests are practice and prepare. (In case you were wondering, the first most important thing is to prepare, and the second is to practice.)

## *Questions without a calculator*

You can fool everybody at the GED tests by bringing the calculator you were born with — that's right, your brain. You're given scratch paper on the test, but the more questions you practice in your head, the easier the non-calculator test questions will be. Here are some tips for solving problems in your head:

- ✔ When you go shopping, add up the items as they go in the cart.
- ✔ Calculate discounts when you shop.
- ✔ Be the first at your table in a restaurant to figure out the tip.

Sometimes, for multiple-choice questions, it is easier and faster to estimate the answer to a question. For example, $4.2 \times 8.9$ is almost $4 \times 9$, which equals 36. If you see one answer that's close to 36 and the rest aren't, that answer is probably correct. If you see five answers that are near 36, however, you need to spend time calculating the answer.

# Testing Your Math Skills

What's being tested on the Mathematics Tests? The short answer is, mathematics.

The Mathematics Tests assess your knowledge in the following areas:

- ✔ Measurement
- ✔ Algebra
- ✔ Geometry
- ✔ Number relations
- ✔ Data Analysis

Now is the time to chant the prime directive: Don't panic! These areas are discussed in detail in the following sections.

Basic arithmetic is everywhere in the Mathematics Tests. While you don't see "arithmetic" listed as one of the areas in which you should have knowledge, you can't pass the Mathematics Tests without knowing how to add, subtract, multiply, and divide numbers, decimals, and fractions. To do this requires practice. If someone wakes you in the middle of the night and asks, "What's 3 times 7?" your first words should be "21!" Your second words may be much stronger, but we leave that up to you.

If you aren't confident and fast with the multiplication tables, use flashcards. Either buy them or make your own. You can also make flashcards for fractions, if that's not a strong area for you.

Without good arithmetic skills, you stand little chance of passing the GED exams.

## Measurement

You use measurement every day. You can measure your height, your weight, or your waistline. You can measure your age in years, months, or days. When you cook, you may use measurement to reproduce a recipe exactly. When you want to paint a room, measuring helps you decide how much paint to buy.

---

## Reviewing equivalent measures

The GED Mathematics Test uses English (not metric) measurements. You may want to memorize the following equivalent measures:

- ✔ 12 inches = 1 foot
- ✔ 3 feet = 1 yard
- ✔ 5,280 feet = 1 mile
- ✔ 1,760 yards = 1 mile

- ✔ 16 ounces = 1 pound
- ✔ 2,000 pounds = 1 ton
- ✔ 8 ounces = 1 cup
- ✔ 2 cups = 1 pint
- ✔ 2 pints = 1 quart
- ✔ 4 quarts = 1 gallon

In the Mathematics Tests, you encounter problems having to do with measuring things and calculating answers from the measurements. In these problems, double-check that the answer makes sense in real life.

1. A wall is 20 feet long and 8 feet high. If all of it is to be painted with two coats of blue paint, how many square feet of wall have to be covered?

    (1) 56

    (2) 160

    (3) 230

    (4) 320

    (5) 40

*Correct answer:* **4.** The area of the wall is $20 \times 8 = 160$ square feet. Each coat requires 160 square feet, but because it's going to be painted with two coats, the answer is $2 \times 160 = 320$.

## Number relations

You use number relations all the time. Number relations are the ways that numbers relate to one another. They include the basic operations of addition, subtraction, multiplication, and division and include estimation in both academic settings and real-life settings (going to the grocery store, dealing with a bank account, and so on).

2. Barry earns $1,730 per month, after taxes. Each month, he spends $900 for rent and $600 for living expenses, like food and utilities. How much does he have left over to buy luxuries and spend on entertainment?

    (1) $170

    (2) $230

    (3) $390

    (4) $320

    (5) $180

*Correct answer:* **2.** Barry spends $900 + $600 = $1500 for rent and living expenses. He has $1730 − $1500 = $230 left over.

## Data analysis

Data analysis is the favorite occupation of sports fans. If you analyze numbers, read statistics, or figure out average scores, you have analyzed data. Have you ever done any of the following?

  ✔ Argued over a player's batting average

  ✔ Asked about the odds on a game

  ✔ Looked at a graph in an ad for interest rates on a loan

  ✔ Worried about your average in school

If so, you've analyzed data.

3. On Monday, Mary walked 12 blocks. On Tuesday, she walked 10 blocks, and on Wednesday, she walked 14 blocks. If she wants to beat her average trip for those three days on Thursday, at least how many blocks must she walk?

    (1) 10

    (2) 11

    (3) 12

    (4) 13

    (5) 14

*Correct answer:* **4.** Her average trip for those three days was $(12 + 10 + 14) \div 3 = 36 \div 3 = 12$ blocks. In order to beat her average, she has to walk 13 blocks. If she walks 12 blocks, she will *equal* (not beat) her average trip.

## Algebra

Algebra lets you solve puzzles. Just to make solving these puzzles easier for you, algebra has sets of rules (or patterns). You get to work with *variables,* quantities (often called $x$) that can assume any value, and solve *equations,* expressions of the equality of two mathematical numbers or variables. In a world where not too much ever gets solved, equations can be a lot of fun.

Keep the following simple rules of algebra in mind:

> ✔ You can represent an unknown quantity with a variable. For example, if you know that 3 times the cost of an item is $15, you can represent the cost of the item by $x$.

> ✔ You can write a statement in algebra the same way you write it in English. If the cost of an item is $x$ and 3 times the cost is $15, you can write $3x = 15$.

> ✔ Whatever you do to one side of an equation, you must do to the other side. If you write the equation $4x = 16$, you can also write $8x = 32$. They're the same because you multiplied both sides by 2.

4. Solve the following equation for $x$: $3x + 12 = 24$

    (1) 12

    (2) 24

    (3) 3

    (4) 4

    (5) 36

*Correct answer:* **4.** If $3x + 12 = 24$, you can subtract 12 from both sides so that $3x = 24 - 12$, or $3x = 12$, or $x = 4$.

## Algebra rules!

People have been using algebra for about 4,000 years. Ancient Babylonians, Egyptians, Hindus, and Greeks solved algebraic problems. And they had to solve them without calculators, computers, or ball-point pens. You have it easy!

## Geometry

People have used geometry to construct buildings and measure land for thousands of years. Like most other things mathematical, geometry has rules and formulas. After you understand these rules and formulas, using them becomes easier. It takes only time and practice.

Keep these basic rules of geometry in mind:

- ✔ The study of geometry is also the study of formulas, theorems, and postulates. To find out more about them, borrow a good high-school geometry book from your local library or high school. On the Mathematics Test, however, if you need to reference any of these rules, they're given to you.

- ✔ You can draw pictures of geometric problems using a graph.
  - The horizontal line is called the *x*-axis.
  - The vertical line is called the *y*-axis.

- ✔ The location of any point on the graph is described by writing down its distance to the right or left of the *y*-axis (along the *x*-axis), followed by its distance above or below the *x*-axis (along the *y*-axis). (–3,6) means 3 units to the left of the *y*-axis and 6 units above the *x*-axis.

5. Where would all the points with an *x*-coordinate of –4 be located?

    (1) 4 units above the *x*-axis

    (2) 4 units to the left of the *x*-axis

    (3) 4 units from the *y*-axis

    (4) 4 units above the *y*-axis

    (5) 4 units to the left of the *y*-axis

*Correct answer:* **5.** All points with *x*-coordinates that are negative are located to the left of the *y*-axis (the vertical axis). If a point has an *x*-coordinate of –4, it's located on a line 4 units to the left of the *y*-axis.

# Preparing for This Test

You can do some specific tasks that help prepare you for the Mathematics Tests:

- ✔ **Master arithmetic fundamentals.** About half the test depends on basic arithmetic (addition, subtraction, multiplication, division, decimals, and fractions). The better you know the fundamentals, the better you can handle this test.

- ✔ **Understand how to solve problems.** You can solve mathematical problems using a few rules. The more problems you solve, the more natural solving problems will become. Borrow or buy as many math books as you can and use the sample questions in them. (Be sure to get one that has answers in the back.) Check every answer immediately after you work the question. If you answered it wrong, figure out why. If you can't answer it, ask someone to explain it to you. It's never silly to let people know that you want to learn.

- ✔ **Understand the rules of math.** Textbooks are full of rules, theorems, hypotheses, and so on. Read them over and try to explain each one to a friend. If you can explain the Pythagorean Relationship to a friend or significant other and he or she understands it, you have mastered the relationship. If you can't explain it, ask someone to help you.

✔ **Take practice tests.** See Chapters 16 and 26 for two full-length practice tests. If that's not enough, buy or borrow additional test-prep books that include sample Mathematics Tests. Be strict about time. After checking your answers, figure out the correct answers for any mistakes you made.

The only part of the test you can't duplicate is the feeling of sitting in the examination room just before you start the test. But the more practice tests you take, the more comfortable you will become.

# Reviewing a Few Rules of the Road

Here are a few rules that will serve you well in this test. For several more general rules about the GED tests, see Chapter 1.

✔ **Knowing what to do with extra information:** Some mathematics questions provide you with extra information. Just use what you need and ignore the rest.

✔ **Handling questions with not enough information:** Some mathematics questions don't give you enough information to answer the question. Then your only answer can be "not enough information given." If this answer isn't available, you missed something. Go back and try again.

✔ **Making assumptions:** Don't assume something is true on this test just because it looks that way in a figure. If something is true, you're specifically told that it's true.

# Part III
# A Set of Full-Length Practice Tests

The 5th Wave    By Rich Tennant

I'm always surprised at the amount of Language Arts inspired by the Mathematics Test of the GED.

# In this part . . .

In this part, you find questions, questions, and more questions — but you also get answers and explanations to those questions.

Before taking the actual GED tests, take these as practice to determine how well you've mastered the required skills. Pretend they're real tests by timing yourself, following the instructions, and (if you can find someone willing to help), asking someone to act as the test administrator to keep you honest. The closer you come to mimicking the real test conditions, the more you get out of practicing.

# Chapter 8

# The Language Arts, Writing Test: Parts I and II

## Language Arts, Writing Test: Part 1

### Directions

The Language Arts, Writing Test measures your ability to use clear and effective English. It is a test of English as it should be written, not as it may be spoken. This test includes both multiple-choice questions and an essay. The following directions apply only to the multiple-choice section; a separate set of directions is given for the essay.

The multiple-choice section consists of documents with lettered paragraphs and numbered sentences. Some of the sentences contain an error in sentence structure, usage, or mechanics (punctuation and capitalization). After reading the numbered sentences, answer the multiple-choice questions that follow. Some questions refer to sentences that are correct as written. The best answer for these questions is the one that leaves the sentence as originally written. The best answer for some questions is the one that produces a document that is consistent with the verb tense and point of view used throughout the text.

You have 120 minutes (two hours) to complete both parts of the test. You can spend up to 75 minutes on the 50 multiple-choice questions, leaving the remaining time for the essay. Work carefully, but do not spend too much time on any one question. Answer every question. You will not be penalized for incorrect answers. You may begin working on the essay section of this test as soon as you complete the multiple-choice section.

Do not mark in this test booklet. Record your answers on the separate answer sheet provided. To record your answers, fill in the numbered circle on the answer sheet that corresponds to the answer you select for each question in the test booklet.

Go on to next page

**EXAMPLE:**

Sentence 1: **We were all honored to meet governor Phillips and his staff.**

Which correction should be made to sentence 1?

(1)  change <u>were</u> to <u>was</u>

(2)  insert a comma after <u>honored</u>

(3)  change <u>governor</u> to <u>Governor</u>

(4)  insert a comma after <u>Phillips</u>

(5)  no correction is necessary

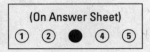

In this example, the word "governor" should be capitalized;
therefore, answer space 3 would be marked on the answer sheet.

Do not rest the point of your pencil on the answer sheet while you are considering your answer. Make no stray or unnecessary marks. If you change an answer, erase your first mark completely. Mark only one answer space for each question; multiple answers will be scored as incorrect. Do not fold or crease your answer sheet. All test materials must be returned to the test administrator.

**DO NOT BEGIN TAKING THIS TEST UNTIL TOLD TO DO SO**

**WRITING TEST: Part I**

1  ① ② ③ ④ ⑤

2  ① ② ③ ④ ⑤

3  ① ② ③ ④ ⑤

4  ① ② ③ ④ ⑤

5  ① ② ③ ④ ⑤

6  ① ② ③ ④ ⑤

7  ① ② ③ ④ ⑤

8  ① ② ③ ④ ⑤

9  ① ② ③ ④ ⑤

10 ① ② ③ ④ ⑤

11 ① ② ③ ④ ⑤

12 ① ② ③ ④ ⑤

13 ① ② ③ ④ ⑤

14 ① ② ③ ④ ⑤

15 ① ② ③ ④ ⑤

16 ① ② ③ ④ ⑤

17 ① ② ③ ④ ⑤

18 ① ② ③ ④ ⑤

19 ① ② ③ ④ ⑤

20 ① ② ③ ④ ⑤

21 ① ② ③ ④ ⑤

22 ① ② ③ ④ ⑤

23 ① ② ③ ④ ⑤

24 ① ② ③ ④ ⑤

25 ① ② ③ ④ ⑤

26 ① ② ③ ④ ⑤

27 ① ② ③ ④ ⑤

28 ① ② ③ ④ ⑤

29 ① ② ③ ④ ⑤

30 ① ② ③ ④ ⑤

31 ① ② ③ ④ ⑤

32 ① ② ③ ④ ⑤

33 ① ② ③ ④ ⑤

34 ① ② ③ ④ ⑤

35 ① ② ③ ④ ⑤

36 ① ② ③ ④ ⑤

37 ① ② ③ ④ ⑤

38 ① ② ③ ④ ⑤

39 ① ② ③ ④ ⑤

40 ① ② ③ ④ ⑤

41 ① ② ③ ④ ⑤

42 ① ② ③ ④ ⑤

43 ① ② ③ ④ ⑤

44 ① ② ③ ④ ⑤

45 ① ② ③ ④ ⑤

46 ① ② ③ ④ ⑤

47 ① ② ③ ④ ⑤

48 ① ② ③ ④ ⑤

49 ① ② ③ ④ ⑤

50 ① ② ③ ④ ⑤

Questions 1 through 10 refer to the following business letter.

**BETA Café Equipment, Inc.**
**700 Millway Avenue, Unit 6**
**Concord, MA 12345**

John Charles
Executive Director
American Specialty Coffee Association
425 Pacific Drive, Suite 301
San Diego, CA 56789

Dear Mr. Charles:

(A)

(1) Thank you for you're interest in our new company, which serves the rapidly expanding specialty coffee industry. (2) BETA Café Equipment, Inc. were formed in 2002 to provide an affordable source of reconditioned Italian espresso/cappuccino machines for new businesses entering the industry.

(B)

(3) During our first year of operation BETA plans to repair and recondition 500 machines for use in restaurants and cafés. (4) This will generate revenue of more then $1,000,000. (5) Almost half a million dollars will be created for returning thirteen jobs to the local economy.

(C)

(6) BETA will purchase used equipement, which will be shipped to our centralized repair and reconditioning depot. (7) After total rebuilding, equipment will be forwarded to regional sales offices to be sold to local restaurants and cafés at a much lower price than comparable new equipment. (8) Entrepreneurs wishing to start new specialty coffee businesses particularly should be interested in our products.

(D)

(9) To learn more about BETA please consult our Web site at www.betace.com or give us a call at our toll-free number, 1-800-TRY-BETA. (10) Any assistence you can provide in sharing this information with your membership will be very much appreciated.

Yours truly,

Edwin Dale, President

*Go on to next page*

1.  Sentence 1: **Thank you for you're interest in our new company, which serves the rapidly expanding specialty coffee industry.**

    What is correction should be made to sentence 1?

    (1) change you're to your

    (2) place a comma after serves

    (3) change interest to concern

    (4) insert but after rapidly

    (5) place expanding before rapidly

2.  Sentence 2: **BETA Café Equipment, Inc. were formed in 2002 to provide an affordable source of reconditioned Italian espresso/cappuccino machines for new businesses entering the industry.**

    What is the best way to write the underlined portion of this sentence?

    (1) was being formed

    (2) had formed

    (3) was formed

    (4) is formed

    (5) have been formed

3.  Sentence 3: **During our first year of operation BETA plans to repair and recondition 500 machines for use in restaurants and cafés.**

    What correction should be made to sentence 3?

    (1) insert a colon after operation

    (2) insert a comma after operation

    (3) insert a comma after recondition

    (4) insert a semi colon after machines

    (5) place a question mark after cafés

4.  Sentence 4: **This will generate revenue of more then $1,000,000.**

    What correction should be made to sentence 4?

    (1) change $1,000,000 to $100,000

    (2) change generate to genarate

    (3) insert about after will

    (4) replace will with may

    (5) change then to than

5.  Sentence 5: **Almost half a million dollars will be created returning thirteen new jobs to the local economy.**

    The most effective revision of sentence 5 would begin with which group of words?

    (1) Thirteen new jobs will be created, returning

    (2) Half a million dollars will be created almost

    (3) Created will be thirteen new jobs almost

    (4) Almost half a million jobs will be created

    (5) no correction needed

6.  Sentence 6: **BETA will purchase used equipement, which will be shipped to our centralized repair and reconditioning depot.**

    What correction should be made to sentence 6?

    (1) change repair to repare

    (2) insert a colon after purchase

    (3) change equipement to equipment

    (4) replace depot with depote

    (5) insert a comma after repair

7.  Sentence 7: **After total rebuilding, equipment will be forwarded to regional sales offices to be sold to local restaurants and cafés at a much lower price than comparable new equipment.**

    Which is the best way to rewrite the underlined portion of this sentence?

    (1) will forward

    (2) be forwarded

    (3) forwarded

    (4) will be

    (5) no correction needed

*Go on to next page*

8.  Sentence 8: **Entrepreneurs wishing to start new specialty coffee <u>businesses particularly should be interested</u> in our products.**

    What correction should be made to the underlined portion?

    (1) businesses should particularly be interested

    (2) businesses should be particularly interested

    (3) businesses particularly should be interested

    (4) businesses should be interested particularly

    (5) particularly businesses should be interested

9.  Sentence 9: **To learn more about BETA please consult our Web site at** `www.betace.com` **or give us a call at our toll-free number, 1-800-TRY-BETA.**

    Which addition should be made to sentence 9?

    (1) no correction required

    (2) insert a colon after web-site

    (3) insert a comma after please

    (4) insert a comma after BETA

    (5) insert a period after `www.betace.com`

10. Sentence 10: **Any assistence you can provide in sharing this information with your membership will be very much appreciated.**

    Which correction should be made to sentence 10?

    (1) change <u>membership</u> to <u>member</u>

    (2) insert a comma after <u>provide</u>

    (3) change <u>appreciated</u> to <u>appreciate</u>

    (4) change <u>assistence</u> to <u>assistance</u>

    (5) change <u>you</u> to <u>I</u>

*Go on to next page*

Questions 11 through 20 refer to the following prospectus.

**Marketing**

(A)

(1) BETAs product is reconditioned Italian café equipment.

(2) The initial's priority will be espresso/cappuccino machines.

(3) There are four ways of marketing the reconditioned machines

    (a) direct sales

    (b) sales through a network of distributors

    (c) leasing directly

    (d) leasing through a network of distributors

(4) Direct sales and leasing will take time, because establishing a network of distributors will be the priority in year one.

(5)   In order for BETA to be successful, a trained workforce are essential.

(6)   A secondary business will be reconditioning machines too order.

**Sales**

(B)

(7) All estimates for potential units reconditioned and soled or leased are conservative.

(8) The initial mix of leasing and sales is estimated to be 20 percent leasing and 80 percent sales for the first year.

**Raw Material**

(C)

(9) The average trade-in for an espresso machine will be $75, while the average price for used machines will be $250.

(10) Twenty percent of the machines acquired will be trade-ins, the balance will be purchased.

*Go on to next page*

11.  Sentence 1: **BETAs product is recondi-
     tioned Italian café equipment.**

     Which correction should be made to
     sentence 1?

     (1)  insert an apostrophe before the s in
          BETAs

     (2)  change <u>Italian</u> to <u>italian</u>

     (3)  replace <u>is</u> with <u>are</u>

     (4)  insert a comma after <u>reconditioned</u>

     (5)  change <u>reconditioned</u> to <u>recondition</u>.

12.  Sentence 2: **The initial's priority will be
     espresso/cappuccino machines.**

     Which change should be made to
     sentence 2?

     (1)  insert <u>to</u> after <u>will</u>

     (2)  replace <u>will</u> with <u>may</u>

     (3)  change <u>priority</u> to <u>prior</u>

     (4)  change <u>initial's</u> to <u>initial</u>

     (5)  no correction needed

13.  Sentence 3: **There are four ways of market-
     ing the reconditioned machines
     (a) direct sales
     (b) sales through a network of distributors
     (c) leasing directly
     (d) leasing through a network of
         distributors.**

     Which punctuation should be added to
     sentence 3?

     (1)  add a colon after <u>machines</u>

     (2)  add a semicolon after <u>ways</u>

     (3)  add a comma after <u>directly</u>

     (4)  add a comma after <u>ways</u>

     (5)  add a colon after <u>marketing</u>

14.  Sentence 4: **Direct sales and marketing
     will take time, because establishing a net-
     work of distributors will be the priority in
     year one.**

     The most effective revision of sentence 5
     would begin with?

     (1)  Because establishing a network of dis-
          tributors will be the priority in year one,

     (2)  Direct sales and marketing since estab-
          lishing a network,

     (3)  The priority in year one will take time,

     (4)  A network of distributors will take time,

     (5)  Because direct sales and marketing will
          take time,

15.  Sentence 5: **In order for BETA to be suc-
     cessful, a trained workforce are essential.**

     Which correction should be made to
     sentence 5?

     (1)  replace <u>to be</u> with <u>being</u>

     (2)  remove the comma after <u>successful</u>

     (3)  change <u>are</u> to <u>is</u>

     (4)  change <u>for</u> to <u>four</u>

     (5)  replace <u>trained</u> with <u>train</u>

16.  Sentence 6: **A secondary business will be
     reconditioning machines too order.**

     Which change should be made to
     sentence 6?

     (1)  change <u>would be</u> to <u>will be</u>

     (2)  change <u>reconditioning</u> to <u>recondition</u>

     (3)  change <u>machines</u> to <u>machine</u>

     (4)  replace <u>too</u> with <u>to</u>

     (5)  change <u>secondary</u> to <u>second</u>

17.  Sentence 7: **All estimates for potential
     units reconditioned and soled or leased
     are conservative.**

     Which correction should be made to
     sentence 7?

     (1)  change <u>for</u> to <u>four</u>

     (2)  change <u>soled</u> to <u>sold</u>

     (3)  replace <u>are</u> with <u>is</u>

     (4)  change <u>estimates</u> to <u>estimate</u>

     (5)  place a comma after <u>reconditioned</u>

18.  Sentence 8: **The initial mix of leasing and
     sales is estimated to be 20 percent leasing
     and 80 percent sales for the first year.**

     Which revision should be made to
     sentence 8?

     (1)  move <u>for the first year</u> between <u>sales</u>
          and <u>is</u>

     (2)  change <u>is</u> to <u>are</u>

     (3)  change <u>sales</u> to <u>sails</u>

     (4)  move <u>is estimated</u> to between <u>mix</u>
          and <u>of</u>

     (5)  change <u>first</u> to <u>1st</u>

*Go on to next page*

19. Sentence 9: **The average trade-in for an espresso machine will be $75, while the average price for used machines will be $250.**

    Which revision should be made to sentence 9?

    (1) remove the comma after <u>$75</u>
    (2) change <u>an</u> to <u>a</u>
    (3) change <u>will be</u> to <u>should be</u>
    (4) change <u>paid</u> to <u>payed</u>
    (5) insert <u>price</u> after trade-in

20. Sentence 10: **Twenty percent of the machines acquired will be <u>trade-ins, the balance</u> will be purchased.**

    Which is the best way to improve the underlined portion of sentence 10?

    (1) remove the comma after <u>trade-ins</u>
    (2) change to <u>trade-ins, while the balance</u>
    (3) change to <u>traded, the balance</u>
    (4) change to <u>trade-ins the balance</u>
    (5) no correction needed

*Go on to next page*

Questions 21 through 30 refer to the following executive summary.

**Marketing**

**Drycleaning and Laundering Industry Adjustment Committee
Report on the Local Labor Market Partnership Project
April 1998 – August 2000**

Executive Summary

(A)

(1) Over the past two years, the Drycleaning and Laundering Industry Adjustment Committee has worked hard to become a cohesive group focused on assessing and addressing the human resource implications associated with changes in the fabricare industry. (2) As of August 2000, the Committee has an active membership of over 15 individuals involved in all aspects of the project. (3) The Committee, which has great difficulty speaking with one voice, has taken responsibility for undertaking actions that will benefit this large, highly fragmented industry.

(B)

(4) During the initial period that the Committee was in existence, its work focused on out-reaching to and building a relationship with key individuals within the industry. (5) One of its first steps was to undertake a Needs Assessment Survey within the industry.

(C)

(6) During the first year, the Committee explored ways of meeting the needs identified in the Needs Assessment Survey, including raising the profile of the industry and offering on-site training programs, particularly in the areas of spotting and pressing. (7) A great deal of feasi-bility work was undertaken during this phase yet each possible training solution proved to be extremely difficult and costly to implement.

(D)

(8) As the Committee moved into its second year, it officially established a joint project with the National Fabricare Association to achieve goals in two priority areas: mentorship, training, and profile building.

(E)

(9) During this passed year, much effort and vision has gone into achieving the goals estab-lished by the Industry Adjustment Committee and the Association. The new priority areas have provided an opportunity for the industry to do the following

- Introduce technology
- Build capacity and knowledge
- Enhance skills
- Build partnerships and networks

*Go on to next page*

21. Sentence 1: **Over the past two years, the Drycleaning and Laundering Industry Adjustment Committee has worked hard to become a cohesive group focused on assessing and addressing the human resource implications in the fabricare industry.**

    Which is the best way to improve sentence 1?

    (1) remove the comma after <u>years</u>

    (2) place a period after <u>group</u> and start a new sentence beginning with <u>It has focused on</u>

    (3) place a comma after <u>group</u>

    (4) change <u>focused</u> to <u>focussed</u>

    (5) place a period after <u>group</u> and start a new sentence beginning with <u>To become focused</u>

22. Sentence 2: **As of August 2000, the Committee has an active membership of over 15 individuals involved in all aspects of the project.**

    Which revision should be made to sentence 2?

    (1) change <u>has</u> to <u>have</u>

    (2) remove the comma after <u>2000</u>

    (3) change <u>individuals</u> to <u>individual's</u>

    (4) change <u>aspects</u> to <u>aspect</u>

    (5) remove <u>over</u>

23. Sentence 3: **The Committee, which has great difficulty speaking with one voice, has taken responsibility for undertaking actions that will benefit this large, highly fragmented industry.**

    Which revision is required to improve sentence 3?

    (1) remove the comma after <u>large</u>

    (2) change <u>Committee</u> to <u>committee</u>

    (3) move <u>,which has great difficulty speaking with one voice,</u> to the end of the sentence after <u>industry</u>

    (4) change <u>has taken</u> to <u>have taken</u>

    (5) no correction needed

24. Sentence 4: **During the initial period that the Committee was in existence, its work focused on outreaching to and building a relationship with key individuals within the industry.**

    Which correction should be made to sentence 4?

    (1) change <u>its</u> to <u>it's</u>

    (2) change <u>outreaching to</u> to <u>reaching out to</u>

    (3) place a comma after <u>period</u>

    (4) change <u>outreaching</u> to <u>out-reaching</u>

    (5) change <u>with</u> to <u>between</u>

25. Sentence 5: **One of its first steps was to undertake a Needs Assessment Survey within the industry.**

    Which change should be made to sentence 5?

    (1) change <u>its</u> to <u>it's</u>

    (2) change <u>first</u> to <u>1st</u>

    (3) change <u>within</u> to <u>with</u>

    (4) change <u>was</u> to <u>were</u>

    (5) no correction needed

26. Sentence 6: **During the first year, the Committee explored ways of meeting the needs identified in the Needs Assessment Survey including raising the profile of the industry and offering on-site training programs, particularly in the areas of spotting and pressing.**

    Which is the best way to improve sentence 6?

    (1) insert a comma after <u>including</u>

    (2) place a period after Survey and start a new sentence with, <u>These included</u>

    (3) place a period after <u>industry</u> and start a new sentence with <u>offering on-site</u>

    (4) remove the comma after <u>programs</u>

    (5) no correction needed

*Go on to next page*

27. Sentence 7: **A great deal of feasibility work was undertaken during this phase yet each possible training solution proved to be extremely difficult and costly to implement.**

    Which correction should be made to sentence 7?

    (1) change <u>was</u> to <u>were</u>
    (2) change <u>proved</u> to <u>prove</u>
    (3) insert a comma after <u>undertaken</u>
    (4) insert a comma after <u>phase</u>
    (5) change <u>difficult</u> to <u>difficulty</u>

28. Sentence 8: **As the Committee moved into its second year, it officially established a joint project with the National Fabricare Association to achieve goals in two priority areas: mentorship, training, and profile building.**

    What correction should be made to sentence 8?

    (1) change <u>its</u> to <u>it's</u>
    (2) change <u>Association</u> to <u>association</u>
    (3) change <u>with</u> to <u>between</u>
    (4) change <u>two</u> to <u>three</u>
    (5) no correction needed

29. Sentence 9: **During this passed year, much effort and vision has gone into achieving the goals established by the Industry Adjustment Committee and the Association.**

    What correction should be made to sentence 9?

    (1) insert a comma after <u>Committee</u>
    (2) change <u>passed</u> to <u>past</u>
    (3) change <u>into</u> to <u>in</u>
    (4) change <u>goals</u> to <u>goal</u>
    (5) remove the comma after <u>year</u>

30. Sentence 10: **The new priority areas have provided an opportunity for the industry to do the following**

    • **Introduce technology**
    • **Build capacity and knowledge**
    • **Enhance skills**
    • **Build partnerships and networks**

    What punctuation should be added to sentence 10?

    (1) place a semicolon after <u>technology</u>
    (2) place a semicolon after <u>knowledge</u>
    (3) place a semicolon after <u>skills</u>
    (4) place a semicolon after <u>following</u>
    (5) place a colon after <u>following</u>

*Go on to next page*

Questions 31 through 40 refer to the following information piece.

**Prior Learning Assessment and Recognition**

**Introduction**

**(A)**

(1) This course is based on a Prior Learning Assessment and Recognition (PLAR) model, as a component of the PLAR, which utilizes preparation for a standardized challenge examination. (2) In addition candidates are guided through the creation of a portfolio, which can be evaluated by a college for admission or advanced standing. (3) This is an opportunity for adults, who have learned in non-formal as well as formal venues to document and assess their prior learning. (4) The course is intents and concentrated and is not meant for every applicant.

**(B)**

(5) Candidates, who score low in the pre-test, should be directed to remedial programs before beginning such a rigorous course. (6) Those who extremely score well in a pre-test may be advised to arrange immediately to take a challenging test, such as one of the GED tests. (7) This course is meant for candidates who will gain from review and re-mediation but do not require extensive teaching.

**Rationale**

**(C)**

(8) This course is designed to help adult learners gain acknowledgement and accreditation of their prior learning in preparation for post secondary study. (9) Students will learn methods for documenting prior knowledge and will develop skills while becoming reacquainted with educational environments and developing the skills needed to succeed in such environments. (10) Through the use of assessment tools and counciling, students will gain a realistic understanding of their levels of competence, personal strengths, weaknesses, and learning styles.

*Go on to next page*

31. Sentence 1: **This course is based on a Prior Learning Assessment and Recognition (PLAR) model, as a component of the PLAR, which utilizes preparation for a standardized challenge examination.**

    Which is the best way to improve sentence 1?

    (1) no improvement required
    (2) delete <u>, as a component of the PLAR,</u>
    (3) change <u>is</u> to <u>has</u>
    (4) change <u>utilizes</u> to <u>utilized</u>
    (5) place a comma after <u>Assessment</u>

32. Sentence 2: **In addition candidates are guided through the creation of a portfolio, which can be evaluated by a college for admission or advanced standing.**

    Which addition should be made to sentence 2?

    (1) insert a comma after <u>candidates</u>
    (2) change <u>are guided</u> to <u>is guided</u>
    (3) change <u>by</u> to <u>through</u>
    (4) insert a comma after <u>addition</u>
    (5) change <u>portfolio</u> to <u>port-folio</u>

33. Sentence 3: **This is an opportunity for adults, who have learned in non-formal as well as formal venues to document and assess there prior learning.**

    Which correction should be made in sentence 3?

    (1) change <u>there</u> to <u>their</u>
    (2) remove the comma after <u>adults</u>
    (3) change <u>an</u> to <u>a</u>
    (4) change <u>venues</u> to <u>venue</u>
    (5) no correction needed

34. Sentence 4: **The course is intents and concentrated and is not meant for every applicant.**

    Which correction should be made to sentence 4?

    (1) <u>is not</u> to <u>are not</u>
    (2) change <u>not</u> to <u>only</u>
    (3) change <u>meant</u> to <u>mend</u>
    (4) <u>place a comma after</u>
    (5) change <u>intents</u> to <u>intense</u>

35. Sentence 5: **Candidates, who score low in the pre-test, should be directed to remedial programs before beginning such a rigorous course.**

    Which improvement should be made to Sentence 5?

    (1) remove the comma after <u>candidates</u>
    (2) remove the comma after <u>pre-test</u>
    (3) remove both the comma after <u>candidates</u> and the comma after <u>pre-test</u>
    (4) change <u>before</u> to <u>after</u>
    (5) change <u>pre-test</u> to <u>post-test</u>

36. Sentence 6: **<u>Those who extremely score well</u> in a pre-test may be advised to arrange immediately to take a challenging test, such as one of the GED tests.**

    Which is the best way to write the underlined portion of this sentence?

    (1) Extremely those who score well
    (2) Those who score well extremely
    (3) Those who score extremely well
    (4) Those extremely who score well
    (5) no correction needed

37. Sentence 7: **The course is meant for candidates who will gain from review and re-mediation but do not require extensive teaching.**

    Which correction should be made to sentence 7?

    (1) change <u>review</u> to <u>revue</u>
    (2) remove the comma after <u>candidates</u>
    (3) remove the comma after <u>re-mediation</u>
    (4) change <u>re-mediation</u> to <u>remediation</u>
    (5) no correction needed

*Go on to next page*

38. Sentence 8: **This course is designed to help adult learners gain acknowledgement and accreditation of their prior learning in preparation for post secondary study.**

    Which change should be made to sentence 8?

    (1) change <u>post secondary</u> to <u>post-secondary</u>

    (2) change <u>acknowledgement</u> to <u>acknowledge</u>

    (3) change <u>post-secondary</u> to <u>post secondary</u>

    (4) change <u>their</u> to <u>there</u>

    (5) no correction needed

39. Sentence 9: **Students will learn methods for documenting prior knowledge and will develop skills while becoming reacquainted with educational environments and developing skills needed to succeed in such environments.**

    Which is the best way to improve sentence 9?

    (1) remove <u>of documentation</u>

    (2) remove <u>and developing skills needed to succeed in such environments</u>

    (3) remove <u>of prior knowledge</u>

    (4) remove <u>with educational environments</u>

    (5) no correction needed

40. Sentence 10: **Through the use of assessment tools and counciling, students will gain a realistic understanding of their levels of competence, personal strengths, weaknesses, and learning styles.**

    Which correction should be made to sentence 10?

    (1) change <u>realistic</u> to <u>real</u>

    (2) change <u>levels</u> to <u>level</u>

    (3) change <u>weaknesses</u> to <u>weeknesses</u>

    (4) change <u>students</u> to <u>students'</u>

    (5) change <u>counciling</u> to <u>counseling</u>

*Go on to next page*

Questions 41 through 50 refer to the following business letter.

**CanLearn Study Tours, Inc.**
**2500 Big Beaver Road**
**Troy, MI 70523**

Dr. Dale Worth, Ph.D.
Registrar
BEST Institute of Technology
75 Ingram Drive
Concord, MA 51234

Dear Dr. Worth:

(A)

(1) Our rapidly changing economic climate has meant both challenges never before known. (2) It has been said that only those organizations who can maintain loyalty and commitment among their employees, members, and customers will continue to survive and prosper in this age of continuous learning and globalization.

(B)

(3) Since 1974, CanLearn Study Tours, Inc. have been working with universities, colleges, school districts, voluntary organizations, and businesses to address the unique learning needs of their staff and clientele. (4) These have included educational travel programs that explore the following, artistic and cultural interests, historic and archeological themes, environmental and wellness experiences, and new service patterns. (5) Professional development strategies have been organized to enhance international understanding and boost creativity. (6) Some organizations have used study tours to build and maintain their membership or consumer base. (7) Other organizations discover a new soarce of revenue in these difficult economic times.

(C)

(8) The formats has varied from a series of local seminars to incentive conferences or sales promotion meetings. (9) Our professional services, including the best possible transportation and accommodation at the most reasonable rates, have insured the success of these programs.

(D)

(10) We would appreciate the opportunity to share our experiences in educational travel and discuss the ways we may be of service to your organization.

Yours sincerely,

Todd Croft, M.A., President
CanLearn Study Tours, Inc.

*Go on to next page*

41. Sentence 1: **Our rapidly changing economic climate has meant both challenges never before known.**

    Which improvement should be made to sentence 1?

    (1) insert <u>and opportunities</u> between <u>challenges</u> and <u>never</u>

    (2) change <u>has meant</u> to <u>have meant</u>

    (3) change <u>known</u> to <u>none</u>

    (4) change <u>challenges</u> to <u>challenge</u>

    (5) no correction needed

42. Sentence 2: **It has been said that only those organizations who can maintain loyalty and commitment among their employees, members, and customers will continue to survive and prosper in this age of continuous learning and globalization.**

    Which change should be made to sentence 2?

    (1) insert a comma after <u>commitment</u>

    (2) change <u>has been</u> to <u>had been</u>

    (3) change <u>who</u> to <u>that</u>

    (4) change <u>those</u> to <u>these</u>

    (5) no correction needed

43. Sentence 3: **Since 1974, CanLearn Study Tours, Inc. <u>have been working</u> with universities, colleges, school districts, voluntary organizations, and businesses to address the unique learning needs of their staff and clientele.**

    Which is the best way to write the underlined portion of sentence 3?

    (1) had been working

    (2) has been working

    (3) will be working

    (4) shall be working

    (5) no correction needed

44. Sentence 4: **These have included educational travel programs that explore the following, artistic and cultural interests, historic and archeological themes, environmental and wellness experiences, and new service patterns.**

    Which addition should be made to sentence 4?

    (1) insert a comma after <u>have included</u>

    (2) change the comma after <u>following</u> to a colon

    (3) change the comma after <u>interests</u> to a colon

    (4) change the comma after <u>themes</u> to a colon

    (5) change the comma after <u>experiences</u> to a colon

45. Sentence 5: **Professional development strategies have been organized to enhance international understanding and boost creativity.**

    Which changes should be made to sentence 5?

    (1) change <u>strategies</u> to <u>strategy</u>

    (2) change <u>boost</u> to <u>boast</u>

    (3) change <u>have been organized</u> to <u>has been organized</u>

    (4) change <u>enhance</u> to <u>enhancing</u>

    (5) no correction needed

46. Sentence 6: **Some organizations' have used study tours to build and maintain their membership and consumer base.**

    Which correction should be made to sentence 6?

    (1) change <u>Some</u> to <u>All</u>

    (2) change <u>their</u> to <u>there</u>

    (3) change <u>have used</u> to <u>has used</u>

    (4) change <u>organizations'</u> to <u>organizations</u>

    (5) change <u>base</u> to <u>bays</u>

*Go on to next page* ➡

47. Sentence 7: **Other organizations discover a new soarce of revenue in these difficult economic times.**

    Which change should be made to sentence 7?

    (1) place an apostrophe after <u>others</u>
    (2) change <u>soarce</u> to <u>source</u>
    (3) change <u>these</u> to <u>this</u>
    (4) change <u>discover</u> to <u>discovering</u>
    (5) no correction needed

48. Sentence 8: **The formats has varied from a series of local seminars to incentive conferences or sales promotion meetings.**

    Which revision should be made to sentence 8?

    (1) add a comma after <u>seminars</u>
    (2) add an apostrophe after <u>sales</u>
    (3) change <u>formats</u> to <u>format</u>
    (4) add a period after <u>seminars</u>
    (5) no correction needed

49. Sentence 9: **Our professional services, including the best possible transportation and accommodation at the most reasonable rates, have insured the success of these programs.**

    Which correction should be made to sentence 9?

    (1) change <u>services</u> to <u>service</u>
    (2) replace <u>insured</u> with <u>ensured</u>
    (3) remove the comma after <u>services</u>
    (4) remove the comma after <u>rates</u>
    (5) no correction needed

50. Sentence 10: **We would appreciate the opportunity to share our experiences in educational travel and discuss the ways we may be of service to your organization.**

    Which revision should be made to sentence 10?

    (1) change <u>would appreciate</u> to <u>appreciate</u>
    (2) insert a comma after <u>share</u>
    (3) insert a comma after <u>ways</u>
    (4) change <u>may</u> to <u>will</u>
    (5) no correction needed

*Go on to next page*

# Language Arts, Writing: Part II

### Essay Directions and Topic

Look at the box on the following page. In the box, you find your assigned topic and the letter of that topic.

You must write on the assigned topic **ONLY.**

Mark the letter of your assigned topic in the appropriate space on your answer sheet booklet.

You have 45 minutes to write on your assigned essay topic. If you have time remaining in this test period after you complete your essay, you may return to the multiple choice section. Do not return the Language Arts, Writing Test booklet until you finish both Parts I and II of the Language Arts, Writing Test.

Two evaluators will score your essay according to its overall effectiveness. Their evaluation will be based on the following features:

- Well-focused main points
- Clear organization
- Specific development of your ideas
- Control of sentence structure, punctuation, grammar, word choice, and spelling

**REMEMBER, YOU MUST COMPLETE BOTH THE MULTIPLE-CHOICE QUESTIONS (PART I) AND THE ESSAY (PART II) TO RECEIVE A SCORE ON THE LANGUAGE ARTS, WRITING TEST. To avoid having to repeat both parts of the test, be sure to observe the following rules:**

- Before you begin writing, jot notes or outline your essay on the sheets provided.
- For your final copy, write legibly <u>in ink</u> so that the evaluators will be able to read your writing.
- Write on the assigned topic. If you write on a topic other than the one assigned, you will not receive a score for the Language Arts, Writing Test.
- Write your essay on the lined pages of the separate answer sheet booklet. Only the writing on these pages will be scored.

Note that if you do not pass one portion of the test, you must take both parts over again.

*Go on to next page*

**Topic C**

Many people enjoy a hobby or special interest in their spare time.

Write an essay that encourages someone else to enjoy a hobby or special interest. Use your personal experiences, knowledge gained, relationships formed, and so on to develop your ideas.

Part II is a test to determine how well you can use written language to explain your ideas.

In preparing for your essay, you should take the following steps:

- ✔ Read the DIRECTIONS and the TOPIC carefully.
- ✔ Plan your essay before you write. Use the scratch paper provided to make any notes. These notes will be collected but not scored.
- ✔ Before you turn in your essay, reread what you have written and make any changes that will improve your essay.

Your essay should be long enough to develop the topic adequately.

**END OF EXAMINATION**

**WRITING TEST: Part II**

Use a No. 2 pencil to write the letter of your essay topic in the box,
then fill in the corresponding circle.

TOPIC  Ⓐ Ⓑ Ⓒ Ⓓ Ⓔ Ⓕ Ⓖ Ⓗ Ⓘ Ⓙ Ⓚ Ⓛ Ⓜ Ⓝ Ⓞ Ⓟ Ⓠ Ⓡ Ⓢ Ⓣ Ⓤ Ⓥ Ⓦ Ⓧ Ⓨ Ⓩ

**USE A BALLPOINT PEN TO WRITE YOUR ESSAY**

_____

_____

_____

_____

_____

_____

_____

_____

_____

_____

_____

_____

_____

_____

_____

_____

_____

_____

_____

_____

_____

_____

_____

_____

Continue your essay on the next page

# Chapter 9

# Answers and Explanations for the Language Arts, Writing Tests

· · · · · · · · · · · · · · · · · · · · · · · · · · · · · · · · · · · · · · · · · · · · · · · · · · · · · · ·

## Answer Key (for Part 1)

After taking the Language Arts, Writing, Part I Test in Chapter 8, use this section to check your answers.

| | | |
|---|---|---|
| 1. 1 | 18. 1 | 35. 3 |
| 2. 3 | 19. 5 | 36. 3 |
| 3. 2 | 20. 2 | 37. 4 |
| 4. 5 | 21. 2 | 38. 1 |
| 5. 1 | 22. 5 | 39. 2 |
| 6. 3 | 23. 3 | 40. 5 |
| 7. 5 | 24. 2 | 41. 1 |
| 8. 2 | 25. 5 | 42. 3 |
| 9. 4 | 26. 2 | 43. 2 |
| 10. 4 | 27. 4 | 44. 2 |
| 11. 1 | 28. 4 | 45. 5 |
| 12. 4 | 29. 2 | 46. 4 |
| 13. 1 | 30. 5 | 47. 2 |
| 14. 1 | 31. 2 | 48. 3 |
| 15. 3 | 32. 4 | 49. 2 |
| 16. 4 | 33. 1 | 50. 5 |
| 17. 2 | 34. 5 | |

# Analysis of the Answers for Part 1

If you aren't sure why an answer was incorrect, use this section to get quick explanations of the answers.

1. **1.** Change "you're" (which means "you are") to "your." "Your" indicates ownership of the new company, which is the meaning you want. The other choices are either grammatically incorrect or do nothing to make the sentence clearer.

2. **3.** The verb tense must be the singular "was," not the plural "were." Singular subjects always take singular verbs.

3. **2.** The sentence needs a comma after "operation" to separate the introductory adverb clause.

4. **5.** Homonyms are words that sound alike but are spelled differently and have different meanings, such as "then" and "than." The correct word to use in this sentence is "than."

5. **1.** While this sentence can be revised in many ways, the answer that makes the most sense is, "Thirteen new jobs will be created, returning half a million dollars to the local economy." This change will improve the organization of the sentence.

6. **3.** "Equipment" is the correct spelling.

To improve your spelling skills, read as much as you can before you take the GED Language Arts, Writing, Part I test. Seeing words spelled correctly (as you do when reading published works) is a great tool for recognizing when words are misspelled on this test.

7. **5.** The sentence is correct. No changes are needed, so no correction is necessary.

Some sentences on the test are correct. Don't correct grammar and punctuation if the sentence looks right to you.

8. **2.** To improve the sentence structure, insert "particularly" (an adverb modifying "interested") before "interested." This makes the sentence easier to read and understand.

9. **4.** You need a comma after "BETA" to separate the introductory adverb phrase.

10. **4.** Correct the spelling error: Change "assistence" to "assistance."

11. **1.** Apostrophes have two uses: to take the place of a missing letter or to indicate possession. An apostrophe is required before the "s" in BETA, because it is a singular possessive.

12. **4.** There is an extra apostrophe in this sentence. The correct form is "initial."

13. **1.** You need a colon to indicate to readers that a list is coming.

14. **1.** The sentence, "Direct sales and marketing will take time, because establishing a network of distributors will be the priority in year one" is not a good one. Good sentences should be easy to understand and flow easily off the tongue. Phrases starting with "because" usually make more sense at the beginning of the sentence. You can then write, "Because establishing a network of distributors will be the priority in year one, direct sales and marketing will take time." Because the meaning of the second section flows from the meaning of the first section, this sentence is an improvement over the original.

15. **3.** The singular noun "workforce" doesn't belong with the plural verb "are." The subject and verb in a sentence must always agree.

16. **4.** "Too" means also, which is not what you need in this sentence. Replace "too" with "to."

Before taking the GED Language Arts, Writing, Part I test, study a list of homonyms: words that sound the same but are spelled differently and have different meanings. Several incorrect homonyms are thrown into the test to test your ability to differentiate them.

17. **2.** Correct the homonym spelling error, from "soled" to "sold." "Sold," the word you want, is the past tense of "sell."

18. **1.** The sentence, "The initial mix of leasing and sales is estimated to be 20 percent leasing and 80 percent sales for the first year," has a problem because it could be misunderstood. The best way to correct this sentence is to change it around to read, "The initial mix of leasing and sales for the first year is estimated to be 20 percent leasing and 80 percent sales." When you read a sentence and words are out of order or make reading awkward, go back and correct them.

19. **5.** Because the sentence is talking about price, add the word "price" to clarify the meaning.

20. **2.** Changing the sentence to read "trade-ins, while the balance" improves the sentence structure. Another way to correct the original sentence is to replace the comma with a semi-colon; however, because that's not an answer given, you must choose answer 2.

21. **2.** Avoid the overly long and complex sentence, "Over the past two years, the Drycleaning and Laundering Industry Adjustment Committee has worked hard to become a cohesive group focused on assessing and addressing the human resource implications in the fabricare industry." To improve it, create two new sentences, such as the following: "Over the past two years, the Drycleaning and Laundering Industry Adjustment Committee has worked hard to become a cohesive group. It has focused on assessing and addressing the human resource implications in the fabricare industry."

22. **5.** Remove "over" to clarify the meaning. If you know that the group has 29 members (or however many it has over 15), say so.

23. **3.** The sentence in question says that the *committee* has great difficulty speaking in one voice, which may be true. However, a more accurate statement is that the *industry* has great difficulty speaking in one voice. You know this because it is described as "fragmented." A better organization for the sentence is, "The Committee has taken responsibility for undertaking actions that will benefit this large, highly fragmented industry, which has great difficulty speaking with one voice."

24. **2.** "Outreaching" isn't a verb; "reaching out" is.

25. **5.** No correction is required because none of the other options improves the sentence.

Are you thinking that we made a mistake in the sentence just above? Nope, it's correct. The noun "none" goes with the verb "improves." The prepositional phrase "of the other options" does not determine how the noun and verb agree. "None" is singular and, therefore, goes with "improves," not "improve." If this comes up on your test, replace "none" with "not one" (in your head), ignore any prepositional phrases between "none" and the verb, and see whether "not one" agrees with the verb given.

26. **2.** The sentence, "During the first year, the Committee explored ways of meeting the needs identified in the Needs Assessment Survey including raising the profile of the industry and offering on-site training programs, particularly in the areas of spotting and pressing," is simply too long to be understood. Find a logical place to break it into two sentences. The first part of the sentence discusses the uses of the Needs Assessment Survey; the second discusses the type of training. You can split the sentence into two smaller, more easily understood, sentences, as follows: "During the first year, the Committee explored ways of meeting the needs identified in the Needs Assessment Survey. These included raising the profile of the industry and offering on-site training programs, particularly in the areas of spotting and pressing."

27. **4.** Insert a comma after "phase" to improve the sentence structure.

28. **4.** This is a gimme: Three areas are listed, not two.

29. **2.** Correct the homonym spelling error, from "passed" to "past."

30. **5.** The introductory clause needs a colon at the end.

    If you thought that the items in the list needed semi-colons, they can have them or not, depending on *house style* (the style used and followed religiously by the company or publishing house writing or editing the text). However, if you used semi-colons, you would use them at the end of each component in the list, and this wasn't an option.

31. **2.** The phrase, "as a component of the PLAR" is unnecessary.

32. **4.** You need a comma after "in addition."

    Not sure about commas? Get a copy of *English Grammar For Dummies* by Geraldine Woods (Wiley Publishing, Inc.) for the lowdown on this sometimes tricky form of punctuation.

33. **1.** "Their" is a possessive (showing belonging) and is the correct choice in this sentence. Correct the spelling error, from "there" to "their."

    The homonyms, "there," "their," and "they're" probably trip up more high-school and college students than any other. Before heading into the GED Language Arts, Writing, Part I Test, know the differences between these three words!

34. **5.** "Intense" and "concentrated" are synonyms used in this sentence for emphasis, but "intense" is misspelled as "intents." "Intents" is where you sleep on a camping trip.

35. **3.** The clause "who score low in the pre-test" is a *dependent clause*, which means that the sentence needs it to make sense to readers. Contrast this with an *independent clause*, which you can take out of a sentence and still fully understand the meaning of the sentence.

36. **3.** "Those who score extremely well" is the best order of the words. "Extremely," an adverb, is best placed next to the word it is modifying, "well."

37. **4.** Correct the error in the spelling of "re-mediation."

    Although exceptions exist, when a prefix that ends in a vowel (as *re–* does) precedes a consonant, no hyphen is used. In many (but not all) cases, when a prefix that ends in a vowel precedes another vowel, a hyphen is used.

38. **1.** When two adjectives (like "post-secondary" in the example) combine to modify one noun, they are almost always hyphenated. Keep in mind, however, that when an adverb and adjective (such as "newly formed") combine to modify a noun, they are never hyphenated.

    If you have trouble remembering this rule, just keep in mind that words ending in *–ly* and forming two-word adjectives are almost never hyphenated.

39. **2.** The sentence, "Students will learn methods for documenting prior knowledge and will develop skills while becoming reacquainted with educational environments and developing skills needed to succeed in such environments," is complex and redundant. Delete the entire phrase, "and developing skills needed to succeed in such environments."

    Unless you're being paid by the word, always try to say what you mean in as few words as possible.

40. **5.** This sentence contains a spelling error. Correct the spelling error, from "counciling" to "counseling."

41. **1.** While the word "both" refers to two options, here, you're given but one option, "challenges." If you insert "and opportunities" between "challenges" and "never," you include a second option and correct the sentence.

42. **3.** An organization is never a "who"; only people can be referred to as "who."

    While the sentence may appear long and, therefore, benefit from rewriting, the sentence isn't technically incorrect. While commas do serve to make sentences clearer, don't insert them unless punctuation rules make them correct.

43. **2.** CanLearn Study Tours is a single entity because it's one company. Therefore, it is singular and needs a singular verb "has" instead of the plural "have."

    People like to refer to companies as "them" when, in fact, a company is always an "it." Even though a company is made up of a lot of people, it is still a singular entity.

44. **2.** A colon is needed before the list to introduce it.

45. **5.** The options presented either make the sentence difficult to understand or introduce errors.

46. **4.** A stray apostrophe has landed on this sentence. The one after "organizations'" is unnecessary because you're not trying to show possession here.

    Get comfortable with the uses of apostrophes — especially those used for possession — before taking the GED Language Arts, Writing, Part I test.

47. **2.** Correct the spelling error, from "soarce" to "source."

48. **3.** "Formats" is plural, but "has" is a singular verb. Verbs and their subjects must agree.

    Study both subject/verb agreement and pronoun/antecedent agreement before taking the Language Arts, Writing Test.

49. **2.** Correct the spelling error by changing "insured" to "ensured."

    Using "insure" is a common error. Use "insure" only when you mean the thing you buy to protect your car, house, health, life, and so on. This example has nothing to do with insurance, so use "ensure," instead.

50. **5.** No correction is required. The other answers don't improve or correct the sentence.

# Sample Essay (for Part II)

The topic for the practice test in Chapter 8 is as follows:

> Many people enjoy a hobby or special interest in their spare time. Write an essay that encourages someone else to enjoy a hobby or special interest. Use personal experiences, knowledge gained, relationships formed, and so on to develop your ideas.

Although every essay will be unique, we provide a sample here to give you an idea of what the test graders will expect. Compare the structure of this essay to yours.

> Hiking is a hobby I can recommend to anyone. Being outdoors, getting exercise, and spending quiet time alone are all facets of hiking that make it unique in today's mostly indoor, sedentary — and yet overly busy — life. Many areas — even large cities — offer parks with dirt or grass paths that are perfect for a daily hike.
>
> Hiking gets me outdoors, away from potentially harmful indoor air. Too much time indoors cuts humans off from the sun, which is vital to mental health, and can also lead to allergies or other illnesses from too much exposure to chemicals and other products that are trapped indoors. Just an hour per day of hiking can counteract many of the effects of spending too much time indoors.

Hiking is also great exercise, because it works the heart, lungs, and leg muscles without adding stress to the knees and other joints. You can hike in your street clothes (although a good pair of hiking boots is a good idea), so hiking does not require the investment in gear that many forms of exercise do.

Perhaps the best — and most unique — feature of hiking, however, is that it provides solace from our loud, fast-paced, materialistic world. When hiking — even in or near a large, metropolitan area — I see deer, listen to birdsongs, and watch squirrels busy with their work. Without the constant sound of a TV or radio in the background, I can focus on my own thoughts instead of on what is expected by society and promoted by advertisers. While on the trail, I can focus on the natural beauty around me instead of worrying about bills or comparing myself to others. This quiet disconnection from society helps me remember what is important in life.

In short, hiking helps me break free of the work-a-day world by getting me outside to appreciate nature, encouraging me to exercise, and giving me long periods of restful silence. I recommend hiking to anyone.

# Tips and Ideas for Mastering Part II

Keep the following tips and ground rules in mind about writing an essay for Part II of the Language Arts, Writing Test:

- ✔ You must write an essay in 45 minutes of about 250 words based on a single topic.

- ✔ The topic is always a brief one about an issue or situation that's familiar to you.

- ✔ The essay tests your ability to write about an issue that has positive or negative implications but about which you have some general knowledge.

- ✔ The essay doesn't test how much you know; instead, it tests your ability to express yourself in writing.

- ✔ An essay usually consists of a number of paragraphs, each of which contain a topic sentence stating a main idea or thought. Be sure each paragraph relates to the overall topic of the essay.

- ✔ A topic sentence is usually (but not always) placed at the beginning of the paragraph and focuses on the main point you want the readers to understand.

- ✔ Effective paragraphs use a variety of sentence types: statements, questions, commands, exclamations, and even quotations.

- ✔ Some sentences may be short, others long to catch the readers' attention. Vary your sentence structure and choice of words to spark the reader's interest.

- ✔ Paragraphs create interest in several ways: by developing details, by using illustrations and examples, by presenting events in a time or space sequence, by providing definitions, by classifying persons or objects, by comparing and contrasting, or by demonstrating reasons and proof. Organize your paragraphs and sentences in a sequence that expresses your ideas.

- ✔ Specific examples and details support your point of view, so use them liberally.

- ✔ The readers are checking whether you can express your ideas clearly and logically.

# Chapter 10

# The Social Studies Test

· · · · · · · · · · · · · · · · · · · · · · · · · · · · · · · · · · · · · · · · · · · · · · · · ·

### Directions

The Social Studies Test consists of multiple-choice questions that measure general social studies concepts. The questions are based on short readings that often include a map, graph, chart, cartoon, or figure. Study the information given and then answer the question(s) following it. Refer to the information as often as necessary in answering the questions.

You have 70 minutes to answer the 50 questions in this booklet. Work carefully, but do not spend too much time on any one question. Be sure you answer every question.

Do not mark in this test booklet. Record your answers on the separate answer sheet provided. Be sure that all requested information is properly recorded on the answer sheet.

To record your answers, fill in the numbered circle on the answer sheet that corresponds to the answer you select for each question in the test booklet.

---

**EXAMPLE:**

Early colonists of North American looked for settlement sites with adequate water supplies and access by ship. For this reason, many early towns were built near

(1) mountains

(2) prairies

(3) rivers

(4) glaciers

(5) plateaus

(On Answer Sheet)

① ② ● ④ ⑤

The correct answer is "rivers"; therefore, answer space 3 would be marked on the answer sheet.

---

Do not rest the point of your pencil on the answer sheet while you are considering your answer. Make no stray or unnecessary marks. If you change an answer, erase your first mark completely. Mark only one answer space for each question; multiple answers will be scored as incorrect. Do not fold or crease your answer sheet. All test materials must be returned to the test administrator.

**DO NOT BEGIN TAKING THIS TEST UNTIL TOLD TO DO SO**

## SOCIAL STUDIES TEST

| | | |
|---|---|---|
| 1 ① ② ③ ④ ⑤ | | 26 ① ② ③ ④ ⑤ |
| 2 ① ② ③ ④ ⑤ | | 27 ① ② ③ ④ ⑤ |
| 3 ① ② ③ ④ ⑤ | | 28 ① ② ③ ④ ⑤ |
| 4 ① ② ③ ④ ⑤ | | 29 ① ② ③ ④ ⑤ |
| 5 ① ② ③ ④ ⑤ | | 30 ① ② ③ ④ ⑤ |
| 6 ① ② ③ ④ ⑤ | | 31 ① ② ③ ④ ⑤ |
| 7 ① ② ③ ④ ⑤ | | 32 ① ② ③ ④ ⑤ |
| 8 ① ② ③ ④ ⑤ | | 33 ① ② ③ ④ ⑤ |
| 9 ① ② ③ ④ ⑤ | | 34 ① ② ③ ④ ⑤ |
| 10 ① ② ③ ④ ⑤ | | 35 ① ② ③ ④ ⑤ |
| 11 ① ② ③ ④ ⑤ | | 36 ① ② ③ ④ ⑤ |
| 12 ① ② ③ ④ ⑤ | | 37 ① ② ③ ④ ⑤ |
| 13 ① ② ③ ④ ⑤ | | 38 ① ② ③ ④ ⑤ |
| 14 ① ② ③ ④ ⑤ | | 39 ① ② ③ ④ ⑤ |
| 15 ① ② ③ ④ ⑤ | | 40 ① ② ③ ④ ⑤ |
| 16 ① ② ③ ④ ⑤ | | 41 ① ② ③ ④ ⑤ |
| 17 ① ② ③ ④ ⑤ | | 42 ① ② ③ ④ ⑤ |
| 18 ① ② ③ ④ ⑤ | | 43 ① ② ③ ④ ⑤ |
| 19 ① ② ③ ④ ⑤ | | 44 ① ② ③ ④ ⑤ |
| 20 ① ② ③ ④ ⑤ | | 45 ① ② ③ ④ ⑤ |
| 21 ① ② ③ ④ ⑤ | | 46 ① ② ③ ④ ⑤ |
| 22 ① ② ③ ④ ⑤ | | 47 ① ② ③ ④ ⑤ |
| 23 ① ② ③ ④ ⑤ | | 48 ① ② ③ ④ ⑤ |
| 24 ① ② ③ ④ ⑤ | | 49 ① ② ③ ④ ⑤ |
| 25 ① ② ③ ④ ⑤ | | 50 ① ② ③ ④ ⑤ |

**Directions:** Choose the one best answer to each question.

Questions 1 through 4 refer to the following passage.

### The First Inhabitants of the Western Hemisphere

In telling the history of the United States and also of the nations of the Western Hemisphere in general, historians have wrestled with the problem of what to call the hemisphere's first inhabitants. Under the mistaken impression he had reached the "Indies," explorer Christopher Columbus called the people he met "Indians." This was an error in identification that has persisted for more than five hundred years, for the inhabitants of North and South America had no collective name by which they called themselves.

Historians, anthropologists, and political activists have offered various names, none fully satisfactory. Anthropologists have used "aborigine," but the term suggests a primitive level of existence inconsistent with the cultural level of many tribes. Another term, "Amerindian," which combines Columbus's error with the name of another Italian explorer, Amerigo Vespucci (whose name was the source of "America"), lacks any historical context. Since the 1960s, "Native American" has come into popular favor, though some activists prefer "American Indian." In the absence of a truly representative term, descriptive references such as "native peoples" or "indigenous peoples," though vague, avoid European influence. In recent years, some argument has developed over whether to refer to tribes in the singular or plural — Apache or Apaches — with supporters on both sides demanding political correctness.

*Excerpted from P. Soifer and A. Hoffman,* CliffsQuickReview U.S. History I *(Wiley Publishing, Inc.)*

1. Why did Columbus call the native inhabitants "Indians"?
   (1) they were in the western hemisphere
   (2) he thought he'd reached the Indies
   (3) North and South America had not been discovered
   (4) they were the hemisphere's first inhabitants
   (5) he liked the sound of the name

2. Who used the term "aborigine"?
   (1) historians
   (2) political activists
   (3) Columbus
   (4) anthropologists
   (5) explorers

3. What name has been favored since 1960?
   (1) Amerindian
   (2) Native American
   (3) native peoples
   (4) indigenous peoples
   (5) Indian

4. How was America named?
   (1) after an Italian explorer
   (2) after its first inhabitants
   (3) because of the European influence
   (4) after the native peoples
   (5) because of political correctness

*Go on to next page*

Questions 5 through 9 refer to the following passage.

### The Voyages of Christopher Columbus

Christopher Columbus, a Genoese sailor, believed that sailing west across the Atlantic Ocean was the shortest sea route to Asia. Ignorant of the fact that the Western Hemisphere lay between Europe and Asia and assuming the earth's circumference to be a third less than it actually is, he was convinced that Japan would appear on the horizon just three thousand miles to the west. Like other seafarers of his day, Columbus was untroubled by political allegiances; he was ready to sail for whatever country would pay for his voyage. Either because of his arrogance (he wanted ships and crews to be provided at no expense to himself) or ambition (he insisted on governing the lands he discovered), he found it difficult to find a patron. The Portuguese rejected his plan twice, and the rulers of England and France were not interested. With influential supporters at court, Columbus convinced King Ferdinand and Queen Isabella of Spain to partially underwrite his expedition. In 1492, Granada, the last Muslim stronghold on the Iberian Peninsula, had fallen to the forces of the Spanish monarchs. With the *Reconquista* complete and Spain a unified country, Ferdinand and Isabella could turn their attention to overseas exploration.

*Excerpted from P. Soifer and A. Hoffman,* CliffsQuickReview U.S. History I *(Wiley Publishing, Inc.)*

**5.** Which direction did Columbus sail to reach Asia?

(1) east

(2) south

(3) north

(4) west

(5) northwest

**6.** What did he assume the earth's circumference to be?

(1) three thousand miles

(2) between Europe and Asia

(3) thirty-three percent less than it was

(4) shortest sea route to Asia

(5) across the Atlantic Ocean

**7.** How did Columbus feel about politics?

(1) he did not care

(2) he was troubled

(3) he was ready to sail

(4) he was arrogant

(5) he was ambitious

**8.** Which country finally agreed to fund his plan?

(1) Portugal

(2) England

(3) France

(4) Japan

(5) Spain

**9.** How were Ferdinand and Isabella convinced?

(1) they now had a unified country

(2) the Muslims were defeated

(3) the English and French were not interested

(4) they were convinced by influential supporters

(5) they were ready for overseas exploration

*Go on to next page*

Questions 10 through 15 refer to the following passage.

## Social Structure of the Thirteen Colonies

At the bottom of the social ladder were slaves and indentured servants; successful planters in the south and wealthy merchants in the north were the colonial elite. In the Chesapeake area, the signs of prosperity were visible in brick and mortar. The rather modest houses of even the most prosperous farmers of the seventeenth century had given way to spacious mansions in the eighteenth century. South Carolina planters often owned townhouses in Charleston and would probably have gone to someplace like Newport to escape the heat in summer. Both in their lifestyles and social pursuits (such as horse racing), the southern gentry emulated the English country squire.

Large landholders were not confined just to the southern colonies. The descendants of the Dutch patrons and the men who received lands from the English royal governors controlled estates in the middle colonies. Their farms were worked by tenant farmers, who received a share of the crop for their labor. In the northern cities, wealth was increasingly concentrated in the hands of the merchants; below them was the middle class of skilled craftsmen and shopkeepers. Craftsmen learned their trade as apprentices and became journeymen when their term of apprenticeship (as long as seven years) was completed. Even as wage earner, a journeyman often still lived with his former master and ate at his table. Saving enough money to go into business for himself was the dream of every journeyman.

*Excerpted from P. Soifer and A. Hoffman,* CliffsQuickReview U.S. History I *(Wiley Publishing, Inc.)*

10. Who was at the top of the social ladder in the Colonies?
    (1) slaves and servants
    (2) apprentices and journeymen
    (3) horse racers
    (4) tenant farmers
    (5) planters and merchants

11. What were the South Carolina planters?
    (1) prosperous farmers
    (2) wealthy merchants
    (3) indentured servants
    (4) spacious mansions
    (5) city squires

12. Why would they go to Newport?
    (1) horse racing
    (2) modest houses
    (3) to be near the sea
    (4) escape the heat
    (5) social pursuits

13. Who were the tenant farmers?
    (1) large landholders
    (2) those who worked for a share of the crops
    (3) royal governors who were appointed
    (4) Dutch patrons
    (5) southern colonials who inherited wealth

14. Who comprised the middle class?
    (1) noblemen
    (2) squires
    (3) merchants
    (4) patrons
    (5) shopkeepers

15. What did a journeyman dream of?
    (1) seven years of apprenticeship
    (2) eating at the master's table
    (3) going into business himself
    (4) becoming a wage earner
    (5) saving his money

*Go on to next page*

Questions 16 through 20 refer to the following passage.

### Declaration of Independence

We hold these truths to be self-evident: that all men are created equal; that they are endowed by their Creator with certain inalienable rights; that among these are life, liberty, and the pursuit of happiness. That to secure these rights, governments are instituted among men, deriving their just powers from the consent of the governed; that whenever any form of government becomes destructive of these ends it is the right of the people to alter or to abolish it, and to institute a new government, laying its foundation on such principles, and organizing its powers in such form, as to them shall seem most likely to effect their safety and happiness. Prudence, indeed, will dictate that governments long established should not be changed for light and transient causes; and accordingly, all experience hath shown, that mankind are more disposed to suffer, while evils are sufferable, than to right themselves by abolishing the forms to which they are accustomed. But when a long train of abuses and usurpations, pursuing invariably the same object, evinces a design to reduce them under absolute despotism, it is their right, it is their duty, to throw off such government, and to provide new guards for their future security. Such has been the patient sufferance of these colonies; and such is now the necessity which constrains them to alter their former system of government. The history of the present king of Great Britain is a history of repeated injuries and usurpations, all having in direct object the establishment of an absolute tyranny over these states. To prove this, let facts be submitted to a candid world.

16. What truths were self evident?

    (1) that all men are not created equal

    (2) that men don't have rights

    (3) that men are suffering

    (4) the men must exercise prudence

    (5) that men have certain rights

17. From where do governments get their power?

    (1) from the people

    (2) from the Creator

    (3) among men

    (4) from a new foundation

    (5) from the king

18. Why should a new government be instituted?

    (1) there were light and transient reasons

    (2) it was long established

    (3) the people were suffering

    (4) there was concern for safety and happiness

    (5) they needed to abolish the accustomed forms

19. How does the Declaration of Independence describe the thirteen Colonies?

    (1) king's injuries and usurpations

    (2) suffering patiently

    (3) absolute despotism

    (4) pursuing the same object

    (5) providing new guards

20. How does the Declaration of Independence describe the king of Great Britain?

    (1) he caused injuries

    (2) he was a kindly ruler

    (3) he was an absolute tyrant

    (4) he was a friend of the people

    (5) he guarded them securely

*Go on to next page*

Questions 21 through 23 refer to the following political cartoon.

21. How does the cartoon depict the use of cellphones?

    (1) wonderful invention

    (2) aid to communication

    (3) medical breakthrough

    (4) useful appliance

    (5) injurious to health

22. How would you best describe the cellphone user in the cartoon?

    (1) foolhardy

    (2) talkative

    (3) considerate

    (4) courageous

    (5) cowardly

23. How do we know that cellphones represent a risk to health?

    (1) going to the movies

    (2) scientific research

    (3) urban legends

    (4) popular opinion

    (5) crime reports

*Go on to next page* ⟹

Questions 24 through 26 refer to the following passage.

## Resistance to Slavery

Resistance to slavery took several forms. Slaves would pretend to be ill, refuse to work, do their jobs poorly, destroy farm equipment, set fire to buildings, and steal food. These were all individual acts rather than part of an organized plan for revolt, but the objective was to upset the routine of the plantation in any way possible. On some plantations, slaves could bring grievances about harsh treatment from an overseer to their master and hope that he would intercede on their behalf. Although many slaves tried to run away, few succeeded for more than a few days, and they often returned on their own. Such escapes were more a protest — a demonstration that it could be done — than a dash for freedom. As advertisements in southern newspapers seeking the return of runaway slaves made clear, the goal of most runaways was to find their wives or children who had been sold to another planter. The fabled underground railroad, a series of safe houses for runaways organized by abolitionists and run by former slaves like Harriet Tubman, actually helped only about a thousand slaves reach the North.

*Excerpted from P. Soifer and A. Hoffman,* CliffsQuickReview U.S. History I *(Wiley Publishing, Inc.)*

24. Why did the slaves refuse to work?

    (1) they were ill

    (2) they did their jobs poorly

    (3) they destroyed farm equipment

    (4) they longed to be free

    (5) they stole food

25. What did running away represent?

    (1) a form of protest

    (2) a grievance about ill treatment

    (3) an upset to the routines

    (4) an appeal to the master

    (5) being sold to another planter

26. Who organized the underground railroad?

    (1) Harriet Tubman

    (2) former slaves

    (3) abolitionists

    (4) runaways

    (5) southern newspapers

*Go on to next page*

Questions 27 through 30 refer to the following report.

**Weather and Traffic Report**

Good morning and welcome to America's weather and traffic on WAWT, the voice of the world in the ear of the nation. Today is going to be hot. That's H-O-T, and we all know what that means. The big "P" is coming back for a visit. We are going to have pollution today for sure. With our record heat today on each coast, there is a problem. If you think that it's hot here, it's even hotter up higher. And that means unhealthy air leading to unhealthy people. I can hear the coughs and sneezes coast to coast. I think I hear a whole series of gasps from our nation's capital, good ol' Washington D.C., and it's not Congress that is producing all that hot air. And out in western California, it's just as bad. Just the other day, I looked up "poor air quality" in the dictionary, and it said "see California." Lots of luck breathing out there.

This morning, once again, there's a layer of hot air just above ground level. That's where we live — ground level. This air acts like a closed gate, and it keeps the surface air from going up and mixing. Of course, we are all going to drive our cars all day in heavy traffic, and some of us will go to work in factories. And, surprise — by afternoon all those pollutants from the cars mix with the emissions from the factories and get trapped by the layer of hot air, and it's try-to-catch-your-breath time. Unhealthy air is here again. Tomorrow and every day after, we'll probably have more of the same until we learn to take care of our environment.

Well, I'll see you tomorrow, if the air's not too thick to see through.

27. When is the worst time for pollution?
    (1) in the morning
    (2) in the afternoon
    (3) late at night
    (4) before breakfast
    (5) after dinner

28. What causes pollution?
    (1) record heat
    (2) air rising and mixing
    (3) unhealthy air quality
    (4) exhausts and emissions
    (5) warmer air aloft

29. Where will pollution be most serious?
    (1) Midwest
    (2) deep south
    (3) up north
    (4) east and west coasts
    (5) near the Great Lakes

30. What is the best way to prevent pollution?
    (1) change the temperature
    (2) reduce emissions
    (3) get rid of hot air layer
    (4) prevent air from rising
    (5) keeping warmer temperatures aloft

*Go on to next page*

Questions 31 through 35 refer to the following passage.

### The End of the Cold War

In July 1989, Gorbachev repudiated the Brezhnev Doctrine, which had justified the intervention of the Soviet Union in the affairs of communist countries. Within a few months of his statement, the Communist regimes in Eastern Europe collapsed — Poland, Hungary, and Czechoslovakia, followed by Bulgaria and Romania. The Berlin Wall came down in November 1989, and East and West Germany were reunited within the year. Czechoslovakia eventually split into the Czech Republic and Slovakia with little trouble, but the end of the Yugoslav Federation in 1991 led to years of violence and *ethnic cleansing* (the expulsion of an ethnic population from a geographic area), particularly in Bosnia-Herzegovina. The Soviet Union also broke up, not long after an attempted coup against Gorbachev in August 1991, and the Baltic states of Latvia, Estonia, and Lithuania were the first to gain their independence. That December, Gorbachev stepped down, and the old Soviet Union became the Commonwealth of Independent States (CIS). The CIS quickly disappeared, and the republics that had once made up the Soviet Union were recognized as sovereign nations. The end of the Cold War led directly to major nuclear weapons reduction agreements between President Bush and the Russian leaders, as well as significant cutbacks in the number of troops the United States committed to the defense of NATO.

*Excerpted from P. Soifer and A. Hoffman,* CliffsQuickReview U.S. History II *(Wiley Publishing, Inc.)*

31. Who or what caused the end of the Cold War?
    (1) the Soviet Union
    (2) communist regimes
    (3) Gorbachev
    (4) Brezhnev
    (5) Eastern Europe

32. How were East and West Germany reunited?
    (1) fall of the Berlin Wall
    (2) intervention of the Soviet Union
    (3) Brezhnev Doctrine
    (4) regimes collapsed
    (5) intervention of the United States

33. What is ethnic cleansing?
    (1) years of violence
    (2) end of Yugoslav Federation
    (3) expelling populations
    (4) split-up of Czechoslovakia
    (5) break-up of the Soviet Union

34. What happened to the republics of the Soviet Union?
    (1) they quickly disappeared
    (2) they joined NATO
    (3) they became the CNS
    (4) they joined the Baltic states
    (5) they became sovereign nations

35. What was one of the results of the end of the Cold War?
    (1) more nuclear weapons
    (2) more tension between the United States and the former Soviet Union
    (3) no agreements between leaders
    (4) increase in troops
    (5) cutbacks in troops

*Go on to next page*

Questions 36 through 40 refer to the following passage.

### The Panic of 1873

During his second term, Grant was still unable to curb the graft in his administration, Secretary of War William Belknap was impeached by the House, and he resigned in disgrace for taking bribes from dishonest Indian agents. The president's personal secretary was involved with the Whiskey Ring, a group of distillers who evaded paying internal revenue taxes. A much more pressing concern though was the state of the economy.

In 1873, over-speculation in railroad stocks led to a major economic panic. The failure of Jay Cooke's investment bank was followed by the collapse of the stock market and the bankruptcy of thousands of businesses; crop prices plummeted and unemployment soared. Much of the problem was related to the use of greenbacks for currency. Hard-money advocates insisted that paper money had to be backed by gold to curb inflation and level price fluctuations, but farmers and manufacturers, who needed easy credit, wanted even more greenbacks put in circulation, a policy that Grant ultimately opposed. He recommended and the Congress enacted legislation in 1875 providing for the redemption of greenbacks in gold. Because the Treasury needed time to build up its gold reserves, redemption did not go into effect for another four years, by which time the longest depression in American history had come to an end.

*Excerpted from P. Soifer and A. Hoffman,* CliffsQuickReview U.S. History I *(Wiley Publishing, Inc.)*

**36.** What was the main problem President Grant had in his second term?

(1) problems with his administration

(2) problems with whiskey

(3) problems with the IRS

(4) problems with personal bankruptcy

(5) problems with his wife

**37.** What was the cause of the Panic of 1873?

(1) investment failure

(2) bankruptcy

(3) over-speculation

(4) tax evasion

(5) economic panic

**38.** What type of money was used for investment?

(1) British pounds

(2) silver

(3) gold

(4) inflation

(5) greenbacks

**39.** What followed the failure of Jay Cooke's bank?

(1) collapse of the stock market

(2) increase in market value

(3) business profitability

(4) rising crop prices

(5) soaring employment

**40.** How did Congress end the depression?

(1) easy credit

(2) level prices

(3) built up gold reserves

(4) hoarding of greenbacks

(5) curbed inflation

*Go on to next page*

Questions 41 through 45 refer to the following tables.

**Comparison of Gross Domestic Product**

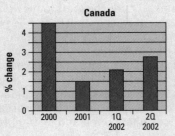

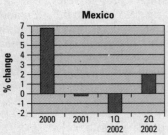

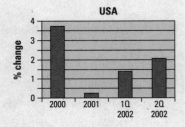

**Comparison of Major Indexes**

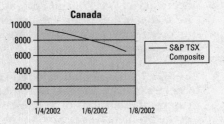

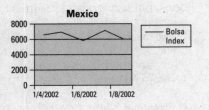

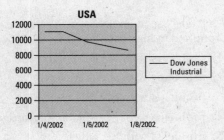

**Comparison of Value of Canadian Dollar and Mexican Peso in American Dollars**

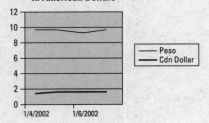

*Go on to next page*

41. By how much did the Mexican gross domestic product (GDP) outperform the U.S. GDP in the year 2000?

    (1) 8.4 percentage points

    (2) 2.8 percentage points

    (3) 0.7 percentage points

    (4) 5.9 percentage points

    (5) 1.3 percentage points

42. Why does Canada's GDP appear healthy as compared to that of the United States and Mexico?

    (1) has consistently performed well

    (2) performed better than in 2Q

    (3) performed better in 1Q

    (4) performed better in 2001

    (5) performed better in 2000

43. How did the Canadian dollar perform against the U.S. dollar, according to the graph?

    (1) moved higher

    (2) stayed the same

    (3) lost ground

    (4) finished even

    (5) no change

44. How did the S&P TSX Composite Index compare on 1/4/2002 and 1/8/2002?

    (1) down almost 2,000

    (2) up about 1,000

    (3) about the same

    (4) up less than 300

    (5) down more than 3,000

45. According to the graph, where is the Dow Jones as compared to January 2001?

    (1) down more than 5,000

    (2) up more than 1,000

    (3) about the same

    (4) up more than 300

    (5) down more than 2,000

*Go on to next page*

Questions 46 through 50 refer to the following political cartoon.

46. What is the setting for the cartoon?

    (1) living room

    (2) laboratory

    (3) playroom

    (4) library

    (5) kitchen

47. What problem has the researcher been studying?

    (1) the common cold

    (2) a rare lung disease

    (3) vision

    (4) hearing

    (5) limited patents for medicines

48. How does the cartoonist depict drug companies?

    (1) dangerous

    (2) religious

    (3) greedy

    (4) scary

    (5) curious

49. Why is this solution important for the drug companies?

    (1) to share with all people

    (2) to make their employees famous

    (3) for good public relations

    (4) to make them look good to their customers

    (5) to increase their profits

50. What is the theme of the cartoon?

    (1) greed

    (2) inventing

    (3) curiosity

    (4) diligence

    (5) patience

**END OF EXAMINATION**

# Chapter 11

# Answers and Explanations for the Social Studies Test

· · · · · · · · · · · · · · · · · · · · · · · · · · · · · · · · · · · · · · · · · ·

## Answer Key

After taking the Social Studies Test in Chapter 10, use this section to check your answers.

| | | |
|---|---|---|
| 1. 2 | 18. 3 | 35. 5 |
| 2. 4 | 19. 2 | 36. 1 |
| 3. 2 | 20. 3 | 37. 3 |
| 4. 1 | 21. 5 | 38. 5 |
| 5. 4 | 22. 1 | 39. 1 |
| 6. 3 | 23. 2 | 40. 3 |
| 7. 1 | 24. 4 | 41. 2 |
| 8. 5 | 25. 1 | 42. 1 |
| 9. 4 | 26. 3 | 43. 2 |
| 10. 5 | 27. 2 | 44. 5 |
| 11. 1 | 28. 4 | 45. 5 |
| 12. 4 | 29. 4 | 46. 2 |
| 13. 2 | 30. 2 | 47. 5 |
| 14. 5 | 31. 3 | 48. 3 |
| 15. 3 | 32. 1 | 49. 5 |
| 16. 5 | 33. 3 | 50. 1 |
| 17. 1 | 34. 5 | |

# Analysis of the Answers

If you aren't sure why an answer was incorrect, use this section to get quick explanations of the answers.

1. **2.** Columbus thought he had reached the Indies when he landed in North America so he called the natives "Indians". The other answers — such as western hemisphere, discovery of the Americas, first inhabitants, or liking the sound — just don't make sense as reasons.

2. **4.** Anthropologists coined the term "aborigine." Historians, activists, Columbus, or explorers may also have used the term, but according to the passage, "anthropologists" is the correct answer.

3. **2.** In the 1960s, after much debate, "Native American" was chosen as the name for the indigenous peoples. Other terms, such as Indian, Amerindian, native peoples, and indigenous peoples, were discarded.

4. **1.** According to the passage, America was named after Italian explorer Amerigo Vespucci.

5. **4.** According to the passage, Columbus sailed west in search of Asia.

6. **3.** Columbus thought the circumference was 33 percent less than it really was. The other answers are incorrect, according to the passage.

7. **1.** Columbus didn't really care about political allegiances. He would sail for any country that was willing to pay for the trip. Other choices — troubled, arrogant, ready to sail or ambitions — don't relate to politics.

8. **5.** Columbus finally got funding from the king and queen of Spain. Portugal, England, France, or Japan didn't provided funding.

9. **4.** Ferdinand and Isabella were convinced by influential supporters to fund the voyage. The other answers — they had a unified country, the Muslims were defeated, the English and French weren't interested, and they were ready for exploration — aren't the best answers.

10. **5.** The passage states that planters and merchants were the colonial elite. Slaves, servants, apprentices, journeymen, and tenant farmers were lower on the ladder. Horse racers are not mentioned in the passage.

11. **1.** South Carolina planters were prosperous farmers. "Planters" refers to a way of making a living, so they weren't merchants or servants, which are other occupations. "City squires" aren't mentioned in the passage. Mansions are buildings, not people.

12. **4.** They went to Newport to escape the summer's heat. Other possible choices, such as horse racing, modest houses, to be near the sea, or social pursuits, may make sense (and may even be true), but they aren't given as the best reason in the passage.

13. **2.** Tenant farmers worked for a share of the crops they produced. They weren't land-holders, governors, patrons, or colonials.

14. **5.** You must read the passage slowly and carefully to determine that shopkeepers and skilled craftsmen were in the middle class. (Note that skilled craftsman is then broken into two categories: apprentices, who worked with another skilled craftsman for as long as seven years, and journeymen, craftsmen who had completed their apprenticeships.)

15. **3.** Each journeyman dreamed of having his own business someday. Other choices, such as apprenticeship, master's table, wage earner, and saving money, may have some validity, but going only by the passage, are not best answers.

16. **5.** The passage lists two self-evident truths: that all men are created equal and that the Creator endowed men with certain rights. (*Self-evident* means evident without need of explanation or proof.)

17. **1.** According to the passage, governments were to get their power from the people.

18. **3.** The people were suffering because of evils of the old government.

19. **2.** The Colonies had been suffering patiently. Other choices — king's injuries, despotism, same object, and new guards — don't refer directly to the Colonies.

20. **3.** George III had become an absolute tyrant. He was neither a kindly ruler nor a friend of the people. "Caused injuries" and "guarded securely" are not the best answers.

21. **5.** Some researchers believe cell phones are injurious to your health, particularly if they cause accidents while driving. The other answers (wonderful invention, aid to communication, medical breakthrough and useful appliance are all factors), but not the ones depicted in the cartoon.

22. **1.** The cell phone user is foolhardy in that he is operating dangerously. Other choices, such as considerate and courageous, are incorrect. Talkative and cowardly are not the best answers.

23. **2.** Some scientific research indicates that cell phones represent a risk to health. Movies, legends, opinion, and reports are not correct choices.

24. **4.** Refusing to work was the main way slaves showed that they longed to be free. Illness, poor jobs, destroyed equipment, and stolen food may have been other ways they showed their frustration, but those answers aren't as important.

25. **1.** Running away represented a form of protest. Other factors, including grievances, upset routines, appealing to the master, or being sold, were not nearly as strong as forms of protest.

26. **3.** The underground railway was organized by the abolitionists. Other possible players, such as Harriet Tubman, former slaves, runaways, and southern newspapers, may have been involved, but according to the passage, weren't the organizers.

27. **2.** Pollution tends to be at its worst in the afternoon when exhausts and emissions are trapped.

28. **4.** Exhausts and emissions are sources of pollution. Other answers, such as record heat, air rising, unhealthy air, and warmer air, are factors but aren't the most important answers.

29. **4.** Pollution tends to be most serious on the east and west coasts. The other locations — Midwest, deep south, up north, and near the Great Lakes — are incorrect according to the passage.

30. **2.** Pollution can best be prevented by reducing emissions. The other choices (temperature change, hot air layer, air rising, and warmer temperatures) may contribute, but aren't the best answers.

31. **3.** Gorbachev ended the cold war when he repudiated the Brezhnev Doctrine. Communist regimes and Brezhnev are incorrect answers. Eastern Europe and Soviet Union refer to locations, not people.

32. **1.** When the Berlin Wall fell, East and West Germany were once again united. Soviet intervention, the Brezhnev Doctrine, regimes collapsing, and U.S. intervention may have existed, but weren't the best answers.

33. **3.** According to the passage, "ethnic cleansing" refers to the expulsion of minority populations.

34. **5.** The former Soviet republics became sovereign nations. According to the passage, the Soviet republics have not disappeared, been invited to join NATO, or become the Baltic States. Nothing called CNS is mentioned in the passage.

35. **5.** All of the factors except 5 are the *opposite* of what the last sentence of the passage states, so 5 is the only correct answer.

36. **1.** President Grant was faced with "graft in his administration," which means that members of his administration faced all sorts of problems and left their jobs under pressure.

37. **3.** Over-speculation in railroad stocks led to the Panic of 1873. Other factors, such as investment failure, bankruptcy, tax evasion, and economic panic may have also happened, but they were not a direct cause of the Panic of 1873.

38. **5.** Greenbacks — not British pounds, gold, or silver — were used as a source of investment capital. "Inflation" has nothing to do with the question.

39. **1.** The failure of Cooke's bank was followed by a collapse of the stock market. The other answers are the opposite of what happened.

40. **3.** Congress ended the depression by building up its gold reserves. Credit, prices, greenbacks, and inflation didn't have much to do with the end of the depression.

41. **2.** The Mexican GDP was 2.8 percentage points higher than the U.S. GDP. The other answers are simply not correct, according to the graphs.

42. **1.** According to the GDP graphs, Canada's economy has consistently performed well when compared to the economies of the United States and Mexico.

43. **2.** The value of the Canadian dollar is a straight line, which means its value stayed the same.

44. **5.** On 1/4/2002, the index was just under 10,000, and on 1/8/2002, it was above 6,000. The answer, "down more than 3,000" is closest.

45. **5.** The Dow Jones was down by more than 2,000 points, from around 11,000 to around 9,000.

46. **2.** The setting for the cartoon is a laboratory, not a living room, playroom, library, or kitchen.

47. **5.** The researcher has been studying limited patents for medicines. You can tell this from the phrase, "perpetual patents."

48. **3.** The cartoonist depicts drug companies as greedy. Drug companies may also be dangerous or scary, but the cartoon doesn't suggest this. Drug companies certainly aren't religious. "Curious" just doesn't make sense.

49. **5.** The solution is important for the drug companies because it will increase their profits. Other potential effects — sharing with people, making employees famous, improving public relations, and looking good — may all be important to people, but they aren't the primary reason for wanting the solution.

50. **1.** The overall theme of the cartoon is the greed of the drug companies.

# Chapter 12

# The Science Test

● ● ● ● ● ● ● ● ● ● ● ● ● ● ● ● ● ● ● ● ● ● ● ● ● ● ● ● ● ● ● ● ● ● ● ● ● ● ● ● ● ● ● ● ● ● ● ● ● ● ● ● ● ● ●

### Directions

The Science Test consists of multiple-choice questions intended to measure general concepts in science. The questions are based on short readings that may include a graph, chart, or figure. Study the information given and then answer the question(s) following it. Refer to the information as often as necessary in answering the questions.

You have 80 minutes to answer the 50 questions in this booklet. Work carefully, but do not spend too much time on any one question. Be sure you answer every question.

Do not mark in this test booklet. Record your answers on the separate answer sheet provided. Be sure that all requested information is properly recorded on the answer sheet.

To record your answers, fill in the numbered circle on the answer sheet that corresponds to the answer you select for each question in the test booklet.

---

**EXAMPLE:**

Which of the following is the smallest unit in a living thing?

(1)   tissue

(2)   organ

(3)   cell

(4)   muscle

(5)   capillary

(On Answer Sheet)

① ② ● ④ ⑤

The correct answer is "cell"; therefore, answer space 3 would be marked on the answer sheet.

---

Do not rest the point of your pencil on the answer sheet while you are considering your answer. Make no stray or unnecessary marks. If you change an answer, erase your first mark completely. Mark only one answer space for each question; multiple answers will be scored as incorrect. Do not fold or crease your answer sheet. All test materials must be returned to the test administrator.

**DO NOT BEGIN TAKING THIS TEST UNTIL TOLD TO DO SO**

**SCIENCE TEST**

| | | | | | | | | | | | |
|---|---|---|---|---|---|---|---|---|---|---|---|
| 1 | ① | ② | ③ | ④ | ⑤ | | 26 | ① | ② | ③ | ④ | ⑤ |
| 2 | ① | ② | ③ | ④ | ⑤ | | 27 | ① | ② | ③ | ④ | ⑤ |
| 3 | ① | ② | ③ | ④ | ⑤ | | 28 | ① | ② | ③ | ④ | ⑤ |
| 4 | ① | ② | ③ | ④ | ⑤ | | 29 | ① | ② | ③ | ④ | ⑤ |
| 5 | ① | ② | ③ | ④ | ⑤ | | 30 | ① | ② | ③ | ④ | ⑤ |
| 6 | ① | ② | ③ | ④ | ⑤ | | 31 | ① | ② | ③ | ④ | ⑤ |
| 7 | ① | ② | ③ | ④ | ⑤ | | 32 | ① | ② | ③ | ④ | ⑤ |
| 8 | ① | ② | ③ | ④ | ⑤ | | 33 | ① | ② | ③ | ④ | ⑤ |
| 9 | ① | ② | ③ | ④ | ⑤ | | 34 | ① | ② | ③ | ④ | ⑤ |
| 10 | ① | ② | ③ | ④ | ⑤ | | 35 | ① | ② | ③ | ④ | ⑤ |
| 11 | ① | ② | ③ | ④ | ⑤ | | 36 | ① | ② | ③ | ④ | ⑤ |
| 12 | ① | ② | ③ | ④ | ⑤ | | 37 | ① | ② | ③ | ④ | ⑤ |
| 13 | ① | ② | ③ | ④ | ⑤ | | 38 | ① | ② | ③ | ④ | ⑤ |
| 14 | ① | ② | ③ | ④ | ⑤ | | 39 | ① | ② | ③ | ④ | ⑤ |
| 15 | ① | ② | ③ | ④ | ⑤ | | 40 | ① | ② | ③ | ④ | ⑤ |
| 16 | ① | ② | ③ | ④ | ⑤ | | 41 | ① | ② | ③ | ④ | ⑤ |
| 17 | ① | ② | ③ | ④ | ⑤ | | 42 | ① | ② | ③ | ④ | ⑤ |
| 18 | ① | ② | ③ | ④ | ⑤ | | 43 | ① | ② | ③ | ④ | ⑤ |
| 19 | ① | ② | ③ | ④ | ⑤ | | 44 | ① | ② | ③ | ④ | ⑤ |
| 20 | ① | ② | ③ | ④ | ⑤ | | 45 | ① | ② | ③ | ④ | ⑤ |
| 21 | ① | ② | ③ | ④ | ⑤ | | 46 | ① | ② | ③ | ④ | ⑤ |
| 22 | ① | ② | ③ | ④ | ⑤ | | 47 | ① | ② | ③ | ④ | ⑤ |
| 23 | ① | ② | ③ | ④ | ⑤ | | 48 | ① | ② | ③ | ④ | ⑤ |
| 24 | ① | ② | ③ | ④ | ⑤ | | 49 | ① | ② | ③ | ④ | ⑤ |
| 25 | ① | ② | ③ | ④ | ⑤ | | 50 | ① | ② | ③ | ④ | ⑤ |

Questions 1 and 2 refer to the following passage.

### Insulation

During the winter, you need something to keep warmth in the house and cold air out. In the summer, you need something to keep heat outside and cooler air inside. What you need is insulation.

Insulation reduces or prevents the transfer of heat (called *thermal transfer*) from the inside out or the outside in. Fiberglass and plastic foam provide such insulation because they contain trapped air. Normally, air is not a good insulator because the currents in air transfer the heat from one place to another. Trapping the air in small places, however, slows or prevents the transfer of heat. Think about these little packets of air the next time you sit in a warm house, safe from the frigid air of winter.

1. Why does a cinder block provide less thermal transfer than a window?

    (1) cinder blocks are thicker

    (2) windows have little insulation value

    (3) you can't see through cinder blocks

    (4) there is no air in a cinder block

    (5) windows are necessary for safety

2. Which would keep you warmest during the winter?

    (1) silk underwear

    (2) silk trousers

    (3) trousers padded with cotton

    (4) cotton underwear

    (5) fiberglass trousers

*Go on to next page*

Questions 3 through 5 refer to the following passage.

## Metabolism

Every cell must have a chemical mechanism for obtaining and distributing energy — the process of metabolism. Plants absorb light from the sun and convert this energy into chemical energy by the process of photosynthesis. Animals must eat food with chemical energy. These foods are primarily carbohydrates, such as glucose, that were originally derived from plants.

The first step in getting energy from glucose is *glycolysis*, a series of chemical reactions that takes place in mitochondria, by which the glucose molecule is split into pyruvic acids. In the process of fermentation, pyruvic acids are broken down into molecules, such as ethanol and lactic acid, and the energy is used to keep fermentation going. In the process of respiration, pyruvic acid molecules are broken down to carbon dioxide and water, liberating much more energy in the process.

*Adapted from James Trefil and Robert M. Hazen,* The Sciences: An Integrated Approach, 3rd Edition *(Wiley Publishing, Inc.)*

3. How do animals depend on plants to stay alive?

   (1) plants provide animals with protective cover

   (2) animals need the shade provided by plants

   (3) cures for some diseases originate in plants

   (4) plants provide a comfortable environment for animals

   (5) plants provide animals with chemical potential energy

4. What would happen to a plant if you covered it with a cloth that does not allow light to pass through it?

   (1) the plant would stop growing

   (2) the leaves would shrivel

   (3) the flower would fall off

   (4) the plant would starve to death

   (5) the roots would die

5. Which chemical is key to providing animals with energy?

   (1) pyruvic acid

   (2) carbon dioxide

   (3) chlorophyll

   (4) ethanol

   (5) lactic acid

*Go on to next page*

Questions 6 and 7 refer to the following passage.

**Velocity and Speed**

There is a difference between speed and velocity, although sometimes you see the words used interchangeably. The velocity of a body is its rate of motion in a specific direction, such as a bicycle traveling 34 miles per hour due east. Because velocity has both magnitude (34 miles per hour) and direction (due east), it can be represented by a *vector*.

Speed has a magnitude only. If a bicycle travels at a speed of 28 miles per hour, you know its magnitude (28 miles per hour), but not its direction. Because speed has a magnitude but not a direction, it can be represented as a *scalar*.

6. If *force* is defined as that which is required to change the state or motion of an object in magnitude and direction, how should it be represented?

   (1) wavy lines
   (2) straight line
   (3) grams
   (4) scalar
   (5) vector

7. If a person travels seven blocks at 3 miles per hour, but you do not know in which direction, what would represent his or her path?

   (1) kilometers
   (2) scalar
   (3) yards
   (4) vector
   (5) linear measure

*Go on to next page*

Questions 8 and 9 refer to the following diagram

**Newcomen's Steam Engine**

From C. Lon Enloe, Elizabeth Garnett, Jonathan Miles, and Stephen Swanson;
Physical Science: What the Technology Professional Needs to Know *(Wiley Publishing, Inc.)*

8. What properties of water and steam allow Newcomen's steam engine to operate?

   (1) water is heavier than steam

   (2) steam condenses when cooled, occupying less space

   (3) the boiler provides the energy to move the pump

   (4) the pump rod is heavy enough to pull the arm down

   (5) the cistern provides a positive pressure

9. What effect does the condensation of steam in the cylinder with the piston have on the pump which fills the cistern?

   (1) controls the fire in the boiler

   (2) pumps water from the cistern to the boiler

   (3) causes the pump to fill the cistern with water

   (4) forces the piston down

   (5) sprays cold water into the main pump

*Go on to next page*

Question 10 refers to the following figure.

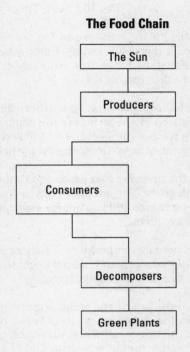

**The Food Chain**

The Sun

Producers

Consumers

Decomposers

Green Plants

10. If the number of consumers in an ecosystem
    began to multiply without control, what
    would happen to the balance of the
    ecosystem?

    (1) the green plants would increase

    (2) the herbivores would increase

    (3) consumers would starve for lack of
        food

    (4) the decomposers would go out of
        business

    (5) the sun would stop shining

Questions 11 through 14 refer to the following passage.

## The Big Bang Theory

It is hard enough to imagine the universe as it is now and even harder to create a theory about how it all began. In the 1940s, George Gamow began to develop such a theory. Georges Lemaitre, another scientist, had also been working on the problem, and Gamow used some of the ideas of Lemaitre to develop his theory.

Gamow proposed the following theory: Somewhere between 10 and 21 billion years ago, there was a giant explosion in space. Before the explosion, the universe was the size of an atomic nucleus, with a temperature of about 10 billion degrees. The explosion started the expansion of the universe. *Quarks,* or elemental particles, existed in huge numbers.

Within a millisecond, the universe had expanded to the size of a grapefruit. The temperature cooled to one billion degrees. The quarks began to clump into protons and neutrons. Minutes later, the universe was still too hot for electrons and protons to form into atoms: a super-hot, fog-like environment.

With passing time and cooling temperatures, nuclear reactions took place, and within 300,000 years, atoms of hydrogen and helium begin to emerge. As the atoms formed, light began to shine. The universe was taking shape.

Gravity began to act on the atoms and transform them into galaxies. Within one billion years of that first great explosion, galaxies and stars began to form. Within 15 billion years, planets began to emerge from the heavy elements thrown off by the dying of stars. The universe started with a big bang and continues to grow and change according to this theory.

11. The temperature of the first tiny particles was thought to be

    (1) 1 billion degrees
    (2) 20 billion degrees
    (3) 10 billion degrees
    (4) 30 billion degrees
    (5) 15 billion degrees

12. Atoms were transformed into galaxies by

    (1) heat
    (2) pressure
    (3) centrifugal force
    (4) light
    (5) gravity

13. Quarks are

    (1) atoms
    (2) 1 billion degrees
    (3) elemental particles
    (4) hydrogen
    (5) helium

14. How is the formation of hydrogen and helium atoms related to the possible destruction from an atomic bomb?

    (1) both use hydrogen
    (2) no relation
    (3) both are scientific principles
    (4) both result from explosions
    (5) both are nuclear reactions

*Go on to next page*

Questions 15 through 17 refer to the following passage

## The Jellyfish

One of the creatures living in all the world's oceans is the jellyfish. Although it lives in the ocean, it is not a fish. The jellyfish is an invertebrate; that is, an animal lacking a backbone. Not only does it lack a backbone, the jellyfish has no heart, blood, brain, or gills and is over 95 percent water.

The jellyfish has a body and tentacles. These tentacles are the long tendrils around the bell that contain stinging cells, which they use to capture prey. The movement of the prey triggers the sensory hair in the stinging cell, and the prey is then in trouble.

Unfortunately, people are also in trouble if they get too close to the tentacles of a jellyfish. The stings are not fatal to humans but can cause a great deal of discomfort.

15. Why is a jellyfish considered an invertebrate?

(1) it has tentacles

(2) it has a small brain

(3) it has a primitive circulatory system

(4) it has no backbone

(5) it swims in the ocean

16. Why do swimmers not like to be near jellyfish?

(1) they look weird

(2) swimmers can get caught in the tentacles

(3) swimmers may accidentally swallow a jellyfish

(4) the stings are painful

(5) swimmers don't like to be near ocean creatures

17. Why do most small ocean creatures try to avoid jellyfish?

(1) jellyfish get in the way of the fish when they are feeding

(2) jellyfish sting and eat small ocean creatures

(3) the fish are afraid of the strange looking creatures

(4) jellyfish and ocean creatures compete for the same food sources

(5) fish cannot swim as fast as jellyfish

*Go on to next page*

Questions 18 through 25 refer to the following passage.

**Laws of Conservation**

You are faced with laws every day. You cannot speed on the roads, and you cannot park wherever you choose.

Science has its laws, as well. One such law is that energy cannot be created or destroyed. This law of conservation of energy makes sense, because you cannot create an electrical charge, for example, from nothing. And if you have an electrical charge, you cannot simply make it disappear.

A further law of conservation is the law of conservation of matter, which says that matter cannot be created or destroyed. This means that when a chemical change occurs, the total mass of an object remains constant. For example, when you melt an ice cube, the water that results is neither heavier nor lighter than the original ice cube.

18. When lightning strikes a tree, much damage is done to the tree, but the lightning ceases to exist. What has happened to the lightning?

    (1) it disappears

    (2) the energy in the lightning is transformed into somthing else

    (3) the tree absorbs the lightning

    (4) striking the tree creates new energy to damage the tree

    (5) it is still there, but invisible

19. Why does science have laws?

    (1) science is an ordered discipline

    (2) to keep scientists honest

    (3) science needs rules to operate carefully

    (4) it makes it easier to study science

    (5) lawyers like laws

20. When a magician makes a rabbit appear in a hat, it is an example of

    (1) physics

    (2) conservation of matter

    (3) entertainment

    (4) illusion

    (5) biology

21. When an iceberg melts, what is the result?

    (1) global warming

    (2) the ocean gets warmer

    (3) nothing

    (4) fish have more food

    (5) the ocean has more water

22. When you take a dead battery out of your flashlight, what has happened to its original charge?

    (1) it has been converted into light

    (2) it has disappeared

    (3) the battery is worn out

    (4) the energy was destroyed

    (5) it went into the flashlight

23. If you add 3 ounces of water to 1 ounce of salt, what is the effect on the final mass?

    (1) the salt will absorb the water

    (2) you will get 1 ounce of salty water

    (3) nothing

    (4) the total mass will remain the same

    (5) the salt will disappear

24. A ball rolling down a hill cannot stop by itself. What would explain this?

    (1) there is a bump on the road

    (2) the ball has no brakes

    (3) the energy from rolling down the hill can't disappear

    (4) the theory of conservation of laws

    (5) the ball always weighs the same

25. Conservation of energy is an example of what?

    (1) something you have to memorize

    (2) a battery commercial

    (3) a statement by a famous scientist

    (4) a law of science

    (5) the title of an article in a magazine

*Go on to next page*

Questions 26 through 28 refer to the following passage.

### Why Do Birds Fly South for the Winter?

Every fall, the sky is full of birds flying south for the winter. However, you can see a few birds in the northern part of the country during the winter. Scientists have advanced theories about this phenomenon.

Some birds eat insects for food. In winter, many species of birds fly south, because that's where the food exists. In southern states, insects are available all year long, providing a banquet for the birds, whereas in the northern parts of the country, insects (as well as other food sources, such as seeds and berries) are scarce or even nonexistent during the winter. The birds fly south for winter to follow the food. In the spring, as insects once again become plentiful in the northern states, the birds still follow the food, this time to the north.

26. Why do migratory birds return to the northern states in the spring?

    (1) they miss their homes

    (2) it gets too hot in the southern states

    (3) they are able to find food again

    (4) habit

    (5) birds like to fly long distances

27. Why are insects responsible for the migration of some birds?

    (1) insects bite the birds

    (2) the insects lead the birds south

    (3) birds eat insects

    (4) habit

    (5) insects like to chase birds

28. Why are scientists interested in the migration of birds?

    (1) it happens regularly and apparently without explanation

    (2) scientists like to go south

    (3) they like to listen to bird songs

    (4) scientists look for connections between travel and caterpillers

    (5) someone asked the scientists

*Go on to next page*

Questions 29 and 30 refer to the following passage.

## The Lake Victoria Episode

Millions of people who live on the shores of Lake Victoria, the largest freshwater lake in Africa, know firsthand about the law of unintended consequences. What was once a rich fishing ground that provided an excellent source of protein to local people has been radically altered by the introduction of a single new species — the Nile perch.

About 30 years ago, sport fishermen, seeking a greater challenge for the growing tourist market, introduced this large, aggressive predator into the lake. The perch thrived and rapidly ate up populations of smaller fish that not only provided an essential part of the local diet but also controlled populations of algae and parasite-bearing snails. Unchecked, live algae spread over the lake's surface, while dead algae sank, decayed, and consumed oxygen in deeper water where fish used to live. Snails also multiplied and become a serious health hazard, because they carry parasites that affect humans.

*Adapted from James Trefil and Robert M. Hazen,* The Sciences: An Integrated Approach, 3rd Edition *(Wiley Publishing, Inc.)*

29. What destroyed the ecological balance in Lake Victoria?

    (1) local merchants

    (2) shrinking populations of snails

    (3) freshwater lake

    (4) growing populations of smaller fish

    (5) Nile perch

30. It is never a good idea to introduce a foreign species into a stable lake because

    (1) the foreign species has plenty of predators

    (2) the foreign species is too attractive

    (3) the other species in the lake would not have to compete for food

    (4) the foreign species is bad for sport fisherman

    (5) the foreign species can upset the ecological balance

*Go on to next page*

Questions 31 through 34 refer to the following table.

| Space Travel | | |
|---|---|---|
| *Characteristic* | *Moon* | *Mars* |
| Distance from Earth | 239,000 miles | 48,600,000 miles |
| Gravity | $\frac{1}{6}$ earth's gravity | $\frac{1}{3}$ earth's gravity |
| Atmosphere | None | Thin carbon dioxide, 1% air pressure of earth |
| Trip time | 3 days | 1.88 earth years |
| Communication time | 2.6 seconds, round trip | 10 to 41 minutes, round trip |

Adapted from Pam Walker and Elaine Wood, Hands-On General Science Activities with Real-Life Applications
(Wiley Publishing, Inc.)

**31.** If you were an aeronautical engineer planning a journey to Mars, why would you prefer to go to a space station on the moon and then launch the rocket to Mars, rather than going directly from Earth to Mars?

(1) lower gravity on moon means less fuel needed for launch

(2) more space to take off and land on the moon

(3) no atmosphere means easier take off

(4) moon is closer to earth than Mars

(5) not enough information given

**32.** If you were a communications engineer trying to establish a safety network to warn a rocket ship of dangers, where would you place the transmitter for this journey to Mars?

(1) on the moon

(2) on Earth

(3) on Mars

(4) at the space station

(5) not enough information given

**33.** Why would a trip to the moon be a better first choice than a trip to Mars for early space travelers?

(1) you can see the moon from earth without a telescope

(2) the time of the trip is much shorter

(3) the moon has a better atmosphere

(4) there are already space vehicles on the moon

(5) you could phone home from the moon

**34.** If you held a pole-vaulting contest on the moon and Mars, on which planet could the same contestant vault higher with the same expenditure of energy?

(1) the moon

(2) Mars

(3) Earth

(4) no difference

(5) not enough information given

*Go on to next page*

Questions 35 through 37 refer to the following passage.

**Heredity, Then and Now**

How often have you seen a young child and said, "She takes after her parents." Many traits in a child do come from her parents. Physical and other characteristics, such as hair color and nose shape, are transmitted from one generation to the next. These characteristics, passed from one generation to the next, exist because of *genetic code.*

The first scientist to experiment with heredity was Gregor Mendel during the 19th century. Mendel experimented with pea plants and noted that characteristics appearing in "child" plants were similar to the "parent" plants. Mendel hypothesized that these characteristics were carried from generation to generation by "factors." It took many years of research to understand why children often look like their parents, but genetic code is now the basis of the study of heredity.

35. According to the passage, what is a primary determinant for characteristics of the next generation?

    (1) chance
    (2) hair color
    (3) pea plants
    (4) heredity
    (5) nature

36. What are the factors that Mendel hypothesized carried traits from one generation to the next?

    (1) plants
    (2) peas
    (3) traits
    (4) protons
    (5) genetic code

37. If you want to grow monster-sized pumpkins, from what kind of pumpkins do you want to get seeds?

    (1) orange ones
    (2) doesn't matter; I have special fertilizer
    (3) monster-sized pumpkins
    (4) larger than average
    (5) healthy ones

*Go on to next page*

Questions 38 and 39 refer to the following passage.

**The Space Shuttle**

NASA has designed and built six space shuttles: Atlantis, Challenger, Columbia, Discovery, Endeavor, and Enterprise. The space shuttles are made up of two distinct parts: the orbiter and the booster rocket. The booster rocket provides the additional thrust to get the space shuttle away from the gravitational pull of the earth. The orbiter carries the people and payload as well as the workings of the shuttle. In a space flight, the booster is jettisoned after clearing the earth's gravitational pull, and the orbiter continues on its way.

**38.** Why would the booster be jettisoned?

   (1) to have more fuel for later in the trip

   (2) because the shuttle needs to add weight

   (3) to increase the size of the shuttle

   (4) to make the shuttle less maneuverable for landing

   (5) because it is no longer needed

**39.** Which part of a shuttle carries the payload?

   (1) booster

   (2) cockpit

   (3) orbiter

   (4) rocket

   (5) Challenger

*Go on to next page*

Questions 40 and 41 refer to the following figure.

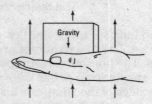

*From C. Lon Enloe, Elizabeth Garnett, Jonathan Miles, and Stephen Swanson;*
*Physical Science: What the Technology Professional Needs to Know (Wiley Publishing, Inc.)*

40. IWork is defined as the product of force times displacement. Consider the diagram. If the force of gravity is greater than the forces being exerted by the muscles controlling the hand, what would happen?

    (1) nothing

    (2) the hand would move downward

    (3) the hand would move to the right

    (4) the hand would move upwards

    (5) the hand would move to the left

41. If an athlete knows that building muscles requires doing work against a weight, what would the athlete want to change in this diagram?

    (1) nothing

    (2) moving the hand upward faster

    (3) adding weight to the hand

    (4) closing the fist as the arm is raised

    (5) exhaling as the arm is raised

*Go on to next page*

Questions 42 and 43 refer to the following passage.

**Copying DNA Sequence**

The polymerase chain reaction (PCR) copies a sequence of DNA. In order to do this, a strand of DNA is mixed with nucleotides (DNA precursors). Nucleotides target a specific piece of DNA, as well as polymerase, an enzyme that helps to assemble DNA. Heat is applied until the temperature reaches 200°F. The energy from the heating separates the DNA strands. The mixture is then cooled to 140°F. At this temperature, the primers attach themselves to the DNA strands. Raising the temperature to 160°F causes the nucleotides to begin to attach to the DNA strands. After all this, two copies of the DNA are created.

*Adapted from James Trefil and Robert M. Hazen,* The Sciences: An Integrated Approach, 3rd Edition *(Wiley Publishing, Inc.)*

42. What process in the polymerase chain reaction separates the DNA strands.

    (1) heating
    (2) chemicals
    (3) pulling
    (4) gravity
    (5) chilling

43. In order to clone an organism, you require an identical DNA blueprint. Why is the PCR something a scientist who is interested in cloning would want to study?

    (1) it creates an identical copy of the DNA
    (2) PCR clones animals
    (3) scientists should know everything
    (4) a duplicate DNA structure cools clones
    (5) the heat destroys clones

*Go on to next page*

Questions 44 and 45 refer to the following passage.

### Dogs and Wolves — Relatives?

Current scientific theory is that the familiar family pet, the dog, descended from the wolf, but the dog has taken a very different path from the wolf. The dog was the first animal to be domesticated, right around the end of the Ice Age.

Dogs are part of an extended family called *Canidae,* which contains 38 different species. Jackals, foxes, wolves, and dogs are all part of this family.

Although they are related, wolves and dogs are different. Wolves have smaller heads for the same body weight. Dogs have smaller teeth, a more curved lower jaw, and eyes that are more rounded and forward looking. At a distance, however, many of these difference are difficult to spot.

44. What feature makes the wolf better adapted to hunting in the wild?

    (1) heavier coat
    (2) larger body
    (3) larger teeth
    (4) larger paws
    (5) deeper growl

45. Of the members of the *Canidae* family that were mentioned, why is the dog the only household pet?

    (1) there are many types of dogs to choose from
    (2) it was domesticated
    (3) dogs are smaller than wolves
    (4) dogs protect people's houses
    (5) dogs can help the visually impaired

*Go on to next page*

Questions 46 and 47 refer to the following passage.

### Isotopes

Isotopes are chemical cousins. They are related to each other, but each isotope has slightly different — but related — atoms. Each of the related atoms has the same number of electrons or protons, but a different number of neutrons. Because the number of electrons or protons determines the atomic number, isotopes have the same atomic number.

The number of neutrons determines the mass number. Because the number of neutrons in each isotope is different, the mass number is different. These cousins all have different mass numbers but the same atomic number. Their chemical properties are similar, but not the same. Like most cousins, they have family resemblances, but each has a unique personality.

46. What determines the atomic number?
    (1) number of isotopes
    (2) number of neutrons
    (3) number of electrons
    (4) number of man
    (5) number of chemicals

47. Isotopes of a chemical have the same
    (1) number of neutrons
    (2) number of atoms
    (3) mass number
    (4) size
    (5) atomic number

48. A scientist has found related atoms in two different substances. If both atoms have the same atomic number but different mass numbers, what preliminary conclusion can be reached about the atoms?
    (1) they are the same substance
    (2) they are isotopes
    (3) they are different substances
    (4) one is a compound of the other
    (5) it is too early to make any decisions

*Go on to next page*

Questions 49 and 50 refer to the following passage.

### How to Survive the Winter

When the temperature drops and the wind blows cold, you may think of animals that don't have homes to keep out the cold and worry about their ability to survive the winter. Not much food is available, temperatures in northern states go into the sub-zero range, and shelter is limited. How do they survive the winter?

Many animals can hibernate for the winter. Hibernation is a sleep-like condition in which the animal's heartbeat, temperature, and metabolism slow down to adapt to the colder temperatures. This dormant condition prevents their starving or freezing during the harsh winters.

49. Bears survive the winter by:

   (1) going south

   (2) living in warm caves

   (3) growing a heavy winter coat

   (4) absorbing the sun's rays to keep warm

   (5) finding a safe shelter and hibernating

50. Why should you not disturb a hibernating animal?

   (1) it gets grouchy when awakened suddenly

   (2) it needs its sleep

   (3) it could have trouble falling asleep again

   (4) you should never bother a wild animal

   (5) it would not be able to find enough food to survive

**END OF EXAMINATION**

# Chapter 13

# Answers and Explanations for the Science Test

## Answer Key

After taking the Science Test in Chapter 12, use this section to check your answers.

| | | |
|---|---|---|
| 1. 2 | 18. 2 | 35. 4 |
| 2. 3 | 19. 1 | 36. 5 |
| 3. 5 | 20. 4 | 37. 3 |
| 4. 4 | 21. 5 | 38. 5 |
| 5. 1 | 22. 1 | 39. 3 |
| 6. 5 | 23. 4 | 40. 2 |
| 7. 2 | 24. 3 | 41. 3 |
| 8. 2 | 25. 4 | 42. 1 |
| 9. 3 | 26. 3 | 43. 1 |
| 10. 3 | 27. 3 | 44. 3 |
| 11. 3 | 28. 1 | 45. 2 |
| 12. 5 | 29. 5 | 46. 5 |
| 13. 3 | 30. 5 | 47. 2 |
| 14. 5 | 31. 1 | 48. 3 |
| 15. 4 | 32. 5 | 49. 5 |
| 16. 4 | 33. 2 | 50. 5 |
| 17. 2 | 34. 1 | |

# Analysis of the Answers

If you aren't sure why an answer was incorrect, use this section to get quick explanations of the answers.

1. **2.** Glass contains no encapsulated air and thus provides neither insulation nor greater thermal flow. Answer 1, that cinder blocks are thicker, can be true, but is not an answer to the question about heat transfer. Answer 2, that windows have little insulation value, is the best of the answers. Answer 3, that you can't see through cinder blocks, is true and interesting but irrelevant to the question. Answer 4, that there is no air in a cinder block, is not accurate. Answer 5, that windows are necessary for safety, is not only irrelevant, but incorrect.

2. **3.** The passage says that insulation is necessary for reduced heat transfer, which would keep you warmer. All of the answers except 3 refer to a piece of clothing made of a single layer of material. The cotton padding acts as insulation for the trousers.

3. **5.** The passage states that animals must eat food with chemical potential energy, which is derived from plants.

   This passage gives you a lot of interesting information, but because you have a time limit, you may want to read the question and look for the answer instead of reading the passage, reading the question, and reading the passage again.

4. **4.** Plants produce food using energy from the sun. If you cut off the energy from the sun, you cut off the food supply.

5. **1.** According to the passage, pyruvic acid is key to energy production.

6. **5.** The passage states that velocity can be represented by a vector because it has both magnitude and direction. Force is defined as changing the state or motion of an object, either in magnitude or direction. Because a force has magnitude and direction, it is represented by a vector.

7. **2.** If a person travels seven blocks from home to school, only the distance is defined. The person can go 4 blocks due east and 3 blocks due west. He or she could take a roundabout path involving all four points of the compass. You really don't know what the person is doing except somehow traveling 7 blocks to school. This activity has only a magnitude and no direction, so it is represented by a scalar.

8. **2.** In the steam engine, water cools the steam, which then condenses, occupying less space. This starts the entire cycle over again. The other answers can be eliminated if guessing is necessary. Answer 1 is incorrect because water and steam are both water, but in different states. Their density may be different, but their weight is the same. Only the volume differs when water turns to steam. Answer 3 is incorrect, because the boiler doesn't provide the energy to move the pump. A close look at the diagram shows you that. Answer 4 is not based on information given. Nowhere are you told the weight of the pump rod. Answer 5 is not based on the diagram, on fact, or on general knowledge.

9. **3.** The pump pushes water into the cistern.

10. **3.** The producers provide food for the consumers. If the producers stay the same but the consumers increase, there will not be enough food, and consumers will starve.

11. **3.** The temperature of the first tiny particles is stated as 10 billion degrees in the passage. This is a good question on which to practice your skimming skills to find an answer. If you skim the passage, you see the words "10 billion degrees." Reading the sentence confirms the answer.

12. **5.** The last paragraph states that gravity transformed the atoms into galaxies.

13. **3.** The passage states that quarks are elemental particles.

14. **5.** An atomic bomb uses a nuclear reaction to produce its massive damage. The passage states that hydrogen and helium atoms were formed by nuclear reactions.

15. **4.** According to the passage, invertebrates have no backbones.

16. **4.** Jellyfish sting swimmers, and the stings are painful.

17. **2.** Small ocean creatures are always on the menu for jellyfish.

18. **2.** The passage states that energy cannot be created or destroyed, thus the energy from the lightning must be transformed into another type of energy. The other answers imply that the energy has somehow disappeared, which the passage says can't happen.

19. **1.** Science is an ordered discipline and, as such, needs laws to maintain its organization.

20. **4.** Matter cannot be created or destroyed. A rabbit cannot appear except by illusion.

21. **5.** When ice melts, it turns into water. Although the amount of water in a melting iceberg is tiny compared to the amount of water in the ocean, it does add some water to the ocean.

22. **1.** Flashlights provide light by using the energy in the battery. The passage says that energy cannot be created or destroyed, so the energy in the battery must have been converted or transformed into something else. In reality, even if you don't use a battery for an extended time, the battery grows weaker because of other reactions inside the cell. But this is not mentioned in the passage and is just a reminder not to leave batteries in your flashlight forever.

23. **4.** If you add 3 ounces of water to 1 ounce of salt, you have 4 ounces of combined ingredients. The combined mass is the same as the sum of the individual masses. The volume may be different but that isn't what the question asks.

24. **3.** The law of conservation of energy states that energy cannot be created or destroyed. The energy developed by the ball rolling down the hill can't disappear.

25. **4.** Conservation of energy is a law of science.

26. **3.** The passage states that the lack of food in the winter months makes most birds fly south to find sources of food. When the food returns to the northern states, so do the birds.

27. **3.** Some birds eat insects for their food supply. If an area has no insects, the birds move to find a new source of food.

28. **1.** Scientists are curious about anything that happens regularly that cannot be easily explained. Migration is one such issue.

29. **5.** This question could have had many answers, from sport fishermen to algae to snails. Of the potential answers given, however, Nile perch is the only correct one.

30. **5.** This question asks you to make a general statement about foreign species of fish. While this question doesn't ask you specifically to consider the Lake Victoria example, you're supposed to think about that example as you answer the question. Using the Lake Victoria example, you can safely say that a foreign species upsets the local balance. You also know from the example that the other four choices are incorrect.

31. **1.** The less fuel you need to launch, the less you have to carry. With the gravity on the moon less than that on Earth, you need less force to break free of gravity.

32. **5.** Not enough information is given about possible options. The only locations mentioned are Mars and the moon.

33. **2.** According to the table, it takes just three days to get to the moon, which is a much better first choice than the 1.88 years needed to get to Mars.

34. **1.** Gravity on the moon is less than that on Mars. Because gravity is the force that attracts you to the moon (or to Earth or to Mars) the less the gravity, the less attraction between you and the surface upon which you are standing. Thus, the higher you can jump.

35. **4.** The passage states that heredity determines the characteristics of the next generation.

36. **5.** The passage states that "These characteristics, passed from one generation to the next, are called the *genetic code*." Thus the best answer is 5, genetic code.

37. **3.** If children inherit the traits of their parents, you would want the desired traits of your pumpkin to be a part of the traits of the parent pumpkins. Monster-sized pumpkin seeds have a better chance of producing extra large pumpkins than do the seeds from a regular-sized pumpkin.

38. **5.** All of the choices are incorrect — in fact, in direct opposition to the passage — except answer 5, that the booster is no longer needed.

39. **3.** Because the booster is jettisoned after takeoff, the orbiter would have to carry anything that is to continue the trip.

40. **2.** If the force pushing down is greater than the force pushing up, the hand would move down.

41. **3.** A larger weight in the hand would produce a greater force downward. The athlete would then be working against this weight.

42. **1.** The passage tells you that heating is the process.

43. **1.** Cloning requires identical DNA. PCR provides identical DNA.

44. **3.** The larger teeth of the wolf are better for hunting. The passage states that dogs have smaller teeth, thus wolves must have bigger teeth.

45. **2.** The passage states that the dog was domesticated very long ago. A domesticated animal is preferable to a wild one for a household pet.

46. **3.** According to the passage, the atomic number is determined by the number of electrons or protons.

47. **5.** The passage states that isotopes have the same atomic number.

In most cases, you don't have to memorize factual information for these tests; the factual information is given in the passage.

48. **2.** The passage states that isotopes have the same atomic numbers.

49. **5.** According to the passage, bears survive the winter by finding a safe shelter and hibernating.

50. **5.** Animals hibernate in the winter when food is scarce. If you wake a hibernating animal, it awakes to a strange environment without its usual sources of food and probably cannot find enough food to survive. The other answers may be right in some circumstances, but they do not relate to the passage. Answer 4 is good advice but not a good answer.

# Chapter 14

# The Language Arts, Reading Test

## Directions

The Language Arts, Reading Test consists of excerpts from fiction and nonfiction. Each excerpt is followed by multiple-choice questions about the reading material.

Read each excerpt first and then answer the questions following it. Refer back to the reading material as often as necessary in answering the questions.

Each excerpt is preceded by a *purpose question*. The purpose question gives a reason for reading the material. Use these purpose questions to help focus your reading. You are not required to answer these purpose questions. They are given only to help you concentrate on the ideas presented in the reading material.

You have 65 minutes to answer the 40 questions in this booklet. Work carefully, but do not spend too much time on any one question. Be sure you answer every question.

Do not mark in this test booklet. Record your answers on the separate answer sheet provided. Be sure that all requested information is properly recorded on the answer sheet.

To record your answers, fill in the numbered circle on the answer sheet that corresponds to the answer you select for each question in the test booklet.

---

**EXAMPLE:**

It was Susan's dream machine. The metallic blue paint gleamed, and the sporty wheels were highly polished. Under the hood, the engine was no less carefully cleaned. Inside, flashy lights illuminated the instruments on the dashboard, and the seats were covered by rich leather upholstery.

The subject ("it") of this excerpt is most likely

(1) an airplane

(2) a stereo system

(3) an automobile

(4) a boat

(5) a motorcycle

(On Answer Sheet)
① ② ● ④ ⑤

The correct answer is "an automobile;" therefore, answer space 3 would be marked on the answer sheet.

---

Do not rest the point of your pencil on the answer sheet while you are considering your answer. Make no stray or unnecessary marks. If you change an answer, erase your first mark completely. Mark only one answer space for each question; multiple answers will be scored as incorrect. Do not fold or crease your answer sheet. All test materials must be returned to the test administrator.

**DO NOT BEGIN TAKING THIS TEST UNTIL TOLD TO DO SO**

**READING TEST**

| | | |
|---|---|---|
| 1 ① ② ③ ④ ⑤ | | 21 ① ② ③ ④ ⑤ |
| 2 ① ② ③ ④ ⑤ | | 22 ① ② ③ ④ ⑤ |
| 3 ① ② ③ ④ ⑤ | | 23 ① ② ③ ④ ⑤ |
| 4 ① ② ③ ④ ⑤ | | 24 ① ② ③ ④ ⑤ |
| 5 ① ② ③ ④ ⑤ | | 25 ① ② ③ ④ ⑤ |
| 6 ① ② ③ ④ ⑤ | | 26 ① ② ③ ④ ⑤ |
| 7 ① ② ③ ④ ⑤ | | 27 ① ② ③ ④ ⑤ |
| 8 ① ② ③ ④ ⑤ | | 28 ① ② ③ ④ ⑤ |
| 9 ① ② ③ ④ ⑤ | | 29 ① ② ③ ④ ⑤ |
| 10 ① ② ③ ④ ⑤ | | 30 ① ② ③ ④ ⑤ |
| 11 ① ② ③ ④ ⑤ | | 31 ① ② ③ ④ ⑤ |
| 12 ① ② ③ ④ ⑤ | | 32 ① ② ③ ④ ⑤ |
| 13 ① ② ③ ④ ⑤ | | 33 ① ② ③ ④ ⑤ |
| 14 ① ② ③ ④ ⑤ | | 34 ① ② ③ ④ ⑤ |
| 15 ① ② ③ ④ ⑤ | | 35 ① ② ③ ④ ⑤ |
| 16 ① ② ③ ④ ⑤ | | 36 ① ② ③ ④ ⑤ |
| 17 ① ② ③ ④ ⑤ | | 37 ① ② ③ ④ ⑤ |
| 18 ① ② ③ ④ ⑤ | | 38 ① ② ③ ④ ⑤ |
| 19 ① ② ③ ④ ⑤ | | 39 ① ② ③ ④ ⑤ |
| 20 ① ② ③ ④ ⑤ | | 40 ① ② ③ ④ ⑤ |

**Directions:** Choose the <u>one best answer</u> to each question.

Questions 1 through 6 refer to the following poem.

### WHAT WAS "THE SHOT HEARD 'ROUND THE WORLD"?

Line

By the rude bridge that arched the flood,
Their flag to April's breeze unfurled,
Here once the embattled farmers stood,
And fired the shot heard round the world.

(05) The foe long since in silence slept;
Alike the conqueror silent sleeps;
And Time the ruined bridge has swept
Down the dark stream which seaward creeps.

On this green bank, by this soft stream,
(10) We set today a votive stone;
That memory may their deed redeem,
When, like our sires, our sons are gone.

Spirit, that made those heroes dare
To die, and leave their children free,
(15) Bid Time and Nature gently spare
The shaft we raise to them and thee.

*Ralph Waldo Emerson, "Concord Hymn," 1886*

1. What is the best phrase to describe where the farmers made their stand?

   (1) by the rough-structured span

   (2) beside the flood

   (3) under the flag

   (4) in April's breeze

   (5) over the arch

2. What were the farmers ready for?

   (1) negotiations

   (2) vacation

   (3) retreat

   (4) war

   (5) celebrations

3. Why are foes and conquerors silent?

   (1) they've gone away

   (2) they've all since died

   (3) they lost the battle

   (4) they won the war

   (5) they live together peacefully

4. What has happened to the bridge?

   (1) it was rebuilt after the battle

   (2) it's not a memory now

   (3) it hasn't been swept away

   (4) it never existed

   (5) only the ruins now remain

5. What does a "votive stone" in line 10 refer to?

   (1) a monument to the fallen

   (2) a new bridge to cross the stream

   (3) a memorial celebration

   (4) a flag-raising ceremony

   (5) a family reunion

6. What does "the shot heard round the world" (line 4) refer to?

   (1) only time will tell

   (2) the unfurling of a flag

   (3) an event about to begin

   (4) the sleeping foes

   (5) the setting of a votive stone

*Go on to next page* →

Questions 7 through 12 refer to the following excerpt.

### WHERE DOES EVIL COME FROM?

Line

**DWIGHT:** (Sitting at table, reading newspaper.) Morning.

**DAD:** You see your brother this morning?

**DWIGHT:** In bed.

**DAD:** I promised Harry Shepherd I'd be over to his place by seven-thirty. He's got a lost
(05) sheep out on the mountain wild and steep.

**DWIGHT:** Says here that fatted calves are down one and three-quarter shekels on the
Damascus market, Dad. Makes me wonder if maybe lean calves wouldn't have a higher profit
margin, and then we could spend more time in the vineyard — Dad, are you listening to me?

**DAD:** I'm worried about your brother.

(10) **DWIGHT:** We can't afford to stand still, Dad. Look at the Stewarts — they're buying up land
left and right! You've got to move ahead or you lose ground . . . .

**WALLY:** (Thickly.) Morning, Dad. Morning, Dwight. (He sits down, groans, puts his head in
his hands.)

**DAD:** You look a little peaked, son.

(15) **WALLY:** I donno — it's some kind of morning sickness, Dad. I feel real good at night and then
I wake up and hurt all over.

**DWIGHT:** I noticed a couple empty wineskins behind the fig tree this morning.

**WALLY:** I dropped them, and they spilled! Honest!

**DAD:** Where were you taking them?

(20) **WALLY:** I was putting them outside! Wine's got to breathe, you know. And so do I, Dad. I've
got a real breathing problem here. I'm worried about my health, Dad. I read an article the
other day in *Assyrian Digest* that says bad feelings may be environmental. I donno. Maybe I
need to get away for a while, Dad. Get my head straight. Work out some things.

*Excerpted from Garrison Keillor, "Prodigal Son," 1989*

7. Why does Wally's father think Wally doesn't
feel well this morning?

   (1) Wally feels badly that he spilled
   some wine

   (2) Wally works on a tree farm in Judea

   (3) Wally drank too much wine

   (4) Wally needs a vacation

   (5) Wally wants to run the business

8. What is the setting for the play?

   (1) breakfast table

   (2) fig tree

   (3) market

   (4) bed

   (5) vineyard

*Go on to next page*

9. Why did Dwight feel it would be better to raise lean calves?

    (1) less profit

    (2) fat is bad for you

    (3) more profit

    (4) more expensive to produce

    (5) better than goats

10. Why isn't Dad paying attention to Dwight?

    (1) he wants to help find a lost sheep

    (2) he wants to spend time in the vineyard

    (3) he wants to buy more land

    (4) he is reading the paper

    (5) he is worried about Wally

11. Why do you think Wally is late for breakfast?

    (1) he is sick

    (2) he has a hangover

    (3) he is doing the chores

    (4) he is reading an article

    (5) he is working in the fields

12. What comparison does Wally make between himself and wine?

    (1) they both are sweet

    (2) they both like to travel

    (3) they both need to breathe

    (4) they are both precious

    (5) they both cause problems

*Go on to next page* ⟶

Questions 13 through 18 refer to the following excerpt.

## HOW CAN I MAKE MY FORTUNE?

Line

When the world rang with the tale of Arctic gold, and the lure of the North gripped the heart-strings of men, Carter Weatherbee threw up his snug clerkship, turned the half of his savings over to his wife, and with the remainder bought an outfit. There was no romance in his nature — the bondage of commerce had crushed all that; he was simply tired of the cease-
(05) less grind, and wished to risk great hazards in view of corresponding returns . . . and there, unluckily for his soul's welfare, he allied himself with a party of men.

There was nothing unusual about this party, except its plans. Even its goal, like that of all the other parties, was the Klondike. But the route it had mapped out to attain that goal took away the breath of the hardiest native, born and bred to the vicissitudes of the Northwest.
(10) Even Jacques Baptiste, born of a Chippewa woman and a renegade voyageur (having raised his first whimpers in a deerskin lodge north of the sixty-fifth parallel, and had the same hushed by blissful sucks of raw tallow), was surprised. Though he sold his services to them and agreed to travel even to the never-opening ice, he shook his head ominously whenever his advice was asked.

(15) Percy Cuthfert's evil star must have been in the ascendant, for he, too, joined this company of Argonauts. He was an ordinary man, with a bank account as deep as his culture, which is saying a good deal. He had no reason to embark on such a venture — no reason in the world, save that he suffered from an abnormal development of sentimentality. He mistook this for the true spirit of romance and adventure.

*Excerpted from Jack London, "In a Far Country," 1898*

13. What caused Carter Weatherbee to leave his job?

(1) arctic gold
(2) a woman
(3) his snug clerkship
(4) half his savings
(5) the heartstrings of men

14. What is meant by "bondage of commerce" in line 4?

(1) the corresponding returns
(2) the romance in his nature
(3) the drudgery of life as a clerk
(4) the risk of great hazards
(5) half of his savings

15. What was the goal of the party?

(1) find the old trails
(2) reach the Klondike
(3) map out a route
(4) tell the tale of the Arctic
(5) buy outfits

16. How would you best describe the chosen route to the Klondike?

(1) blissful
(2) hardy
(3) hushed
(4) ominous
(5) surprising

*Go on to next page*

**17.** Why was Jacques Baptiste important to the party?

(1) he was a native of the Northwest

(2) he was born of a Chippewa woman

(3) he was a renegade voyageur

(4) he was born in a deerskin lodge

(5) he sucked raw tallow

**18.** Why do you think Percy Cuthfert joined the party?

(1) to show that he is an ordinary man

(2) to fill his bank account

(3) to seek romance and adventure

(4) to be able to say a good deal

(5) because of his abnormal development

*Go on to next page*

Questions 19 through 24 refer to the following excerpt.

### WHY DOES SONNY FEEL SORRY?

Line

DEAR BROTHER,

(05) You don't know how much I needed to hear from you. I wanted to write you many a time but I dug how much I must have hurt you and so I didn't write. But now I feel like a man who's been trying to climb up out of some deep, real deep and funky hole and just saw the sun up there, outside. I got to get outside.

(10) I can't tell you much about how I got here. I mean I don't know how to tell you. I guess I was afraid of something or I was trying to escape from something and you know I have never been very strong in the head (smile). I'm glad Mama and Daddy are dead and can't see what's happened to their son and I swear if I'd known what I was doing I would never have hurt you so, you and a lot of other fine people who were nice to me and who believed in me.

(15) I don't want you to think it had anything to do with me being a musician. It's more than that. Or maybe less than that. I can't get anything straight in my head down here and I try not to think about what's going to happen to me when I get outside again. Sometime I think I'm going to flip and *never* get outside and sometime I think I'll come straight back. I tell you one thing, though, I'd rather blow my brains out than go through this again. But that's what they all say, so they tell me.

Your brother,
SONNY

*Excerpted from James Baldwin, "Sonny's Blues," 1957*

**19.** Why didn't Sonny write to his brother (lines 1–5)?

(1) he was lazy

(2) he felt guilty

(3) he was too busy

(4) he was afraid

(5) he was in a hole

**20.** Where do you think Sonny is writing from?

(1) a funky hole

(2) inside the place

(3) a prison cell

(4) another space

(5) a deep place

**21.** What is the meaning of "strong in the head" (line 8)?

(1) physically fit

(2) humorous

(3) happy

(4) intelligent

(5) angry

**22.** Why is Sonny glad his parents are dead (lines 8 and 9)?

(1) they escaped from something that no one knows about

(2) they never have to hurt him

(3) they were afraid of something

(4) they knew a lot of other fine people from the neighborhood

(5) they cannot see what has happened to their son

*Go on to next page*

23. What is Sonny most afraid of while inside?
    (1) flipping before he gets out
    (2) getting anything straight
    (3) being a musician
    (4) coming straight back
    (5) blowing his brains out

24. How does Sonny feel about his brother?
    (1) he blames him
    (2) he hates him
    (3) he likes him
    (4) he likes his music
    (5) he rejects him

*Go on to next page*

Questions 25 through 30 refer to the following excerpt.

## WHAT WERE THE THINGS THEY CARRIED?

Line

First Lieutenant Jimmy Cross carried letters from a girl named Martha, a junior at Mount Sebastian College in New Jersey. They were not love letters, but Lieutenant Cross was hoping, so he kept them folded in plastic at the bottom of his rucksack. In the late afternoon, after a day's march, he would dig his foxhole, wash his hands under a canteen, unwrap the

(05) letters, hold them with the tips of his fingers, and spend the last hour of light pretending. He would imagine romantic camping trips into the White Mountains in New Hampshire. He would sometimes taste the envelope flaps, knowing her tongue had been there. More than anything, he wanted Martha to love him as he loved her, but the letters were mostly chatty, elusive on the matter of love. She was a virgin, he was almost sure. She was an English major

(10) at Mount Sebastian, and she wrote beautifully about her professors and roommates and midterm exams, about her respect for Chaucer and her great affection for Virginia Woolf. She often quoted lines of poetry; she never mentioned the war, except to say, Jimmy, take care of yourself. The letters weighed 10 ounces. They were signed Love, Martha, but Lieutenant Cross understood that Love was only a way of signing and did not mean what he sometimes

(15) pretended it meant. At dusk, he would carefully return the letters to his rucksack. Slowly, a bit distracted, he would get up and move among his men, checking the perimeter, then at full dark he would return to his hole and watch the night and wonder if Martha was a virgin.

*Excerpted from Tim O'Brien, "The Things They Carried," 1990*

**25.** When did Jimmy read Martha's letters?

(1) after a day's march

(2) in his fox hole

(3) under a canteen

(4) at the bottom of his rucksack

(5) in the first light of day

**26.** How would you best describe their relationship?

(1) lovers

(2) strangers

(3) acquaintances

(4) siblings

(5) no relationship

**27.** How did Jimmy demonstrate his affection?

(1) he washed his hands

(2) he wrapped the letters

(3) by the tips of his fingers

(4) at the last hour of light

(5) he tasted the envelope flaps

**28.** What does the phrase "mostly chatty" (line 8) tell you about Martha's feelings toward Jimmy?

(1) she cares deeply

(2) she is just being friendly

(3) she is infatuated

(4) she has a casual interest

(5) she has no feelings for Jimmy at all

*Go on to next page*

29. How do you know Martha enjoyed writing letters?

    (1) her letters were full of news

    (2) her respect for Chaucer

    (3) she was an English major

    (4) she wrote beautifully

    (5) her professors and roommates

30. What do you think the letters really meant to Jimmy?

    (1) an interesting hobby

    (2) a pleasing pastime

    (3) a way to escape boredom

    (4) a sense of hope for the future

    (5) profound disappointment

*Go on to next page*

Questions 31 through 35 refer to the following excerpt.

## WHAT ARE THE SECRETS OF THUNDER BAY?

Line

ABOARD THE R. V. CONNECTICUT — Sunrise glinted off serene Thunder Bay yesterday and clear blue skies offered stunning views of islands, rugged coastline and kilometers of green water.

(05) But the Lake Huron bay didn't earn its name or notorious reputation on balmy late summer days.

The lake bottom off northeast Michigan is a shipping graveyard, littered with hundreds of steamers and schooners that gambled their loads of grain, ore and sailors' lives against the lake's unpredictable late fall weather.

(10) "It was all about money and the ships were competing. One more trip meant more money," said Jeff Gray, manager of the Thunder Bay National Marine Sanctuary and Underwater Preserve.

"It was a risk that owners and captains took, and records often showed it was to be the last trip of the season."

Yesterday, researchers and historians aboard the Research Vessel Connecticut huddled around a bank of video monitors and computer screens and scanned the lake floor 30 meters (15) below, waiting for a glimpse of the 40 meter E. B. Allen.

The three-mast schooner collided with another vessel in heavy fog and sank in September, 1871 while carrying a cargo of grain from Chicago to Buffalo.

Soon the ship appeared through the cold, clear depths — the still-solid oak hull, here-and-there slabs of pine decking, jutting sections of fir masts, the rudder, the anchor hoist.

(20) "It's beautiful imagery," said historian C. Patrick Labadie, retired director of the Canal Park Marine Museum in Duluth, Minn.

"I'm used to seeing wrecks in bits and pieces. The ability to do research of a relatively deep wreck is fantastic."

The Connecticut expedition will study Great Lakes shipping history and is a joint operation (25) that teams researcher and explorer Robert Ballard's staff with the National Oceanic and Atmospheric Administration and Thunder Bay Sanctuary personnel.

Ballard, who found the *Titanic in* 1985 and recently located John F. Kennedy's PT 109, is interested in the Thunder Bay sanctuary in part because it's the newest arrival among 13 U.S. national marine sanctuaries.

(30) Ballard's team from the Institute for Exploration toured the 1,300-square-kilometer Thunder Bay sanctuary last year, where wrecks spanning nearly 200 years rest on the bottom.

*Mike Tyree, Associated Press, August 31, 2002. Reprinted with permission of The Associated Press.*

*Go on to next page*

31. How does the writer describe Thunder Bay?
    (1) it's clear and blue
    (2) it's stunning and rugged
    (3) it has green water
    (4) it is a serene sunrise
    (5) it has balmy summer days

32. How did Thunder Bay earn its name?
    (1) unpredictable fall weather
    (2) competing ships
    (3) northeast Michigan
    (4) the hundreds of steamers
    (5) loads of grain and ore

33. Why do you think it was named a National Marine Sanctuary?
    (1) its stunning views
    (2) the deep water
    (3) it's appealing to visitors
    (4) it's a shipping graveyard
    (5) for the last trip of the season

34. Why do you think Robert Ballard was a good choice for the expedition?
    (1) his shipping history
    (2) he is a researcher and explorer
    (3) he found the Titanic
    (4) he toured the sanctuary
    (5) he knows Thunder Bay

35. What is the most important reason for creating the Sanctuary?
    (1) exploring the area
    (2) encouraging tourism
    (3) getting donations
    (4) studying shipping
    (5) preserving historic wrecks

*Go on to next page*

Questions 36 through 40 refer to the following excerpt.

### HOW MUST EMPLOYEES BEHAVE?

<sup>Line</sup> It is expected that employees behave in a respectful, responsible, professional manner. Therefore, each employee must do the following:

> ✔ Wear appropriate clothing and use safety equipment where needed.

(05)
> ✔ Refrain from the use and possession of alcohol and/or illicit drugs and associated paraphernalia throughout the duration of the work day.

> ✔ Refrain from associating with those who pass, use, and are under the influence of illicit drugs and/or alcohol.

> ✔ Address all other employees and supervisors with courtesy and respect, using non-offensive language.

(10)
> ✔ Accept the authority of supervisors without argument. If you consider an action unfair, inform the Human Resources department.

> ✔ Respect the work environment of this company and conduct oneself in a manner conducive to the growth and the enhancement of our business.

> ✔ Refrain from inviting visitors to our place of work in order to keep the premises secure.

(15)
> ✔ Promote the dignity of all persons, regardless of gender, creed, or culture and conduct oneself with dignity.

If the employee chooses *not* to comply:

> ✔ On the first offense, the employee meets with his or her supervisor. A representative from Human Resources may choose to attend.

(20)
> ✔ On the second offense, the employee meets with the Vice-President of Human Resources before returning to work.

> ✔ On the third offense, the employee is dismissed.

**36.** Which requirement relates to employee appearance?

   (1) the employee must refrain from using alcohol

   (2) the employee must not use associated paraphernalia

   (3) the employee must wear appropriate clothing

   (4) the employee must use courtesy and respect

   (5) the employee must use non-offensive language

**37.** Which requirement addresses relations with supervisors?

   (1) accept authority

   (2) business growth and enhancement

   (3) use non-offensive language

   (4) do not use drugs and alcohol

   (5) refrain from associating

*Go on to next page* ⇨

38. Which requirement is concerned with the growth and enhancement of the business?

    (1) conducive to growth

    (2) enhancement of self

    (3) dressing unprofessionally

    (4) personal conduct

    (5) inviting visitors

39. How are safety and security protected?

    (1) by promoting dignity

    (2) by not inviting others in

    (3) by the types of interaction

    (4) through meetings with supervisors

    (5) by being respectful and responsible

40. What are the penalties for continued non-compliance?

    (1) you meet with the president of the company

    (2) your salary goes up

    (3) you must avoid your supervisor

    (4) you have to take behavior classes

    (5) you are fired

**END OF EXAMINATION**

# Chapter 15

# Answers and Explanations for the Language Arts, Reading Test

• • • • • • • • • • • • • • • • • • • • • • • • • • • • • • • • • • • • • • • • • • • •

## Answer Key

After taking the Language Arts, Reading Test in Chapter 14, use this section to check your answers.

| | | |
|---|---|---|
| 1. 1 | 15. 2 | 29. 1 |
| 2. 4 | 16. 4 | 30. 4 |
| 3. 2 | 17. 1 | 31. 2 |
| 4. 5 | 18. 3 | 32. 1 |
| 5. 1 | 19. 2 | 33. 4 |
| 6. 3 | 20. 3 | 34. 3 |
| 7. 3 | 21. 4 | 35. 5 |
| 8. 1 | 22. 5 | 36. 3 |
| 9. 3 | 23. 1 | 37. 1 |
| 10. 5 | 24. 3 | 38. 4 |
| 11. 2 | 25. 1 | 39. 2 |
| 12. 3 | 26. 3 | 40. 5 |
| 13. 1 | 27. 5 | |
| 14. 3 | 28. 2 | |

# Analysis of the Answers

If you aren't sure why an answer was incorrect, use this section to get quick explanations of the answers.

1. **1.** They stood on the rude span (or rough-hewn bridge) to make their stand. Although a flag and an arch are mentioned in the poem, they are not the best answers. Neither the flood (meaning the river) or April breeze are possible answers.

2. **4.** The farmers were ready for war. The fact that they were embattled (another word for "fighting") and firing shots shows this. They definitely were not having negotiations (instead, they seem resolute) or a vacation, nor were they retreating or celebrating.

3. **2.** They've all since died (sleeping silently). They have not just gone away because they won or lost the war, nor are they living together peacefully.

4. **5.** The bridge has fallen into ruins. The other answers are incorrect: The bridge did exist (obviously), and it was not rebuilt after the battle (as indicated by the fact that it's no longer there), and it was swept away.

5. **1.** The votive stone represents a memorial to the fallen. A new bridge, celebration, ceremony, or reunion are not appropriate answers — they just don't make sense in the context of the poem.

6. **3.** The shot heard round the world refers to the beginning of an event; specifically, the American Revolution. The tone of the poem is what tells you this, in descriptions of the flag as "unfurling" and the farmers as "embattled." You don't, of course, have to know which war it was.

7. **3.** Wally isn't feeling well because he drank too much wine. You have to infer this from Dwight's saying that he "noticed a couple empty wineskins behind the fig tree this morning."

8. **1.** Breakfast table is correct, because the characters had just sat down for breakfast. The other locations — fig tree, market, bedroom, and vineyard — while mentioned in the excerpt, are not the setting of the play.

9. **3.** Dwight felt it would be better to raise lean calves because they would represent more profit. Two of the answers — less profit and more expensive — are the opposite of what's stated in the passage. High fat content may be true, but it isn't mentioned in the passage. Goats aren't mentioned in the passage.

10. **5.** Dad isn't paying attention to Dwight because he is worried about Wally. Lost sheep, time in the vineyard, buying more land, and reading the paper are not the best reasons for Dad's distraction.

11. **2.** Wally had been drinking wine the night before and is suffering from a hangover. The other reasons given — sickness, chores, reading, and working — are not appropriate answers, based on the passage.

12. **3.** Both Wally and the wine need to breathe. Wally says, "Wine's got to breathe, you know. And so do I, Dad."

13. **1.** Carter left his job because he was lured by the promise of Arctic gold. Leaving his snug clerkship may be partially correct, but is not the best answer. "A woman" isn't mentioned in the passage, except his wife, who stays behind. "Half his savings" and "the heartstrings of men" don't answer the question.

14. **3.** He wanted to escape his everyday drudgery in life as a clerk. "Bondage of commerce" refers to his dislike of his day routine in the business world. His need for wealth (returns), romance, risk-taking, and savings are different factors that don't apply to the question.

15. **2.** The text says that, "Even its [the party's] goal . . . was the Klondike."

16. **4.** It was "ominous" because there was a foreboding of ill-fortune. The route certainly was not blissful or hushed. "Surprising" doesn't make sense, and "hardiest" refers to a native of the region.

17. **1.** The fact that Jacques was native-born and raised in the Northwest made him important to the party. The fact that he was a renegade voyageur, born of a Chippewa woman in a deerskin lodge where he sucked tallow, are not as relevant as his knowledge of the area to his importance to the party.

18. **3.** Percy was seeking some romance and adventure in his otherwise mundane life. The fact that he was an ordinary man with a bank account, who spoke a good deal and was abnormally sentimental, all are not as important answers.

19. **2.** Sonny felt guilty at not having written sooner. The other answers — that he was lazy, busy, afraid, and in a hole — may relate to Sonny's behavior, feelings, or location but aren't the best answers.

20. **3.** The passage points out that Sonny has been sent to prison. Other locations, while mentioned in the excerpt, don't adequately describe his location.

21. **4.** "Strong in the head" refers to being smart or intelligent. Humorous, happy, and angry aren't characteristics related to strength or ability. Physically fit relates to the whole body, not the brain.

22. **5.** Sonny would be embarrassed if his parents knew he had been sent to prison.

23. **1.** Sonny is afraid he'll flip (or lose his mind) before being released from prison. Being a musician doesn't refer to his life in prison. "Getting anything straight" doesn't mean anything and is a trick question. The other two — coming straight back and blowing his brains out — refer to things that may happen after he leaves prison, not while inside it.

24. **3.** You know from the first sentence and from line 10 that Sonny likes his brother and appreciates what his brother has done for him.

25. **1.** Jimmy finally got a chance to read Martha's letters after a day's march. The question asks "when" he read the letters. In the first light of day is not correct (the passage refers to the "last hour of light.") The other answers refer to "where," so they can't possibly be correct answers.

26. **3.** Martha saw Jimmy as just an acquaintance, while he wished they could be lovers. Strangers, siblings and no relationship are not correct answers.

27. **5.** He tasted the flaps of envelopes that he knew her tongue had sealed. This shows how much he cared for her. The other actions — washing his hands and wrapping the letters — are other ways, but aren't as strong as demonstrations of affection. Tips of fingers and the last hour of light don't describe his feelings.

28. **2.** Martha enjoyed writing to Jimmy on a purely friendly basis. To say she cared deeply (she didn't), was infatuated (she wasn't), had a casual interest (it was more that casual), or no feelings at all (she does have some feelings) don't correctly describe her interest.

29. **1.** The fact that her letters were thick and newsy indicate that she enjoyed writing letters. Her respect for Chaucer, her status as an English major, and her beautiful writing are not the best answers. Professors and roommates don't relate to her enjoyment.

30. **4.** The letters served as a source of hope for the future. Other answers — an interesting hobby, a pleasing pastime, escape from boredom, and profound disappointment — may all be true but don't indicate the real reason for Jimmy's deep interest in the letters.

31. **2.** Thunder Bay was stunning and rugged. Clear and blue refers to the skies, not the water. Green water is not as good a description. "Serene" refers to the sunrise and "balmy" to summer days.

32. **1.** Unpredictable fall weather gives Thunder Bay its name. Competing ships, northeast Michigan, steamers, and grain and ore are not better factors to influence the name.

33. **4.** The National Marine Sanctuary is a graveyard for ships that's protected by the government. Other answers, such as stunning views, deep-water, appeal to visitors, and the last trip of the season don't relate to a protected sanctuary.

34. **3.** Ballard is a good choice because he found the *Titanic*. The fact that he has shipping history, was a researcher and explorer, toured the sanctuary, and knows the bay are not as strong as the correct answer.

35. **5.** The most important reason for creating the sanctuary was to preserve the historic wrecks. Other reasons, including exploration, tourism, donations, and shipping studies, are relevant, but less important.

36. **3.** Employees should wear appropriate clothing to project a professional appearance and maintain safety standards. Other factors — such as alcohol use, paraphernalia, respect, and language — don't relate to appearance.

37. **1.** Employees must accept the authority of supervisors, as is stated clearly in the passage.

38. **4.** Employees must conduct themselves professionally, so that the business grows and improves.

39. **2.** To ensure safety and security, employees shouldn't invite other people in. The promotion of dignity, interaction, supervisors, and respect don't directly relate to bringing outsiders into the place of work.

40. **5.** Repeated instances of non-compliance leads to dismissal. The other answers are not backed up by the passage.

# Chapter 16

# The Mathematics Test: Parts I and II

## The Mathematics Test, Part 1

### Directions

The Mathematics Test consists of multiple-choice questions intended to measure general mathematics skills or problem-solving ability. The questions are based on short readings that often include a graph, chart, or figure.

You will have 45 minutes to complete the 25 questions in this part. Work carefully, but do not spend too much time on any one question. Be sure to answer every question.

Formulas you may need are given on the page before the first test question. Only some of the questions will require you to use a formula. Not all the formulas given will be needed.

Some questions contain more information that you will need to solve the problem; other questions do not give enough information. If the question does not give enough information to solve the problem, the correct answer choice is "Not enough information given."

**The use of calculators is allowed in Part I only.**

Do not write in this test booklet. The test administrator will give you a blank paper for your calculations. Record your answers on the separate answer sheet provided. Be sure all information is properly recorded on the answer sheet.

To record your answers, fill in the numbered circle on the answer sheet that corresponds to the answer you select for each question in the test booklet.

---

**EXAMPLE:**

If a grocery bill totaling $15.75 is paid with a $20.00 bill, how much change should be returned?

(1)  $5.25

(2)  $4.75

(3)  $4.25

(4)  $3.75

(5)  $3.25

(On Answer Sheet)

① ② ● ④ ⑤

The correct answer is "$4.25"; therefore, answer space 3 would be marked on the answer sheet.

---

Do not rest the point of your pencil on the answer sheet while you are considering your answer. Make no stray or unnecessary marks. If you change an answer, erase your first mark completely. Mark only one answer space for each question; multiple answers will be scored as incorrect. Do not fold or crease your answer sheet. All test materials must be returned to the test administrator.

*Go on to next page*

## Calculator Directions

To prepare the calculator for use the *first* time, press the ON (upper-rightmost) key. "DEG" will appear at the top-center of the screen and "0" at the right. This indicates the calculator is in the proper format for all your calculations.

To prepare the calculator for *another* question, press the ON or the red AC key. This clears any entries made previously.

To do any arithmetic, enter the expression as it is written. Press = (equals sign) when finished.

**EXAMPLE A:** $8 - 3 + 9$

First press ON or AC

Enter the following: 8 , − , 3 , + , 9 , =

The correct answer is 14.

If the expression in parentheses is to be multiplied by a number, press × (multiplication sign) between the number and the parenthesis sign.

**EXAMPLE B:** $6(8 + 5)$

First press ON or AC

Enter the following: 6 , × , ( , 8 , + , 5 , ) , =

The correct answer is 78.

To find the square root of a number

- ↙ Enter the number.
- ↙ Press the SHIFT (upper-leftmost) key ("SHIFT" appears at the top-left of the screen).
- ↙ Press $x^2$ (third from the left on top row) to access its second function: square root.

DO NOT press SHIFT and $x^2$ at the same time.

**EXAMPLE C:** $\sqrt{64}$

First press ON or AC

Enter the following: 6 , 4 , SHIFT , $x^2$ , =

The correct answer is 8.

To enter a negative number, such as −8:

- ↙ Enter the number without the negative sign (enter 8).
- ↙ Press the "change sign" ( +/− ) key, which is directly above the 7 key.

All arithmetic can be done with positive and/or negative numbers.

**EXAMPLE D:** $-8 - (-5)$

First press ON or AC

Enter the following: 8 , +/− , − , 5 , +/− , =

The correct answer is −3.

*Go on to next page* ⟹

### The Standard Grid

Mixed numbers, such as 3½, cannot be entered in the standard grid. Instead, represent them as decimal numbers (in this case, 3.5) or fractions (in this case, ⁷⁄₂). In addition, no answer on a standard grid can be a negative number, such as –8.

To record your answer for a standard-grid question:

- ✔ Begin in any column that will allow your answer to be entered.
- ✔ Write your answer in the boxes on the top row.
- ✔ In the column beneath a fraction bar or decimal point (if any) and each number in your answer, fill in the circle representing that character.
- ✔ Leave blank any unused column.

---

**EXAMPLE:**

The scale on a map indicates that ½ inch represents an actual distance of 120 miles. In inches, how far apart on the map will the two towns be if the actual distance between them is 180 miles?

The answer to the above example is ¾, or 0.75, inches. A few examples of how the answer could be gridded are shown below.

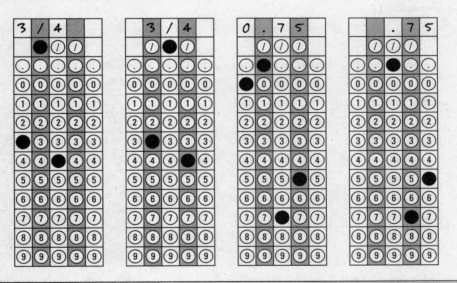

---

Points to remember:

- ✔ The answer sheet will be machine scored. **The circles must be filled in correctly.**
- ✔ Mark no more than one circle in any column.
- ✔ Grid only one answer even if there is more than one correct answer.
- ✔ Mixed numbers, such as 3½, must be gridded as 3.5 or ⁷⁄₂.
- ✔ No answer on a standard grid can be a negative number.

*Go on to next page*

**The Coordinate-Plane Grid**

To record an answer on the coordinate-plane grid, you must have an *x*-value and a *y*-value. No answer for a coordinate-plane question will have a value that is a fraction or decimal.

**Mark only the <u>one</u> circle that represents your answer.**

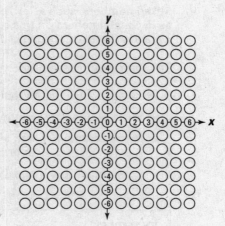

**EXAMPLE:**

The coordinates of point A, shown on the graph below, are (2,–4).

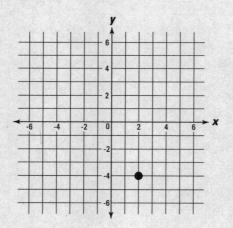

The coordinates of point B, not shown on the graph, are (–3,1). What is the location of point B?

DO NOT MARK YOUR ANSWER ON THE GRAPH ABOVE.

Mark your answer on the coordinate-plane grid on the answer sheet (at right).

**CORRECT RESPONSE:**

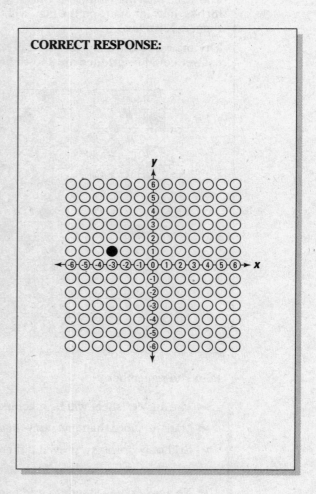

*Go on to next page*

## Formulas

**AREA** of a:

| | |
|---|---|
| square | Area = side$^2$ |
| rectangle | Area = length × width |
| parallelogram | Area = base × height |
| triangle | Area = ½ × base × height |
| trapezoid | Area = ½ × (base$_1$ + base$_2$) × height |
| circle | Area = π × radius$^2$; π is approximately equal to 3.14 |

**PERIMETER** of a:

| | |
|---|---|
| square | Perimeter = 4 × side |
| rectangle | Perimeter = (2 × length) + (2 × width) |
| triangle | Perimeter = side$_1$ + side$_2$ + side$_3$ |

**CIRCUMFERENCE** of a circle — Circumference = π × diameter; π is approximately equal to 3.14

**VOLUME** of a:

| | |
|---|---|
| cube | Volume = side$^3$ |
| rectangular solid | Volume = length × width × height |
| square pyramid | Volume = ⅓ × (base)$^2$ × height |
| cylinder | Volume = π × radius$^2$ × height; π is approximately equal to 3.14 |
| cone | Volume = ⅓ × π × radius$^2$ × height; π is approximately equal to 3.14 |

**COORDINATE GEOMETRY** — distance between points = $\sqrt{(x_2 - x_1)^2 + (y_2 - y_1)^2}$; $(x_1, y_1)$ and $(x_2, y_2)$ are two points in a plane

slope of a line = $\frac{y_2 - y_1}{x_2 - x_1}$; $(x_1, y_1)$ and $(x_2, y_2)$ are two points on the line

**PYTHAGOREAN RELATIONSHIP** — $a^2 + b^2 = c^2$; $a$ and $b$ are legs, and $c$ is the hypotenuse of a right triangle

**MEASURES OF CENTRAL TENDENCY** — **mean** = $\frac{x_1 + x_2 + \cdots + x_n}{n}$; where the $x$'s are the values for which a mean is desired, and $n$ is the total number of values for $x$

**median** = the middle value of an odd number of *ordered* scores, and halfway between the two middle values of an even number of *ordered* scores.

**SIMPLE INTEREST** — interest = principal × rate × time

**DISTANCE** — distance = rate × time

**TOTAL COST** — total cost = (number of units) × (price per unit)

**DO NOT BEGIN TAKING THIS TEST UNTIL TOLD TO DO SO**

**PART I**

1. ① ② ③ ④ ⑤
2. ① ② ③ ④ ⑤

3.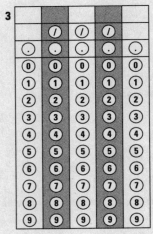

4. ① ② ③ ④ ⑤
5. ① ② ③ ④ ⑤
6. ① ② ③ ④ ⑤
7. ① ② ③ ④ ⑤

8.

9. ① ② ③ ④ ⑤
10. ① ② ③ ④ ⑤
11. ① ② ③ ④ ⑤

12.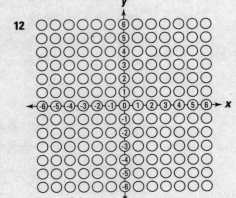

13. ① ② ③ ④ ⑤
14. ① ② ③ ④ ⑤
15. ① ② ③ ④ ⑤
16. ① ② ③ ④ ⑤

17.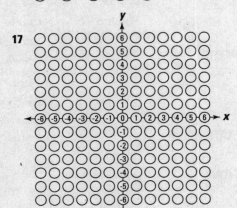

18. ① ② ③ ④ ⑤
19. ① ② ③ ④ ⑤
20. ① ② ③ ④ ⑤
21. ① ② ③ ④ ⑤
22. ① ② ③ ④ ⑤
23. ① ② ③ ④ ⑤
24. ① ② ③ ④ ⑤

25.

**END OF PART I**

*Go on to next page*

1. Dharma is making sale signs for the Super Summer Sale at the Super Saver Swim Shop. Sales tax in Dharma's state is 5%. She makes a series of signs:

   Sign A: ½ off all merchandise

   Sign B: Buy one item, get the second item of equal value free

   Sign C: 50% off all merchandise

   Sign D: Nine times your sales tax back

   What would a shrewd consumer notice about the signs?

   (1) Sign A offers a better buy

   (2) Sign C offers the worst deal

   (3) Sign D offers the worst deal

   (4) Sign B offers a better deal

   (5) All signs offer the same deal

2. Daryl is framing a picture. He draws the following diagram to help him make it:

   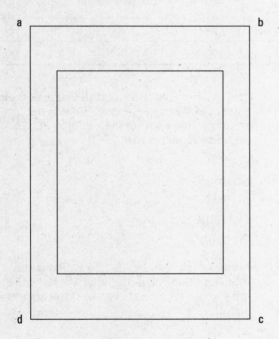

   Which of the following is true about the above diagram?

   (1) *ab* must be perpendicular to *ad*

   (2) *ab* must be parallel to *bc*

   (3) *ad* must be parallel to *ab*

   (4) *ab* and *dc* must be perpendicular

   (5) *ab* and *ad* must be parallel

3. The Hammerhill family is building a deck behind their house. The deck is to be 16 feet long and 21 feet wide, and the decking material was priced at $45.00 a square yard. What would be the cost in dollars of the decking material? Mark the answer on the standard grid on the answer sheet.

4. Margaret Millsford, the Chief Financial Officer of Aggravated Manufacturing Corporation, has to report to the Board of Directors. She has been instructed to analyze the sales of each of the company's product lines and recommend dropping the least profitable line. She found that the per-unit profit of each of their lines was the same. She prepared the following graph to back up her recommendation. What should be her recommendation of the least profitable line to drop?

   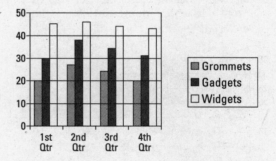

   (1) widgets

   (2) grommets

   (3) gadgets

   (4) grommets and widgets

   (5) gadgets and widgets

*Go on to next page* ⟶

5.  Quan wants to build steps down from the six-foot-high porch behind his house. The bottom step should be seven feet away from the house to allow for a gentle slope. How long, in feet, will the steps be (answer to two decimal places)?

    (1)  8.22

    (2)  13.00

    (3)  2.92

    (4)  13.22

    (5)  9.22

6.  Alice was trying to explain how the length of time she could run each morning had improved each month since she started, except for the month she twisted her ankle. She told Mary and Kevin to look at the graph she had drawn. It showed the average length of time she ran each day that month. In which month did Alice twist her ankle?

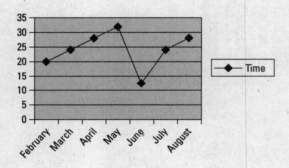

    (1)  June

    (2)  February

    (3)  August

    (4)  September

    (5)  May

7.  Dominic and Paula were comparing their report cards, as follows:

### Dominic's Report Card

| Subject | Grade |
| --- | --- |
| Mathematics | 63 |
| Social Studies | 76 |
| Science | 65 |
| Language Arts | 84 |
| Physical Education | 72 |

### Paula's Report Card

| Subject | Grade |
| --- | --- |
| Mathematics | 80 |
| Social Studies | 64 |
| Science | 76 |
| Language Arts | 72 |
| Physical Education | 88 |

The teacher told them that the ratio of their total marks was very close. What is the ratio of Paula's marks to Dominic's marks on these report cards?

    (1)  9:10

    (2)  18:19

    (3)  10:9

    (4)  19:18

    (5)  2:1

8.  In the series, 4, 6, 10, 18, . . . , which is the first term that is a multiple of 11? Mark the answer on the standard grid on the answer sheet.

*Go on to next page*

9.  Simone follows the stock market very carefully. She has been carefully following Cowardly Corporation the last few months, keeping track of her research in the following table.

| Date | Closing Price |
| --- | --- |
| August 7 | 15.03 |
| August 17 | 16.12 |
| September 1 | 14.83 |
| September 9 | 15.01 |
| September 16 | 14.94 |
| September 20 | 15.06 |
| September 23 | 15.17 |
| September 24 | 15.19 |

She bought shares of the stock on September 24 and wants to make money before selling it. She paid 3% commission to her broker for buying and will pay the same again for selling. What is the lowest price for which Simone can sell each of her shares in order to break even?

(1)  16.48

(2)  16.13

(3)  15.66

(4)  20.00

(5)  15.99

10.  If $22.4 = \dfrac{56a}{5a + 10}$, what is the value of $a$?

(1)  0

(2)  −56

(3)  4

(4)  −4

(5)  56

Questions 11 and 12 refer to the following graph.

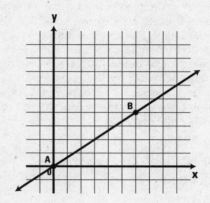

11.  Calculate the slope of the line $AB$.

(1)  ⅔

(2)  ½

(3)  ⅖

(4)  ¼

(5)  −⅗

12.  If the slope of $AB$ remains the same, but it intercepts the $y$-axis at $C(0,4)$, where does it intersect the $x$-axis? Use the coordinate-plane grid on the answer sheet to draw the point where $AB$ intersects the $x$-axis.

13.  If a fire is contained in a square barbeque, where is the safest place to stand?

(1)  at a corner

(2)  along the left side

(3)  along the right side

(4)  six feet from the middle

(5)  not enough information given

*Go on to next page*

14. Lydia and Wayne are shopping for carpets for their home and are looking for the best carpet at the best price. Carnie's Carpets offers them a wool carpet for $21.50 per square yard. Flora's Flooring says they will match that same carpet for only $2.45 per square foot, while Dora's Deep Discount offers them an 8 by 12 foot rug of the same carpet material for $210.24. What is the lowest price per square foot offered to Lydia and Wayne?

    (1) $24.50

    (2) $2.45

    (3) $21.90

    (4) $2.19

    (5) $2.39

15. Miscellaneous Appliances Limited is concerned about its output at Plant A. For its annual report, company officials prepared graphs to show the output for each quarter of the last two years. Which quarter showed a dramatic decrease in production in 2002?

**Output at Plant A – 2001**

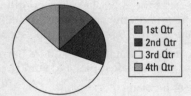

**Output at Plant A – 2002**

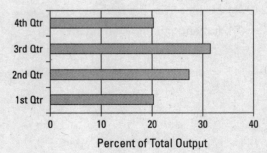

Percent of Total Output

    (1) 3rd quarter

    (2) 1st quarter

    (3) 4th quarter

    (4) 2nd quarter

    (5) no significant change

16. The Ng's are looking to expand their two-story house and have calculated that they need at least another 630 square feet to live comfortably. They want to use the basement level for storage and the rest for living. A contractor quotes them $15.80 per square foot for the renovation without redecoration. A real estate agent tells them that they can increase the value of their home by about $18,000 by building the addition. If they want to add as much additional space as possible for the $18,000 they will recover, how much additional space, in square feet, should they add on?

    (1) 630

    (2) 1,260

    (3) 1620

    (4) 1,140

    (5) 1,329

17. In an experiment involving throws of a 20-sided die, the following results were obtained:

| Throw | Left-Handed | Right-Handed |
| --- | --- | --- |
| 1 | 2 | 4 |
| 2 | 4 | 12 |
| 3 | 5 | 2 |
| 4 | 9 | 6 |
| 5 | 11 | 13 |
| 6 | 10 | 15 |
| 7 | 4 | 17 |
| 8 | 6 | 3 |
| 9 | 7 | 5 |

Using the coordinate-plane grid on the answer sheet, plot the point representing the combined medians of the throws using the median of the left-hand results as the $x$ value and the median of the right-hand throws as the $y$ value.

*Go on to next page*

18. LeeAnne is shopping for a new vehicle. She drives about 18,000 miles per year. She is most concerned about the cost of gasoline and other operating costs, like insurance and maintenance. She expects gasoline to average $1.75 a gallon during the five years she will own the car and is basing her decision on that price. As she shops, she makes the following chart:

| Type of Vehicle | Miles per Gallon | Operating Costs per Mile |
|-----------------|------------------|--------------------------|
| SUV | 12.8 | $.39 |
| Sedan | 19.6 | $.24 |
| 2-door | 19.5 | $.27 |
| All-wheel drive | 17.2 | $.31 |
| Sports car | 18.6 | $.33 |

Based on her criteria, which car should LeeAnne buy?

(1) SUV

(2) sedan

(3) 2 door

(4) all-wheel drive

(5) sports car

19. Tom is worried about getting to the GED tests on time. He knows that he averages 40 miles per hour on the route to the tests. If the test site is 47 miles from Tom's house, and he wants to arrive 20 minutes early, how much time does he have to leave for travel and waiting? Choose the answer that indicates which operations need to be performed and the order in which they need to be performed.

(1) add then divide

(2) multiply then add

(3) divide then add

(4) add then multiply

(5) divide then multiply

20. Leonora has just received her mid-term report card. Her grades are as follows:

| **Leonora's Report Card** | |
|---|---|
| **Subject** | **Grade (%)** |
| English | 84 |
| Geography | 78 |
| Mathematics | 68 |
| Physical Education | 77 |
| Physics | 82 |

Her average grade is 77.8. In order to get into the college of her choice, she needs an average of 80%. English is her best subject. By how many percentage points will her English score have to go up, assuming all her other subjects stay the same, to get into college?

(1) 7

(2) 8

(3) 9

(4) 10

(5) 11

21. Sonia has an amazing recipe for rice. For each 1 cup of rice, she adds 2 cups of vegetable soup and a quarter cup of lentils. This weekend, she is having a large dinner party and figures she needs to cook 3½ cups of rice for her guests. How much of the other two ingredients should she use?

(1) 7 cups of soup and ⅞ cup of lentils

(2) 3½ cups of soup and ½ cup of lentils

(3) 7 cups of soup and 1 cup of lentils

(4) 1 cup of soup and 7 cups of lentils

(5) 6 cups of soup and ⅞ cups of lentils

*Go on to next page*

22. In drawing cards from a deck, any single card has an equal chance of being drawn. After six cards have been drawn and removed, what is the probability of drawing an ace of hearts if it has not yet been drawn?

    (1) 1:52

    (2) 1:50

    (3) 1:48

    (4) 1:46

    (5) 1:44

23. The Symons are redecorating a room in their house. They have some interesting ideas. They want to put a rug on the floor surrounded by a border of tiles. They are considering teak paneling halfway up each wall. In addition, they may cut away part of the ceiling to put in a skylight. This is a diagram of their room.

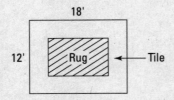

    The rug costs $7.50 a square foot, and tile costs $9.00 a square foot. One rug they like is 16 feet by 10 feet, leaving just a little area around the rug for tiles. At the store, however, they see another rug that is only 12 feet by 8 feet, but it's just the right pattern and colors for their room. Which floor treatment is less expensive?

    (1) both the same cost

    (2) larger rug

    (3) smaller rug without the paneling

    (4) smaller rug

    (5) not enough information given

24. Brad is a secret shopper for the Friendly Furniture store. His job is to go to competitive stores and price a series of items to make sure his employer can advertise that they have the best prices. His boss wants to start a new advertising campaign: "Friendly Furniture — always lower than the average price of our competitors." Brad's job is to shop several stores to make sure the claim is accurate. Brad's results are recorded on the following table:

| Item | Store A | Store B | Store C | Store D | Friendly Furniture |
|------|---------|---------|---------|---------|--------------------|
| Couch | $1,729 | $1,749 | $1,729 | $1,699 | $1,719 |
| Dining room set | $4,999 | $4,899 | $5,019 | $4,829 | $4,899 |
| Loveseat | $1,259 | $1,199 | $1,279 | $1,149 | $1,229 |
| Coffee table | $459 | $449 | $479 | $429 | $449 |
| Reclining chair | $759 | $799 | $739 | $699 | $739 |

Which item cannot be advertised as "lower than the average price?"

    (1) couch

    (2) dining room set

    (3) loveseat

    (4) coffee table

    (5) reclining chair

25. In a pistachio-eating contest, Sarah eats 48 pistachios in 18 minutes. If she could maintain her rate of eating pistachios, how many could she eat in 2 hours? Record your answer on the standard grid on the answer sheet.

*Go on to next page*

# The Mathematics Test, Part II

### Directions

The Mathematics Test consists of multiple-choice questions intended to measure general mathematics skills or problem-solving ability. The questions are based on short readings that often include a graph, chart, or figure.

You will have 45 minutes to complete the 25 questions in this part. Work carefully, but do not spend too much time on any one questions. Be sure to answer every question. If you finish early, you may return to Part I, but without the calculator.

Formulas you may need are given on the page before the first test question. Only some of the questions will require you to use a formula. Not all the formulas given will be needed.

Some questions contain more information that you will need to solve the problem; other questions do not give enough information. If the question does not give enough information to solve the problem, the correct answer choice is "Not enough information given."

**The use of calculators is <u>not</u> allowed in Part II.**

Do not write in this test booklet. The test administrator will give you a blank paper for your calculations. Record your answers on the separate answer sheet provided. Be sure all information is properly recorded on the answer sheet.

To record your answers, fill in the numbered circle on the answer sheet that corresponds to the answer you select for each question in the test booklet.

---

**EXAMPLE:**

If a grocery bill totaling $15.75 is paid with a $20.00 bill, how much change should be returned?

(1)   $5.25

(2)   $4.75

(3)   $4.25

(4)   $3.75

(5)   $3.25

(On Answer Sheet)

① ② ● ④ ⑤

The correct answer is "$4.25"; therefore, answer space 3 would be marked on the answer sheet.

---

Do not rest the point of your pencil on the answer sheet while you are considering your answer. Make no stray or unnecessary marks. If you change an answer, erase your first mark completely. Mark only one answer space for each question; multiple answers will be scored as incorrect. Do not fold or crease your answer sheet. All test materials must be returned to the test administrator.

*Go on to next page* ⟩

## The Standard Grid

Mixed numbers, such as 3½, cannot be entered in the standard grid. Instead, represent them as decimal numbers (in this case, 3.5) or fractions (in this case, ⁷⁄₂). No answer on a standard grid can be a negative number, such as –8.

To record your answer for a standard-grid question:

- ✔ Begin in any column that will allow your answer to be entered.

- ✔ Write your answer in the boxes on the top row.

- ✔ In the column beneath a fraction bar or decimal point (if any) and each number in your answer, fill in the circle representing that character.

- ✔ Leave blank any unused column.

**EXAMPLE:**

The scale on a map indicates that ½ inch represents an actual distance of 120 miles. In inches, how far apart on the map will the two towns be if the actual distance between them is 180 miles?

The answer to the above example is ¾, or 0.75, inches. A few examples of how the answer could be gridded are shown below.

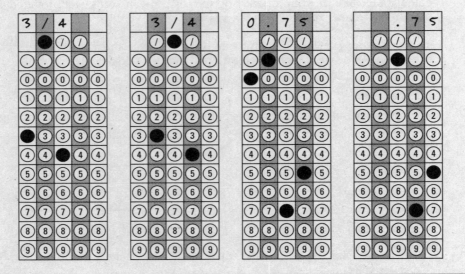

Points to remember:

- ✔ The answer sheet will be machine scored. **The circles must be filled in correctly.**

- ✔ Mark no more than one circle in any column.

- ✔ Grid only one answer even if there is more than one correct answer.

- ✔ Mixed numbers, such as 3½, must be gridded as 3.5 or ½.

- ✔ No answer on a standard grid can be a negative number.

*Go on to next page*

**The Coordinate-Plane Grid**

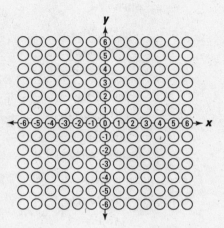

To record an answer on the coordinate-plane grid, you must have an *x*-value and a *y*-value. No answer for a coordinate-plane question will have a value that is a fraction or decimal.

**Mark only the <u>one</u> circle that represents your answer.**

---

**EXAMPLE:**

The coordinates of point A, shown on the graph below, are (2,–4).

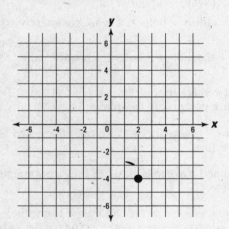

The coordinates of point B, not shown on the graph, are (–3,1). What is the location of point B?

DO NOT MARK YOUR ANSWER ON THE GRAPH ABOVE.

Mark your answer on the coordinate-plane grid on the answer sheet (at right).

**CORRECT RESPONSE:**

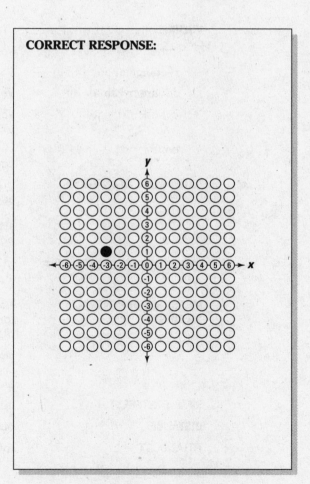

---

*Go on to next page*

## Formulas

**AREA** of a:

| | |
|---|---|
| square | Area = side$^2$ |
| rectangle | Area = length × width |
| parallelogram | Area = base × height |
| triangle | Area = ½ × base × height |
| trapezoid | Area = ½ × (base$_1$ + base$_2$) × height |
| circle | Area = π × radius$^2$; π is approximately equal to 3.14 |

**PERIMETER** of a:

| | |
|---|---|
| square | Perimeter = 4 × side |
| rectangle | Perimeter = (2 × length) + (2 × width) |
| triangle | Perimeter = side$_1$ + side$_2$ + side$_3$ |

**CIRCUMFERENCE** of a circle — Circumference = π × diameter; π is approximately equal to 3.14

**VOLUME** of a:

| | |
|---|---|
| cube | Volume = side$^3$ |
| rectangular solid | Volume = length × width × height |
| square pyramid | Volume = ⅓ × (base)$^2$ × height |
| cylinder | Volume = π × radius$^2$ × height; π is approximately equal to 3.14 |
| cone | Volume = ⅓ × π × radius$^2$ × height; π is approximately equal to 3.14 |

**COORDINATE GEOMETRY**

distance between points = $\sqrt{(x_2 - x_1)^2 + (y_2 - y_1)^2}$; $(x_1, y_1)$ and $(x_2, y_2)$ are two points in a plane

slope of a line = $\frac{y_2 - y_1}{x_2 - x_1}$; $(x_1, y_1)$ and $(x_2, y_2)$ are two points on the line

**PYTHAGOREAN RELATIONSHIP**

$a^2 + b^2 = c^2$; $a$ and $b$ are legs, and $c$ is the hypotenuse of a right triangle

**MEASURES OF CENTRAL TENDENCY**

**mean** = $\frac{x_1 + x_2 + \cdots + x_n}{n}$; where the $x$'s are the values for which a mean is desired, and $n$ is the total number of values for $x$

**median** = the middle value of an odd number of *ordered* scores, and halfway between the two middle values of an even number of *ordered* scores.

**SIMPLE INTEREST** — interest = principal × rate × time

**DISTANCE** — distance = rate × time

**TOTAL COST** — total cost = (number of units) × (price per unit)

**DO NOT BEGIN TAKING THIS TEST UNTIL TOLD TO DO SO**

**PART II**

1. ① ② ③ ④ ⑤
2. ① ② ③ ④ ⑤
3. ① ② ③ ④ ⑤
4. ① ② ③ ④ ⑤
5. ① ② ③ ④ ⑤
6. ① ② ③ ④ ⑤

7.
| | / | / | / | |
|---|---|---|---|---|
| | . | . | . | . | . |
| ⓪ | ⓪ | ⓪ | ⓪ | ⓪ |
| ① | ① | ① | ① | ① |
| ② | ② | ② | ② | ② |
| ③ | ③ | ③ | ③ | ③ |
| ④ | ④ | ④ | ④ | ④ |
| ⑤ | ⑤ | ⑤ | ⑤ | ⑤ |
| ⑥ | ⑥ | ⑥ | ⑥ | ⑥ |
| ⑦ | ⑦ | ⑦ | ⑦ | ⑦ |
| ⑧ | ⑧ | ⑧ | ⑧ | ⑧ |
| ⑨ | ⑨ | ⑨ | ⑨ | ⑨ |

8. ① ② ③ ④ ⑤
9. ① ② ③ ④ ⑤
10. ① ② ③ ④ ⑤

11.
| | / | / | / | |
|---|---|---|---|---|
| . | . | . | . | . |
| ⓪ | ⓪ | ⓪ | ⓪ | ⓪ |
| ① | ① | ① | ① | ① |
| ② | ② | ② | ② | ② |
| ③ | ③ | ③ | ③ | ③ |
| ④ | ④ | ④ | ④ | ④ |
| ⑤ | ⑤ | ⑤ | ⑤ | ⑤ |
| ⑥ | ⑥ | ⑥ | ⑥ | ⑥ |
| ⑦ | ⑦ | ⑦ | ⑦ | ⑦ |
| ⑧ | ⑧ | ⑧ | ⑧ | ⑧ |
| ⑨ | ⑨ | ⑨ | ⑨ | ⑨ |

12. ① ② ③ ④ ⑤

13.
| | / | / | / | |
|---|---|---|---|---|
| | . | . | . | . | . |
| ⓪ | ⓪ | ⓪ | ⓪ | ⓪ |
| ① | ① | ① | ① | ① |
| ② | ② | ② | ② | ② |
| ③ | ③ | ③ | ③ | ③ |
| ④ | ④ | ④ | ④ | ④ |
| ⑤ | ⑤ | ⑤ | ⑤ | ⑤ |
| ⑥ | ⑥ | ⑥ | ⑥ | ⑥ |
| ⑦ | ⑦ | ⑦ | ⑦ | ⑦ |
| ⑧ | ⑧ | ⑧ | ⑧ | ⑧ |
| ⑨ | ⑨ | ⑨ | ⑨ | ⑨ |

14. ① ② ③ ④ ⑤
15. ① ② ③ ④ ⑤

16.

17. ① ② ③ ④ ⑤
18. ① ② ③ ④ ⑤
19. ① ② ③ ④ ⑤

20.
| | / | / | / | |
|---|---|---|---|---|
| . | . | . | . | . |
| ⓪ | ⓪ | ⓪ | ⓪ | ⓪ |
| ① | ① | ① | ① | ① |
| ② | ② | ② | ② | ② |
| ③ | ③ | ③ | ③ | ③ |
| ④ | ④ | ④ | ④ | ④ |
| ⑤ | ⑤ | ⑤ | ⑤ | ⑤ |
| ⑥ | ⑥ | ⑥ | ⑥ | ⑥ |
| ⑦ | ⑦ | ⑦ | ⑦ | ⑦ |
| ⑧ | ⑧ | ⑧ | ⑧ | ⑧ |
| ⑨ | ⑨ | ⑨ | ⑨ | ⑨ |

21. ① ② ③ ④ ⑤
22. ① ② ③ ④ ⑤
23. ① ② ③ ④ ⑤
24. ① ② ③ ④ ⑤
25. ① ② ③ ④ ⑤

**END OF PART II**

*Go on to next page* ➡

1. Kevin wants to paint his room, which is 9 feet 5 inches long, 8 feet 3 inches wide and 8 feet 2 inches high. The label on the paint can cautions that air must be exchanged in the room every 12 minutes. When Kevin looks for exhaust fans to keep the air moving, he finds that they are calibrated in cubic feet per minutes. What operation does Kevin have to perform first to figure out which size fan he needs?

   (1) multiplication
   (2) division
   (3) addition
   (4) subtraction
   (5) square root

2. Which of these shapes has the same relationship to the horizontal after a 90 degree rotation about a point on the perimeter?

   (1) square
   (2) isosceles triangle
   (3) circle
   (4) pentagon
   (5) not enough information given

Question 3 refers to the following figure and chart.

3. In a large company, the top four positions are organized as follows:

Each department has the following budget:

| Department | Budget ($ Millions) |
| --- | --- |
| Operations | 14.7 |
| Human Resources | 2.1 |
| Marketing | 5.6 |

What is the ratio of the largest budget to the smallest budget?

   (1) 7:1
   (2) 14:1
   (3) 5:2
   (4) 7:5
   (5) 14:5

*Go on to next page*

4. A company has doubled its sales from the first to the 3rd quarters. Which graph indicates this pattern?

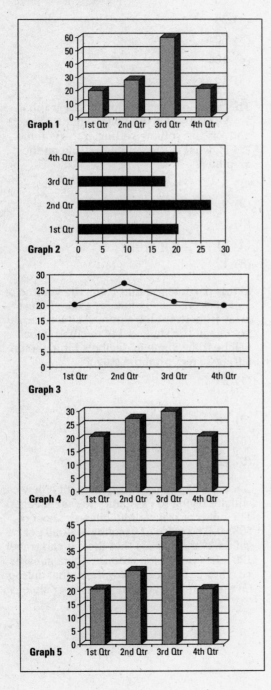

(1) Graph 1

(2) Graph 2

(3) Graph 3

(4) Graph 4

(5) Graph 5

5. A six-foot tall forester standing some 16 feet from a tree uses his digital rangefinder to calculate the distance between his eye and the top of the tree to be 25 feet. How tall is the tree?

(1) $\sqrt{41}$

(2) $\sqrt{881}$

(3) $\sqrt{256}$

(4) $\sqrt{97}$

(5) not enough information given

6. Lawrie is trying to save money and keeps her money in both checking and savings accounts. Each week, she puts $24.00 from her paycheck into her savings account. However, the fourth week she overdraws her checking account by $7.50, and the bank transfers the money from her savings account. For providing this service, the bank charges Lawrie $10.00. What is her savings account balance after week 4?

(1) $88.50

(2) $96.00

(3) $86.00

(4) $78.50

(5) $24.00

7. Sarah is negotiating the price of a chair for her room. The original price was $96.00. Store A offers her ⅓ off. Store B offers her a discount of 30%. How much will she save by taking the lower price? Use the standard grid on the answer sheet to record your answer in dollars.

*Go on to next page*

Questions 8 through 10 are based on the following information and figure.

While a rock band is setting up for a concert, the audio engineer is calibrating the amplifiers used for the concert. He has an instrument that develops and displays a graph for each setting on the amplifier controls. The graph appears like this:

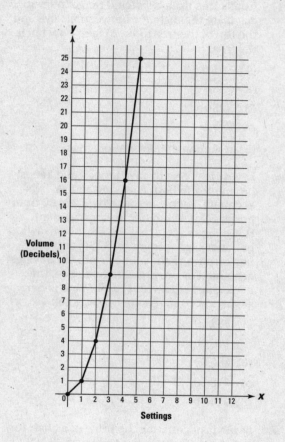

Volume (Decibels)

Settings

8. From the graph, calculate the volume in decibels for a setting of 10 on the amplifier.

(1) 20

(2) 30

(3) 50

(4) 100

(5) 10

9. The equation that produced this graph is $V = S^2$, where $V$ is the volume in decibels and $S$ is the volume setting. If the volume is 144, what is the volume setting on the amplifier?

(1) 8

(2) 9

(3) 10

(4) 11

(5) 12

10. In this particular auditorium, the volume of sound decreases by half for every 10 feet away from the stage a person sits. If the volume at the stage is 144 decibels, what will be the volume in decibels for a person sitting 20 feet from the stage?

(1) 24

(2) 36

(3) 48

(4) 60

(5) 72

11. Gary and Georgina George bought a new car and are trying to estimate the gas mileage. The new car travels 240 miles at a cost of $38.00. The price of gasoline is $1.90 per gallon. Gary guesses that the car can travel 120 miles per gallon, and Georgina guesses 12 miles per gallon. Show the actual mileage on the standard grid on the answer sheet.

*Go on to next page*

Question 12 is based on the following figures:

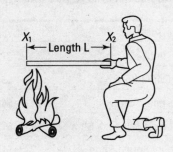

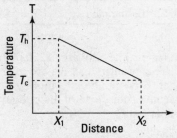

*Reprinted from Physical Science: What the Technology Professional Needs to Know (Wiley Publishing, Inc.)*

12. If the person pictured wants to remain at a constant temperature, what geometrical shape should he follow as a path?

    (1) hexagon

    (2) ellipse

    (3) line

    (4) square

    (5) circle

13. Igor is in charge of the swimming pool at the local recreation center. The pool is 120 feet long and 24 feet wide and holds 12,902 cubic feet of water. What is the average depth of the pool in feet? Record your answer on the standard grid on the answer sheet.

Questions 14 through 16 refer to the following table.

| Vehicle | Mileage (Miles per Gallon) | | Annual Cost ($)* |
| --- | --- | --- | --- |
| | *City* | *Highway* | |
| A | 23 | 28 | 840 |
| B | 21 | 29 | 875 |
| C | 19 | 25 | 1000 |
| D | 18 | 24 | 1050 |
| E | 17 | 22 | 1105 |
| F | 16 | 22 | 1167 |
| G | 15 | 21 | 1235 |
| H | 14 | 19 | 1314 |
| I | 13 | 18 | 1400 |
| J | 12 | 16 | 1823 |

**Average Mileage and Annual Fuel Cost of Selected Vehicles**

*\*Annual cost includes 15,000 miles driven annually; 55% of the miles in the city and 45% on the highway; standard price of fuel*

14. If you were in the market for a car, how much could you save, in dollars, over a three-year period, by buying the most economical car over the least economic car?

    (1) 840

    (2) 983

    (3) 2520

    (4) 5469

    (5) 2949

15. What is the difference in miles per gallon between the mean city mileage and the median of the city mileages for these vehicles?

    (1) 1⅔

    (2) ⅓

    (3) 17

    (4) 2½

    (5) 2

*Go on to next page*

16. Graph the results for Vehicle A, with the difference between city and highway mileage as the appropriate point on the $y$-axis.

17. In order to solve a problem in her mathematics class, Jan had to solve the following set of equations:

    $2x + 3y = 10$

    $5x + 6y = 13$

    What is the correct value of $y$?

    (1) +4

    (2) −8

    (3) −6

    (4) +6

    (5) +8

18. An international survey found the following information about participation in adult education:

    ### Percent of Population over Age 21 Participating in Adult Education in the Year 2003

    | Country | Total Participation Rate |
    | --- | --- |
    | Denmark | 62.3 |
    | Hungary | 17.9 |
    | Norway | 43.1 |
    | Portugal | 15.5 |
    | United States | 66.4 |

    Approximately how many times more adults participate in adult education in the country with the highest participation rate than in the country with the lowest participation rate?

    (1) 2

    (2) 4

    (3) 6

    (4) 8

    (5) not enough information given

19. Gordon has six bills to pay this month:

    | Bill Payable To | Amount |
    | --- | --- |
    | Bedding by Vidalia | $23.00 |
    | Chargealot Credit Corp. | $31.00 |
    | Dink's Department Store | $48.00 |
    | Furniture Fit for a Princess Shoppe | $13.00 |
    | Highest Fidelity Sound Shop | $114.00 |
    | Overpriced Gas Corporation | $39.00 |

    Each month, he allocates $250.00 to pay his bills. This month, his bills are over this budget. How much extra money must he find from other parts of his budget to pay all of his bills?

    (1) $8.00

    (2) $268.00

    (3) $28.00

    (4) $18.00

    (5) $38.00

20. If a flight of stairs is 15 feet long, and the second floor is 9 feet above the floor below, how much floor space in length will the stair case occupy? Use the standard grid on the answer sheet to record your answer.

21. Andrew just bought a small circular swimming pool for his children to play in. The diameter of the pool is 12 feet, and Andrew can fill it safely to a depth of 9 inches. If a cubic foot of water weighs 62.42 pounds, how many pounds does the water in Andrew's pool weigh?

    (1) approximately 27,000

    (2) approximately 2,700

    (3) approximately 53,000

    (4) approximately 1,300

    (5) approximately 5,300

*Go on to next page*

22. If Giorgio borrows $100 for one year and three months and repays $108 dollars including interest, what rate of interest was he charged?

    (1) 6.4%

    (2) 8.0%

    (3) 4.0%

    (4) 4.6%

    (5) 8.4%

23. Chico went shopping for some groceries for his family. His shopping list was as follows:

    ✔ 2 pound of apples

    ✔ 5 bananas

    ✔ 1 container of milk

    ✔ 1 bread

    If apples were $.79 a pound, bananas $.23 each, milk $1.27 a carton, and bread $.98 a loaf, what is the approximate total cost of the groceries?

    (1) $3.90

    (2) $4.10

    (3) $4.90

    (4) $5.50

    (5) $6.00

24. What is the next number in the series: 4, 7, 12, 19, . . . ?

    (1) 28

    (2) 26

    (3) 24

    (4) 32

    (5) 30

25. A rectangle 5 units long and 4 units high is represented on a graph. If three of the corners are placed at (3,2), (3,–2) and (–2,2), where should the fourth corner be placed?

    (1) (–2,2)

    (2) (2,–2)

    (3) (–2,–2)

    (4) (2,2)

    (5) (5,4)

**END OF EXAMINATION**

# Chapter 17

# Answers and Explanations for the Mathematics Tests

· · · · · · · · · · · · · · · · · · · · · · · · · · · · · · · ·

## Answer Key (for Part 1)

After taking the Mathematic Test, Part I in Chapter 16, use this section to check your answers.

1. 3

2. 1

3. 1680 (on standard grid)

4. 2

5. 5

6. 1

7. 4

8. 66 (on standard grid)

9. 3

10. 4

11. 1

12.

13. 5

14. 4

15. 1

16. 4

17.

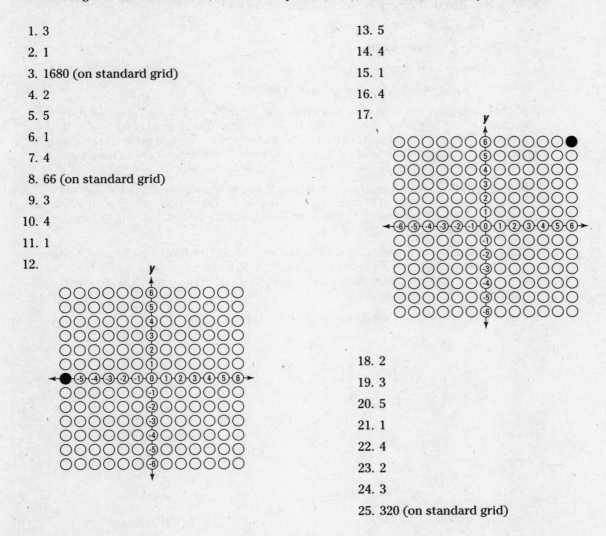

18. 2

19. 3

20. 5

21. 1

22. 4

23. 2

24. 3

25. 320 (on standard grid)

# Analysis of the Answers for Part 1

If you aren't sure why an answer was incorrect, use this section to get quick explanations of the answers.

1. **3.** This problem tests your understanding of numbers and their equivalents (integers, fractions, decimals and percents) in a real-world situation. Signs A, B, and C give customers 50% off. Sign D gives them 45% (9 × 5% sales tax). Sign D offers the least discount.

2. **1.** Frames are rectangles. This problem involves measurement and geometry and tests your understanding of perpendicular and parallel lines in a geometrical figure. Each pair of opposite sides must be parallel for this to be a rectangle.

3. **1680 (on standard grid).** This problem tests your knowledge and mastery of number operations and number sense. Use the calculator, because numerous conversions are involved, as follows:

    The area of the deck is 16 × 21 = 336 square feet.

    9 square feet = 1 square yard

    $^{336}/_9$ = 37⅓ square yards

    1 square yard of decking costs $45.00

    37⅓ square yards of decking costs $1,680.00

4. **2.** This problem tests your data-analysis skills. You're asked to interpret and draw inferences from the bar graph. Because the profit per unit is the same for all products, the product selling the least units provides the lowest profit. In each quarter, according to the bar graph, grommets sold the fewest numbers. Grommets were the least profitable product and, therefore, are recommended as the one to drop.

5. **5.** Measurement and geometry are tested in this problem. You're asked to use the Pythagorean Relationship to calculate a distance. This is a good question on which to use the calculator, because it involves squaring, adding, and calculating the square root.

The Pythagorean Relationship says that the square of the hypotenuse of a right-angle triangle is equal to the sum of the squares of the other two sides. (In your school or study guides, this may have been called the Pythagorean Theorem.) The *hypotenuse* is the side opposite the right angle.

If you draw a sketch for this problem, it looks something like this:

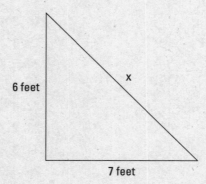

*x* represents the length of the hypotenuse. You know that the square of *x* is equal to the square of 6 plus the square of 7, or

$$6^2 + 7^2 = x^2$$

$$36 + 49 = 85$$

Then $x^2 = 85$

$x = 9.22$

The length of the stairs is 9.22 feet, correct to two decimal places.

6. **1.** Alice has converted her story into a graph, and you are being asked to interpret the line graph in conjunction with her story. The line is telling you what happened, and you must interpret the information.

Because her average daily time had been increasing until May, dropped in June, and recovered in July and August, you can assume that the twisted ankle slowed her down. It likely happened in June.

7. **4.** Number operations are involved in solving this problem. You are asked to average a set of grades for each person and compare them using a ratio. This is a question that can be simplified using the calculator.

The total of Paula's marks is $80 + 64 + 76 + 72 + 88 = 380$.

The total of Dominic's marks is $63 + 76 + 65 + 84 + 72 = 360$

Because you divide each total by 5 to get the average for both students, it is simplest to use the ratio of the totals, because it will equal the ratio of the averages. (Note that if one of the students, for example, had six grades and the other had five, you'd have to use the ratio of the averages, not of the totals.)

The ratio of Paula's marks to Dominic's marks is 380:360.

You can simplify this by dividing top and bottom by 20 to get 19:18. Note that answer 2 is the ratio of Dominic's marks to Paula's marks, but that's not asked for.

8. **66 (on standard grid).** This problem involves algebra, functions, and patterns. The numbers: 4, 6, 10, 18, . . . form a pattern (also called a *series*). From looking carefully, you see that the second term is formed by subtracting 1 from the first term and multiplying by 2. Trying this on the third number: $(6 - 1) \times 2 = 10$. This is your pattern. Continuing the series: 4, 6, 10, 18, 34, 66, . . . , the first term you come to that is a multiple of 11 is 66.

9. **3.** This problem involves data analysis and manipulation of numbers and is best done using the calculator. Most of the information is irrelevant, except to decide that Simone may have bought at a high point. The important price to consider is $15.19. In addition to this price per share, she has to pay her broker 3% commission.

Her final price per share on September 24 is $15.19 + $.03(15.19) = $15.6457. Because this is money, you have to round the number to two decimal places, making her final price per share = $15.65. This is the amount of money that came out of her bank account for each share that she bought.

If she decides to sell the shares at this price, $15.65, she has to pay her broker another 3% commission, or $.03(15.65) = $0.4695. Round to two decimals, and she has to pay a commission of $0.47 per share. She then receives the value of the shares, $15.65, minus the commission of $0.47, for a total of $15.18 per share. That is, for each share she sells, the broker deposit $15.18 into her account. But that is less than she paid for it.

In order to break even, Simone has to *receive* $15.65 per share — after the commission. Set the equation up this way:

$1x - x(.03) = 15.65$, where $x$ is the selling price.

$1x - .03x = 15.65$, where $x$ is the selling price.

$.97x = 15.65$. Now divide both sides by .97 and $x = 16.13$.

10. **4.** This question involves algebra. It lets you solve a linear equation, as follows:

$$22.4 = \frac{56a}{5a + 10}$$

Cross-multiply and write this equation as 22.4(5a + 10) = 56a

Getting rid of the parentheses, the equation looks like this: 112a + 224 = 56a

Bringing all the a's to the left and the numbers to the right, you have: 112a − 56a = −224

Combining the a's, you have: 56a = −224

Divide both sides by 56 to get one a on the left: a = −4

11. **1.** This is a test of your skill in measurement and geometry. You're asked to find the slope of a line drawn for you.

The x-axis runs horizontally across the paper. The y-axis runs vertically, up and down the paper. The origin is where the two *axes* (that's the plural of *axis*) intersect. Points to the left of the y-axis have negative x values. Points below the x-axis have negative y values. The *x-intercept* is the point where the line cuts the y axis. The *y-intercept* is the point where the line cuts the x axis. All lines parallel to the x axis have slopes of 0.

The slope of a line is the rise over the run. The rise is 4 and the run is 6. This means that the slope is ⅚ or ⅔ (divide top and bottom by 2 to simplify).

12. **(−6,0) on coordinate-plane grid.** Measurement and geometry are being tested here. You're asked to identify the x-intercept and the y-intercept and draw a line with slope of ⅔ on the coordinate plane grid. Also note that the second slope is related to the first.

If you draw a line through the point on the y-axis having the same slope, it crosses the x-axis at (−6,0). Simply count over 3 points to the left (the run), down 2 (the rise), and you're at (−3,2). But you're asked for the x-intercept, so repeat this process. Go over 3 more points to the left and down 2 more, and you're at (−6,0).

13. **5.** This question doesn't provide enough information to give an accurate answer. If the fire were rectangular in shape the answer would be different from a circular fire, or an irregularly shaped fire. The question provides information only about the shape of the barbeque.

14. **4.** Consider the price per square foot at each store:

   ✔ Carnie's Carpets: $21.50 per square yard = $21.50 ÷ 9 = $2.39 per square foot

   ✔ Flora's Flooring: $2.45 per square foot

   ✔ Dora's Deep Discount: The area of an 8 by 12 foot rug is 8 × 12 = 96 square feet. The cost for 96 square feet is $210.24 or $210.24 ÷ 96 = $2.19 per square foot

15. **1.** In this question, you're asked to analyze graphs to identify patterns in a workplace situation.

In the first graph for 2001, the 3rd quarter produces about half the output for the year. In the 2nd graph, the 3rd quarter of 2002 produces only a little over 30% of the output. The best answer for this question is the 3rd quarter.

16. **4.** This is a problem involving measurement; specifically, area and money. Assuming that the estimate for renovation is accurate, the number of square feet of renovation that the Ng's can afford for $18,000 is 18,000 ÷ 15.80 = 1,139.24 This is rounded to 1,140, because you usually don't add part of a square foot.

17. **(6,6) on coordinate-plane grid.** This problem involves data analysis, statistics, and probability. You're being asked to graph a point representing the medians of two sets of data. First, find the median (the middle number, when put in order) of the first set of numbers. The median is 6. Then, find the median of the second set of numbers. Again, it is 6.

Neatness doesn't count in your rough work. Don't spend time making beautiful tables. Just sketch out the answer.

18. **2.** This problem is based on measurement using uniform rates and asks you to make a decision based on factual information. To figure the cost of gasoline over the five years, set up the problem this way:

$$18,000\ miles \times \frac{1\ gallon}{12.8\ miles} \times \frac{\$1.75}{gallon} \times 5\ years$$

To figure the operating costs over five years, set up the problem this way:

$$18,000\ miles \times \frac{\$0.39}{mile} \times 5\ years$$

To help you make the decision, create a chart like the following:

| Vehicle Type | Miles/Gallon | Total Gas Costs | Operating Costs/Mile | Total Operating Cost | Total Cost |
|---|---|---|---|---|---|
| SUV | 12.8 | $12,304.69 | $.39 | $35,100.00 | $47,404.69 |
| Sedan | 19.6 | $8,035.71 | $.24 | $21,600.00 | $29,635.71 |
| 2-door | 19.5 | $8,076.92 | $.27 | $24,300.00 | $32,376.92 |
| All-wheel drive | 17.2 | $9,156.98 | $.31 | $27,900.00 | $37,056.98 |
| Sports car | 18.6 | $8,467.74 | $.33 | $29,700.00 | $38,167.74 |

From these figures, the sedan is the best buy.

19. **3.** This problem involves number operations. Instead of asking you for the answer, which is pretty simple, you're asked to answer the operations that are required to solve the problem. First you divide (miles to site ÷ miles per hour), and then add (the amount of time Tom wants to arrive early).

20. **5.** This question tests data analysis. You're asked to apply measures of *central tendency* (the mean) and analyze the effect of changes in data on this measure. If Leonora's present average is 77.8 and she wants to get 80%, she requires enough marks to get an additional 2.2% (80 – 77.8).

Because she is taking five subjects, she requires 5 extra points for each percent increase. Thus, she requires 2.2 × 5 = 11 additional points. The problem says that English is her best subject, so she would need the 11 extra points in English.

21. **1.** This is a test of your ability to figure out how a change in the amount of rice used results in changes to the amount of soup and lentils needed.

Because each cup of rice requires 2 cups of soup, 3½ cups of rice require 2 × 3½ = 7 cups of soup

Because each cup of rice requires ¼ cup of lentils, 3½ cups of rice require 3½ × ¼ = ⅞ × ¼ = ⅞ cup of lentils

22. **4.** This question is a test in probability. You're asked to figure out the probability of an event occurring. If you had an entire deck of 52 cards, the probability of drawing an ace of hearts would be 1:52. If you remove six cards and none of them is the ace of hearts, you may as well have a 46-card deck (52 – 6). The probability of drawing an ace of hearts from a 46-card deck is 1:46.

23. **2.** This problem tests your measurement skills. You're asked to predict the impact of changes in the linear dimensions of the rug on its area and cost. Answer 3 seems logical, but the question never mentions of the cost of the paneling, so it can't be considered as an answer.

Draw a sketch of the room with the larger rug. It will have a tiled area around it. You have to figure how many square feet of tile and carpet you need for this floor treatment, as follows:

The area of the room is $18 \times 12 = 216$ square feet.

The larger rug will cover $16 \times 10 = 160$ square feet of the floor. This leaves 56 square feet (216 – 160) to be covered with tile. The cost of the rug is $\$7.50 \times 160 = \$1,200$. The cost of the tile is $\$9.00 \times 56 = \$504.00$. The total cost is $\$1,200.00 + \$504.00 = \$1,704.00$.

The smaller rug will cover $12 \times 8 = 96$ square feet of the floor. This leaves $216 - 96 = 120$ square feet to be covered with tile. The cost of the rug is $\$7.50 \times 96 = \$720.00$. The cost of the tile is $\$9.00 \times 120 = \$1,080.00$. The total cost is $\$720.00 + \$1,080.00 = \$1,800.00$. The smaller rug will cost more for the entire floor treatment.

Because tile costs more per square foot than carpeting, you know without doing any figuring that having more tile will result in higher costs.

24. **3.** This is an exercise in data analysis. You're asked to compare sets of data on the basis of mean (average) prices of the other four stores. You can summarize the average prices on a sketch table like the one that follows:

| Item | Store A | Store B | Store C | Store D | Average Price | Friendly Furniture |
|------|---------|---------|---------|---------|---------------|--------------------|
| Couch | $1,729.00 | $1,749.00 | $1,729.00 | $1,699.00 | $1,726.50 | $1,719.00 |
| Dining room set | $4,999.00 | $4,899.00 | $5,019.00 | $4,829.00 | $4,936.50 | $4,899.00 |
| Loveseat | $1,259.00 | $1, 199.00 | $1,279.00 | $1,149.00 | $1,221.50 | $1,229.00 |
| Coffee table | $459.00 | $449.00 | $479.00 | $429.00 | $454.00 | $449.00 |
| Reclining chair | $759.00 | $799.00 | $739.00 | $699.00 | $749.00 | $739.00 |

You can see that the only item Friendly Furniture sells for over the average price is the loveseat, which is the answer to the question.

25. **320 (on standard grid).** This is a test of your knowledge of number operation, by asking you to solve a problem involving calculations. Sarah ate $48 \div 18$ pistachios per minute. In 2 hours or 120 minutes, she could eat $120 \times \dfrac{48}{18} = 320$.

# Answer Key (for Part II)

After taking the Mathematic Test, Part II in Chapter 16, use this section to check your answers.

1. 1
2. 5
3. 1
4. 5
5. 5
6. 4
7. 1.20 (on standard grid)
8. 4
9. 5
10. 2
11. 12 (on standard grid)
12. 5
13. 4.48 (on standard grid)
14. 5
15. 1

16.

17. 5
18. 2
19. 4
20. 12 (on standard grid)
21. 5
22. 1
23. 3
24. 1
25. 3

# Analysis of the Answers for Part II

If you aren't sure why an answer was incorrect, use this section to get quick explanations of the answers.

1. **1.** This is a question about number operations in which you're asked to select the appropriate operation to solve a problem. Because the first operation performed is to find the volume of the room, and the formula for volume is length × width × height, the first operation is multiplication.

2. **5.** This question measures your knowledge of measurement and geometry. You're asked to visualize and describe geometrical figures under a 90-degree rotation. Each of the figures is changed by the rotation. Try drawing each of these shapes, picking a point on the perimeter and rotating it 90 degrees. Because this is a timed test, try one or two, noticing that they change quite a bit. Use your imagination to check the rest.

3. **1.** This question tests your data-analysis skills by asking you to interpret a chart and answer a question involving calculation.

   The largest budget is the Operations budget, while the smallest budget is Human Resources. Thus the ration is 14.7 to 2.1 or 7:1 (dividing both sides by 2.1).

   If you wanted to do this in your head, notice that 14:2 is double 7:1.

4. **5.** This question tests your knowledge of patterns by asking you to compare different graphs to extract information. Graph 5 has the first and third quarters in the required ratio.

5. **5.** This problem involves measurement and geometry, asking you to use the Pythagorean Relationship to solve a problem.

   You can't actually solve this problem, however. Because the rangefinder is measuring the distance from the forester's eye and you do not know how high his eye is above the ground, you can't calculate the height of the tree. You can calculate the distance from the forester's eye to the top of the tree by using the Pythagorean Relationship but the question asks for the height of the tree (which is the distance from the *ground* — not the forester's eye — to the top of the tree).

6. **4.** This question tests your knowledge of number operations by asking you to perform several operations to calculate an answer. After week 4, Lawrie would have deposited 4 × $24.00 = $96.00. There would have been two withdrawals totaling $7.50 + $10.00 = $17.50. Her balance after week 4 would be $96.00 − $17.50 = $78.50.

7. **3.20 (on standard grid).** This question tests your skills in using percentage and discounts. Store A offered Sarah ⅓ off or 96 ÷ 3 = $32.00 off the original price. Store B offers her 30% off. 30% is 0.30, so she'll get 96 × 0.30 = $28.80 off the original price. By buying at store A, she would get the chair for $32.00 − $28.80 = $3.20 less. She would save $3.20 and you would mark 3.20 on the Standard Grid.

8. **4.** This question tests your skills by asking you to use information from a graph to solve a problem. From the graph, you can figure out that the volume in decibels is the square of the volume setting. For a volume setting of 4, the volume is 16 decibels. Therefore, for a setting of 10, the volume is 100 decibels.

9. **5.** This question tests your skills in algebra by asking you to solve equations. The equation given is $V = S^2$. If $S^2 = 144$, the square root of 144 is 12. Thus, the answer is 12.

10. **2.** If the volume decreases by half for every ten feet from the stage, a person sitting 10 feet from the stage would hear at a volume of 72 decibels and a person sitting 20 feet from the stage would hear at a volume of 36 decibels.

11. **12 (on standard grid).** This is a test of number operations. You're asked to calculate the average miles per gallon for a vehicle. Rather than provide you with the number of

gallons used, you're given the cost of gasoline and the cost of the 240-mile trip. To calculate the amount of fuel used, you divide $38.00 by $1.90 to get 20 gallons. This can be done mentally to speed things up. Next you divide the miles, 240, by the fuel used, 20, to get the mileage, 12 miles per gallon (240 ÷ 20 = 12).

12. **5.** This question tests your skills in measurement and geometry. To remain at a constant temperature, you have to remain at a constant distance from the fire.

The path of a point that travels a constant distance from a point is a circle.

13. **4.48 (on standard grid).** This problem tests your ability to do calculations and use a formula: Volume = length × width × depth. Substituting, 12,902 = 120 × 24 × average depth. The average depth = $\frac{12,902}{(120 \times 24)}$ = 4.48 (the answer is rounded).

14. **5.** This question tests your ability to make a decision based on data presented in a table, and then use that information to answer a question. The least economical car costs $1,823 to drive for a year, while the most economical car costs $840 for the same time under the same conditions. The difference in cost for one year is $1,823 – $840 = $983. The cost for three years is $983 × 3 = $2,949.

15. **1.** This question tests your ability to analyze data using the mean and median to answer a question about the data given. The mean of the city mileages is the sum of the mileages divided by 10 (the number of entries), which equals 16.8. The median of the mileages is the one midway between the two in the middle, or 16.5. The difference between the two numbers (16.8 – 16.5) is ⅓.

16. **(0,5) on coordinate-plane grid.** This question tests your ability to analyze data by representing data graphically.

For Vehicle A, the difference between the city and highway mileage is 5 mpg (28 – 23). The point you want on the y-axis is (0,5) and that should be marked on the coordinate-plane grid.

17. **5.** This question tests your skill in algebra by asking you to solve a system of linear equations. A *linear equation* is one in which the powers of the variables are all equal to 1.

$$2x + 3y = 10$$

$$5x + 6y = 13$$

To solve this system, you have to eliminate $x$ by multiplying each equation by a number that allows you to subtract one from the other and end up with just $y$s. Here's how:

Multiply the first equation by 5 and the second equation by 2.

$$5(2x + 3y = 10) = 10x + 15y = 50$$

$$2(5x + 6y = 13) = 10x + 12y = 26$$

Subtract the second equation from the first, and you get 3y = 24; y = 8. (Note that you can also multiply the second equation by –2 and add the two equations together. Either way gets you the same answer.)

18. **2.** This question asks you to analyze a situation presented in a table. The table tells you that the country with the highest participation rate is the United States, with a participation rate of 66.4. The country with the lowest participation rate is Portugal, with a participation rate of 15.5. Because you're asked for an approximation, you can say that the participation rate in the United States is 60 and in Portugal is 15. This means that 4 times as many adults participate in adult education in the United States as in Portugal.

19. **4.** This problem tests number operations. The total amount of these bills is $23.00 + $31.00 + $48.00 + $13.00 + $114.00 + $39.00 = $268.00. If Gordon allocates only $250.00 to pay these bills, he ends up $268.00 – $250.00 = $18.00 short. Be wary of answer 2, which is a special trap for people who don't read the question carefully.

20. **12 (on standard grid).** This question tests your ability to use the Pythagorean Relationship to solve a problem.

    If the hypotenuse is 15 feet and the vertical height is 9 feet, the square of the third side is equal to $15^2 - 9^2$: $225 - 81 = 144$. $\sqrt{144} = 12$.

21. **5.** This problem tests your knowledge of measurement and geometry by asking you to solve a problem involving volume and weight. This problem can be done in your head, but we take you through the steps using calculation first.

    The formula for volume of a cylinder (the cylinder is the circular inside of the pool to a height of 9 inches) is $\pi \times r^2 \times h$, where $\pi$ = approximately 3.14, $r$ = radius, and $h$ = height. If the diameter is 12 feet, the radius is 6 feet. If the height is 9 inches, it is $\frac{9}{12}$ feet; simplified, that's ¾ feet.

    In a formula, all units must be the same; that is, feet and feet or inches and inches.

    The volume is $(3.14)(6 \times 6)(\frac{3}{4})$ = 85.59 cubic feet.

    Because 1 cubic foot weighs 62.42 pounds, the weight of 85.59 cubic feet is 85.59 × 62.42 = 5,343 or 5,300 rounded to two decimal places.

    To do this in your head, multiply 6 × 6 to get 36. Multiply 36 by ¾ to get 27, and 27 by 3 is 81. The approximate volume of the pool is 81 cubic feet, which isn't bad for an approximation. For your purposes, say the volume is 80 cubic feet, which is still close. The weight of a cubic foot of water is 62.42 pounds, so round to 60 pounds. Now, 80 by 60 = 4,800, which is closest to answer 5. You can go with that approximation, because it is very close to one of the answers.

22. **1.** This question test your ability to evaluate an answer using a formula. This formula, $I = p \times r \times t$ isn't exactly in the format you want it, because you want to calculate the rate, which means solving for $r$. You can change the equation to $r = \frac{I}{p \times t}$, which allows you to calculate the rate from the information given. Substituting into this equation, you get $r = \frac{8}{100 \times 1.25}$. (Remember that 1 year and 3 months is 1¼ or 1.25 of a year.) Then $r = \frac{8}{125} = 0.064 = 6.4\%$.

23. **3.** This is a test of number operations. You're asked to calculate — in your head — the answer to a problem.

    To do this using mental math, round everything. Consider the apples at $.80 a pound, bananas at $.20 each, milk at $1.30 and a bread at $1.00. The total for this approximation is $(2 \times \$.80) + (5 \times \$.20) + \$1.30 + \$1.00 = \$4.90$. Looking at the other answers, this is the only one close to our approximation.

24. **1.** This series of numbers tests your knowledge of patterns by asking you to figure out the next number in a series. By looking at the series, it looks like each number is the square of the placement of the number in the list, plus 3. That is the first number is 1 squared plus 3, or 4. The second number is 2 squared plus 3, or 7. The third term is 3 squared (9) plus 3, or 12. The fifth term would be 5 squared (25) plus 3, which is 28.

25. **3.** This question tests your skills in geometry by asking you to visualize a graph of an object. Because the object is a rectangle, the opposite sides are equal in length and are parallel, the fourth corner will be 2 units to the left of the $y$-axis, giving it an $x$-coordinate of –2, and 2 units below the $x$-axis, giving it a $y$-coordinate of –2. The point would be (–2,–2).

    The *x-coordinate* is the distance from the $y$-axis, and the *y-coordinate* is the distance from the $x$-axis.

# Part IV

# Once More, with Feeling: Another Set of Full-Length Practice Tests

The 5th Wave     By Rich Tennant

"I wish you'd practice for the Math Test of the GED on your own time and not when you're calculating the tip on three cheeseburger specials and Cokes all around."

# In this part . . .

In this part (as in Part III), you find more questions, along with more answers and explanations to those questions. We recommend that you take these tests after you've studied and brushed up your skills in each of the five tested areas. Mastering this sets of tests tells you that you're ready to take the real GED tests. If you don't do as well as you'd hoped on this set, you know you have a bit more studying to do before you're ready for prime time.

As we suggest for the practice tests in Part III, take these tests seriously and pretend you're taking them under real test conditions.

# Chapter 18

# Language Arts, Writing Tests: Parts I and II

## Language Arts, Writing, Part 1

### Directions

The Language Arts, Writing Test measures your ability to use clear and effective English. It is a test of English as it should be written, not as it may be spoken. This test includes both multiple-choice questions and an essay. The following directions apply only to the multiple-choice section; a separate set of directions is given for the essay.

The multiple-choice section consists of documents with lettered paragraphs and numbered sentences. Some of the sentences contain an error in sentence structure, usage, or mechanics (punctuation and capitalization). After reading the numbered sentences, answer the multiple-choice questions that follow. Some questions refer to sentences that are correct as written. The best answer for these questions is the one that leaves the sentence as originally written. The best answer for some questions is the one that produces a document that is consistent with the verb tense and point of view used throughout the text.

You have 120 minutes (two hours) to complete both parts of the test. You can spend up to 75 minutes on the 50 multiple-choice questions, leaving the remaining time for the essay. Work carefully, but do not spend too much time on any one question. Answer every question. You will not be penalized for incorrect answers. You may begin working on the essay section of this test as soon as you complete the multiple-choice section.

Do not mark in this test booklet. Record your answers on the separate answer sheet provided. To record your answers, fill in the numbered circle on the answer sheet that corresponds to the answer you select for each question in the test booklet.

*Go on to next page*

**EXAMPLE:**

Sentence 1: **We were all honored to meet governor Phillips and his staff.**

Which correction should be made to sentence 1?

(1)    change <u>were</u> to <u>was</u>

(2)    insert a comma after <u>honored</u>

(3)    change <u>governor</u> to <u>Governor</u>

(4)    insert a comma after <u>Phillips</u>

(5)    no correction is necessary

(On Answer Sheet)

① ② ● ④ ⑤

In this example, the word "governor" should be capitalized; therefore, answer space 3 would be marked on the answer sheet.

Do not rest the point of your pencil on the answer sheet while you are considering your answer. Make no stray or unnecessary marks. If you change an answer, erase your first mark completely. Mark only one answer space for each question; multiple answers will be scored as incorrect. Do not fold or crease your answer sheet. All test materials must be returned to the test administrator.

**DO NOT BEGIN TAKING THIS TEST UNTIL TOLD TO DO SO**

**WRITING TEST: Part I**

1 ① ② ③ ④ ⑤        26 ① ② ③ ④ ⑤

2 ① ② ③ ④ ⑤        27 ① ② ③ ④ ⑤

3 ① ② ③ ④ ⑤        28 ① ② ③ ④ ⑤

4 ① ② ③ ④ ⑤        29 ① ② ③ ④ ⑤

5 ① ② ③ ④ ⑤        30 ① ② ③ ④ ⑤

6 ① ② ③ ④ ⑤        31 ① ② ③ ④ ⑤

7 ① ② ③ ④ ⑤        32 ① ② ③ ④ ⑤

8 ① ② ③ ④ ⑤        33 ① ② ③ ④ ⑤

9 ① ② ③ ④ ⑤        34 ① ② ③ ④ ⑤

10 ① ② ③ ④ ⑤       35 ① ② ③ ④ ⑤

11 ① ② ③ ④ ⑤       36 ① ② ③ ④ ⑤

12 ① ② ③ ④ ⑤       37 ① ② ③ ④ ⑤

13 ① ② ③ ④ ⑤       38 ① ② ③ ④ ⑤

14 ① ② ③ ④ ⑤       39 ① ② ③ ④ ⑤

15 ① ② ③ ④ ⑤       40 ① ② ③ ④ ⑤

16 ① ② ③ ④ ⑤       41 ① ② ③ ④ ⑤

17 ① ② ③ ④ ⑤       42 ① ② ③ ④ ⑤

18 ① ② ③ ④ ⑤       43 ① ② ③ ④ ⑤

19 ① ② ③ ④ ⑤       44 ① ② ③ ④ ⑤

20 ① ② ③ ④ ⑤       45 ① ② ③ ④ ⑤

21 ① ② ③ ④ ⑤       46 ① ② ③ ④ ⑤

22 ① ② ③ ④ ⑤       47 ① ② ③ ④ ⑤

23 ① ② ③ ④ ⑤       48 ① ② ③ ④ ⑤

24 ① ② ③ ④ ⑤       49 ① ② ③ ④ ⑤

25 ① ② ③ ④ ⑤       50 ① ② ③ ④ ⑤

Questions 1 through 10 refer to the following excerpt.

## Fix the Problem

(1) This step requires you to listen to each customers assessment of the problem. Your job when she explains the situation from her perspective is to fully absorb what she is saying about her unique set of circumstances. (2) After you identify the customer's problem, the next step, obviously, is to fix it. (3) Sometimes, you can easily remedy the situation by changing an invoice, redoing an order, waving or refunding charges, or replacing a defective product. (4) At other times, fixing the problem is more complex because the damage or mistake cannot be repaired simply. (5) In these instances, mutually exceptable compromises need to be reached.

(6) Whatever the problem, this step begins to remedy the situation and gives the customer what she needs to resolve the source of the conflict. (7) Don't waste time and effort by putting the horse before the cart and trying to fix the wrong problem. (8) Its easy to jump the gun and think that you know what the customer is about to say because you've heard it all a hundred times before. (9) Doing so loses you ground on the recovery front and further annoys the customer. (10) More often than not, what you think the problem is at first glance, is different from what it becomes upon closer examination.

*Karen Leland and Russell Bailey, adapted from* Customer Service For Dummies *(Wiley Publishing, Inc.)*

1. Sentence 1: **This step requires you to listen to each customers assessment of the problem.**

   Which correction should be made to sentence 1?

   (1) change <u>requires</u> to <u>required</u>

   (2) change <u>customers</u> to <u>customers'</u>

   (3) change <u>assessment</u> to <u>assessing</u>

   (4) change <u>customers</u> to <u>customer's</u>

   (5) no correction required

2. Sentence 2: **Your job when she explains the situation from her perspective is to fully absorb what she is saying about her unique set of circumstances.**

   The most effective revision of sentence 2 would begin with which group of words?

   (1) When she explains the situation from her perspective,

   (2) Your job when she explains,

   (3) What she is saying about,

   (4) Her unique set of circumstances,

   (5) no correction required

3. Sentence 3: **Sometimes, you can easily remedy the situation by changing an invoice, redoing an order, waving or refunding charges, or replacing a defective product.**

   Which correction should be made to sentence 3?

   (1) change <u>redoing</u> to <u>re-doing</u>

   (2) change <u>invoice</u> to <u>invoise</u>

   (3) change <u>waving</u> to <u>waiving</u>

   (4) change <u>defective</u> to <u>defected</u>

   (5) no correction required

4. Sentence 4: **At other times fixing the problem is more complex because the damage or mistake cannot be repaired simply.**

   Which is the best way to write the underlined portion of this sentence? If the original is the best way, choose option (1).

   (1) add a comma after <u>because</u>

   (2) add a semicolon after <u>times</u>

   (3) add a comma after <u>times</u>

   (4) add a comma after <u>mistake</u>

   (5) add a semicolon after <u>mistake</u>

*Go on to next page*

5. Sentence 5: **In these instances, mutually exceptable compromises need to be reached.**

   Which correction should be made to sentence 5?

   (1) remove the comma after <u>instances</u>

   (2) change <u>these</u> to <u>those</u>

   (3) change <u>need</u> to <u>needed</u>

   (4) change <u>exceptable</u> to <u>acceptable</u>

   (5) no correction required

6. Sentence 6: **Whatever the problem, this step begins to remedy the situation and gives the customer what she needs to resolve the source of the conflict.**

   Which is the best way to begin sentence 6? If the original is the best way choose option 1.

   (1) Whatever the problem,

   (2) This step begins to remedy,

   (3) What she needs to resolve,

   (4) To resolve the source of the conflict,

   (5) To remedy the situation,

7. Sentence 7: **Don't waste time and effort by putting the horse before the cart and trying to fix the wrong problem.**

   Which change should be made to sentence 7?

   (1) change <u>waste</u> to <u>waist</u>

   (2) revise to read <u>the cart before the horse</u>

   (3) change <u>trying</u> to <u>try</u>

   (4) change <u>don't</u> to <u>doesn't</u>

   (5) no correction required

8. Sentence 8: **Its easy to jump the gun and think you know what the customer is about to say because you've heard it all a hundred times before.**

   What correction should be made to sentence 8?

   (1) replace <u>is</u> with <u>was</u>

   (2) change <u>heard</u> to <u>herd</u>

   (3) replace <u>you've</u> with <u>you had</u>

   (4) change <u>Its</u> to <u>It's</u>

   (5) no correction required

9. Sentence 9: **Doing so loses you ground on the recovery front and farther annoys the customer.**

   Which change should be made to sentence 9?

   (1) replace <u>loses</u> with <u>looses</u>

   (2) change <u>recovery</u> to <u>recover</u>

   (3) replace <u>farther</u> with <u>further</u>

   (4) change <u>you</u> to <u>your</u>

   (5) no correction required

10. Sentence 10: **More often than not, what you think the problem is at first glance, is different from what it becomes upon closer inspection.**

    Which correction should be made to sentence 10?

    (1) remove the comma after <u>not</u>

    (2) remove the comma after <u>glance</u>

    (3) insert a comma after <u>different</u>

    (4) insert a comma after <u>from</u>

    (5) no correction required

*Go on to next page*

Questions 11 through 17 refer to the following business letter.

**BEST Institute of Technology**
75 Ingram Drive
Concord, MA 51234

To whom it may concern:

(1) I am pleased to comment on the relationship of our organization to Peta Jackson of the York Square Employment resource Center. (2) The BEST Institute of Technology has partnered with the York Square ERC in recruiting candidates for our Café Technician and Operator training programs since April 2000.

(3) In support of the partnership, Peta provided the following services to our programs

- Set up information presentations as part of her job readiness seminars
- Distributed print materials
- Counseled applicants
- Expedited meetings with potential candidates
- Arranged five graduating ceremonies held at York Square ERC

(4) Peta has always been a strong advocate for our program, which has trained more than 50 technicians and operators during the past 18 months. (5) The fact that York Square was our primary source of referrals are a tribute to Peta's efforts. (6) She has, with a high degree of professional competence, pursued her responsibilities. (7) On a personal level, it has been a joy to work with Peta and I wish her the very best in her future endeavors.

Dale Worth, Ph.D., Registrar

11. Sentence 1: **I am pleased to comment on the relationship of our organization to Peta Jackson of the York Square Employment resource Center.**

Which revision should be made to sentence 1?

(1) change <u>to Peta Jackson</u> to <u>of Peta Jackson</u>

(2) change <u>pleased</u> to <u>please</u>

(3) change <u>resource</u> to <u>Resource</u>

(4) change <u>Center</u> to <u>Centre</u>

(5) no correction required

12. Sentence 2: **The BEST Institute of Technology has partnered with the York Square ERC in recruiting candidates for our Café Technician and Operator training programs since April 2002.**

Which way should you improve sentence 2?

(1) Move <u>since April 2002</u> to the start of the sentence.

(2) change <u>has partnered</u> to <u>have partnered</u>

(3) change <u>with</u> to <u>between</u>

(4) change <u>in recruiting</u> to <u>while recruiting</u>

(5) no correction required

*Go on to next page*

13. Sentence 3: **In support of the partnership, Peta provided the following services to our programs**

    • **Set up information presentations as part of her job readiness seminars**
    • **Distributed print materials**
    • **Counseled applicants**
    • **Expedited meetings with potential candidates**
    • **Arranged five graduating ceremonies held at York Square ERC**

    Which correction should be made to sentence 3?

    (1) remove the comma after <u>partnership</u>
    (2) add a semicolon after <u>seminars</u>
    (3) add a semicolon after <u>materials</u>
    (4) insert a colon after <u>programs</u>
    (5) insert a comma after <u>services</u>

14. Sentence 4: **Peta <u>has always been</u> a strong advocate for our program, which has trained more than 50 technicians and operators during the past 18 months.**

    Which is the best way to write the underlined portion of this sentence? If the original is the best way choose option (1).

    (1) has always been
    (2) always has been
    (3) has been always
    (4) have always been
    (5) always have been

15. Sentence 5: **The fact that York Square was our primary source of referrals are a tribute to Peta's efforts.**

    Which correction should be made to sentence 5?

    (1) change <u>Peta's</u> to <u>Petas'</u>
    (2) change <u>are</u> to <u>is</u>
    (3) change <u>was</u> to <u>were</u>
    (4) change <u>our</u> to <u>her</u>
    (5) no correction required

16. Sentence 6: **She has, with a high degree of professional competence and efficiency, pursued her responsibilities.**

    Which revision should be made to sentence 6?

    (1) move <u>with a high degree of professional competence,</u> after <u>she</u>
    (2) move <u>with a high degree of professional competence</u> after <u>pursued</u>
    (3) move <u>with a high degree of professional competence</u> to the end of sentence after <u>responsibilities</u>
    (4) place <u>With a high degree of professional competence</u> at the front of the sentence before <u>She</u>
    (5) no correction required

17. Sentence 7: **On a personal level, it has been a joy to work with Peta and I wish her the very best in her future endeavors.**

    Which improvement should be made to sentence 7?

    (1) break sentence 7 into two sentences
    (2) change <u>endeavors</u> to <u>endeavours</u>
    (3) change <u>has been</u> to <u>have been</u>
    (4) move <u>on a personal level</u> to be inserted after <u>Peta</u>
    (5) no correction required

*Go on to next page*

Questions 18 through 28 refer to the following example.

### The Care Token Coupon

(1) A new copy shoppe recently opened near our office. (2) Modern and full of new, stream-lined, state-of-the-art copiers. (3) The store was just what I needed. (4) The first time I went over I waited 45 minutes to get served because of a shortage of trained staff. (5) They bounced back by apologizing, explaining the situation, and gave me a care token coupon that was worth 100 free copies. (6) Okay, I thought, fair enough, they're new and getting their act together, no big deal. (7) A week later, I went back and waited 30 minutes for service. (8) They apologised, explained the situation, and gave me a coupon for 100 free copies. (9) This time I was a little less understanding. (10) Two weeks later, I went back and the same thing happened again. (11) I didn't want another free coupon — they had bounced back just once too often. (12) My opinion of their services were so soured that I began looking for another copy shop.

*Karen Leland and Russell Bailey, adapted from* Customer Service For Dummies *(Wiley Publishing, Inc.)*

18. Sentence 1: **A new copy shoppe recently opened near our office.**

    Which correction should be made to sentence 1?

    (1) change <u>copy</u> to <u>copie</u>

    (2) change <u>shoppe</u> to <u>shop</u>

    (3) change <u>opened</u> to <u>is opening</u>

    (4) change <u>a</u> to <u>an</u>

    (5) no correction required

19. Sentences 2 and 3: **Modern and full of new, streamlined, state-of-the-art copiers. The store was just what I needed.**

    Which improvement should be made to sentences 2 and 3?

    (1) combine the two sentences

    (2) remove the hyphens from <u>state-of-the-art</u>

    (3) change <u>streamlined</u> to <u>streamlining</u>

    (4) change <u>store was</u> to <u>the copiers were</u>

    (5) no correction required

20. Sentence 4: **The first time I went over I waited 45 minutes to get served because of a shortage of trained staff.**

    Which is the best way to begin sentence 4?

    (1) Because to get served . . .

    (2) I waited 45 minutes . . .

    (3) To get served because . . .

    (4) Because of a shortage . . .

    (5) no correction required

21. Sentence 5: **They bounced back by apologizing, explaining the situation, and gave me a care token coupon that was worth 100 free copies.**

    Which correction should be made to sentence 5?

    (1) change <u>apologizing</u> to <u>apologized</u>

    (2) replace <u>explaining</u> with <u>explained</u>

    (3) change <u>gave</u> to <u>giving</u>

    (4) replace <u>was</u> with <u>were</u>

    (5) no correction required

22. Sentence 6: **Okay, I thought, fair enough, they're new and getting their act together, no big deal.**

    Which revision should be made to sentence 6?

    (1) change <u>thought</u> to <u>am thinking</u>

    (2) change to two or three sentence.

    (3) change <u>no</u> to <u>know</u>

    (4) change <u>getting</u> to <u>got</u>

    (5) change the first <u>they're</u> to <u>their</u>

*Go on to next page*

23. Sentence 7: **A week later I went back and waited 30 minutes for service.**

    Which addition should be made to sentence 7?

    (1) add a comma after <u>later</u>

    (2) add a comma after <u>back</u>

    (3) add a colon after <u>back</u>

    (4) add <u>more</u> after <u>minutes</u>

    (5) no correction required

24. Sentence 8: **They apologised, explained the situation, and gave me a coupon for 100 free copies.**

    Which correction is required for sentence 8?

    (1) change <u>apologised</u> to <u>apologising</u>

    (2) change <u>explained</u> to <u>explaining</u>

    (3) change <u>apologised</u> to <u>apologized</u>

    (4) change <u>copies</u> to <u>copys</u>

    (5) no correction required

25. Sentence 9: **This time I was a little less understanding.**

    Which correction should be made to sentence 9?

    (1) insert a comma after <u>time</u>

    (2) change <u>was</u> to <u>am</u>

    (3) change <u>less</u> to <u>least</u>

    (4) change <u>understanding</u> to <u>understood</u>

    (5) no correction required

26. Sentence 10: **Two weeks <u>later, I went back</u> and the same thing happened again.**

    Which is the best way to write the underlined portion of the sentence?

    (1) later, back I went,

    (2) back, later I went

    (3) later, I went back,

    (4) I, later, went back,

    (5) I went back later

27. Sentence 11: **I didn't want another free coupon — they had bounced back just once too often.**

    Which is the best way to revise sentence 11?

    (1) remove <u>once</u>

    (2) insert a period after <u>coupon</u>

    (3) change <u>had</u> to <u>have</u>

    (4) change <u>another</u> to <u>no</u>

    (5) no correction required

28. Sentence 12: **My opinion of their services were so soured that I began looking for another copy shop.**

    Which correction should be made to sentence 12?

    (1) change <u>began</u> to <u>begun</u>

    (2) insert a comma after <u>soared</u>

    (3) replace <u>my</u> with <u>our</u>

    (4) change <u>were</u> to <u>was</u>

    (5) no correction required

*Go on to next page*

Questions 29 through 41 refer to the following executive summary.

**Executive Summary**
**KWIK Stop Auto Center**

**The correct approach for the 21st century**

(1) Back in 1978, Morris James, President and Founder of KWIK Stop Auto Center, foresaw changes necessary for the automotive-service industry. (2) The market was becoming much more sophisticated. (3) Combined with 5 years' experience as a licensed mechanic and owner/operator of a repair facility, this knowledge, led to the opening of KWIK Stop Auto Center's first location.

(4) Morris James analyzed the "fast food" concept of providing high quality merchandize at affordable prices. (5) This concept combined with speedy service helped the industry grow every year. (6) Morris decided that the same principals should be applied to the automotive industry, and he started KWIK Stop as the first logical step.

(7) In 1987, Morris was relocated to Woodbridge and began searching for a new shop site to begin franchising. (8) The opening of a Concord franchise became very profitable and proved Morris's theory to be correct. (9) He then opened the corporate store having established the validity of the concept in Wellesley, in 1991.

(10) Now the challenge is to develop the corporate store in a way that it can not only function in its capacity as a profit center but also be used as a hands-on training center for future franchise owners.

(11) The start up costs will require some initial investment, but will be gained within the first three years. (12) We will look at this situation more in-depth within the plan. (13) The addition of a wide selection of accessories, for the customer, will broaden the impact of this new concept.

29. Sentence 1: **Back in 1978, Morris James, President and Founder of KWIK Stop Auto Center, foresaw changes necessary for the automotive-service industry.**

Which change should be made to sentence 1?

(1) change <u>foresaw</u> to <u>forseen</u>

(2) remove the comma after <u>1978</u>

(3) remove the comma after <u>Center</u> and add one after <u>changes</u>

(4) move <u>necessary</u> and insert between <u>foresaw</u> and <u>changes</u>

(5) no correction required

30. Sentence 2: **The market <u>was becoming</u> much more sophisticated.**

Which is the best way to write the underlined portion of this sentence? If the original is the best way choose option (1).

(1) was becoming

(2) will becoming

(3) were becoming

(4) is becoming

(5) would becoming

*Go on to next page*

31. Sentence 3: **Combined with 5 years' experience as a licensed mechanic and owner/operator of a repair facility, this knowledge, led to the opening of KWIK Stop Auto Center's first location.**

    Which improvement should be made to sentence 3?

    (1) change years' to year's
    (2) remove the comma after knowledge
    (3) change licensed to licenced
    (4) move This knowledge, to the beginning of the sentence
    (5) change Center's to Centers

32. Sentence 4: **Morris James analyzed the "fast food" concept of providing high quality merchandize at affordable prices.**

    What correction should be made to sentence 4?

    (1) change analyzed to analysed
    (2) change merchandize to merchandise
    (3) change concept to consept
    (4) delete of
    (5) no correction required

33. Sentence 5: **This concept combined with speedy service helped the industry grow every year.**

    Which change should be made to sentence 5?

    (1) add commas after concept and service
    (2) change helped to has helped
    (3) change grow to growing
    (4) change service to servicing
    (5) no correction required

34. Sentence 6: **Morris decided that the same principals should be applied to the automotive industry, and he started KWIK Stop as the first logical step.**

    Which correction should be made to sentence 6?

    (1) change principals to principles
    (2) change decided to had decided
    (3) change should be to shouldn't be
    (4) change industry to industries
    (5) no correction required

35. Sentence 7: **In 1987, Morris was relocated to Woodbridge and began searching for a new shop site to begin franchising.**

    Which is the best way to write the underlined portion of this sentence? If the original is the best way, choose option (1).

    (1) was located
    (2) is located
    (3) has located
    (4) relocated
    (5) will locate

36. Sentence 8: **The opening of a Concord franchise became very profitable and proved Morris's theory to be correct.**

    Which revision should be made to sentence 8?

    (1) change concord to Concord
    (2) change franchise to franchize
    (3) change Morris's to Morris'
    (4) change profitable to profiting
    (5) no correction required

37. Sentence 9: **He then opened the corporate store having established the validity of the concept in Wellesley, in 1991.**

    Which is the best way to begin this sentence? If the original is the best way choose option (1).

    (1) He then opened the corporate store
    (2) Having established the validity of the concept
    (3) In Wellesley, in 1991, he then opened
    (4) In 1991, he then opened
    (5) The validity of the concept having established

*Go on to next page*

38. Sentence 10: **Now the challenge is to develop the corporate store in a way that it can not only function in its capacity as a profit center, but can also be used as a hands-on training center for future franchise owners.**

    Which is the best way to improve sentence 10?

    (1) insert , as a profit center, between store and in

    (2) change can not only to only can not

    (3) place a comma after capacity

    (4) change challenges is with challenges are

    (5) no correction required

39. Sentence 11: **The start up costs will require some initial investment but will be regained within the first three years.**

    Which correction should be made to sentence 11?

    (1) change some to any

    (2) change start up to start-up

    (3) add a comma after investment

    (4) change within to between

    (5) no correction required

40. Sentence 12: **We will look at this <u>situation more in-depth</u> within the plan.**

    Which is the best way to improve the underlined? If the original is the best way choose option (1).

    (1) situation more in-depth

    (2) more situation in-depth

    (3) situation in more depth

    (4) more in-depth situation

    (5) in-depth more situation

41. Sentence 13: **The addition of a wide selection of accessories, for the customer, will broaden the impact of this new concept.**

    Which revision should be made to sentence 13?

    (1) move <u>for the customer</u> to the end of the sentence and eliminate the commas

    (2) change <u>will broaden</u> to <u>broaden</u>

    (3) begin the sentence with <u>The impact of this new concept . . .</u>

    (4) begin the sentence with <u>The customer will broaden . . .</u>

    (5) change commas after <u>accessories</u> and <u>customer</u> to semicolons

*Go on to next page*

Questions 42 through 50 refer to the following information.

**The Customer Chain**

(1) The relationship among internal customers and external customers is what forms the customer chain. (2) If you have a back room kind of job where you see the light of day, rarely, you can easily begin to feel that your work has little or no impact on external customers. (3) But if you look at the bigger picture, you can see that everyone in a company plays some part in fulfilling the customers needs. (4) Barely an hour goes by during the day when you are not, in some form or another, providing somebody for something. (5) Each interaction with an internal customer is an important link in a chain of events that always end up at the external customers' feet.

(6) About two years ago, *The Wall Street Journal* ran an article entitled, Poorly treated employees treat the customer just as poorly. (7) We had dealt with a frightening percentage of managers who do not realize that their staffs are their internal customers. (8) That the quality of service that a company provides to its customers — we are convinced — is a direct reflection of how the staff of the company are treated by their managers. (9) View your staff members as some of your most important customers and treat them accordingly.

*Karen Leland and Russell Bailey, adapted from* Customer Service For Dummies *(Wiley Publishing, Inc.)*

42. Sentence 1: **The relationship among internal customers and external customers is what forms the customer chain.**

    Which correction should be made to sentence 1?

    (1) replace <u>among</u> with <u>between</u>

    (2) change <u>relationship</u> to <u>relations</u>

    (3) replace <u>is what</u> with <u>was what</u>

    (4) change <u>customer</u> to <u>customers'</u>

    (5) no correction required

43. Sentence 2: **If you have a back room kind of job, <u>where you see the light of day, rarely,</u> you can easily begin to feel that your work has little or no impact on external customers.**

    Which is the best way to write the underlined portion of this sentence? If the original is the best way choose option (1).

    (1) where you see the light of day rarely

    (2) where the light of day you see rarely

    (3) where you rarely see the light of day

    (4) where you see rarely the light of day

    (5) where rarely you see the light of day

44. Sentence 3: **But if you look at the bigger picture, you can see that everyone in a company plays some part in fulfilling the customers needs.**

    Which correction should be made to sentence 3?

    (1) replace <u>customers</u> with <u>customers'</u>

    (2) change <u>bigger</u> to <u>biggest</u>

    (3) replace <u>everyone</u> with <u>everybody</u>

    (4) change <u>fulfilling</u> to <u>fulfiling</u>

    (5) no correction required

45. Sentence 4: **Barely an hour goes by during the day when you are not, in some form or another, providing somebody for something.**

    Which revision should be made to sentence 4?

    (1) replace <u>barely</u> with <u>about</u>

    (2) change <u>somebody for something</u> to <u>something for somebody</u>

    (3) replace <u>during</u> with <u>over</u>

    (4) change <u>providing</u> to <u>provided</u>

    (5) no correction required

*Go on to next page*

46. Sentence 5: **Each interaction with an internal customer is an important link in a chain of events that always end up at the external customer's feet.**

Which correction should be made to sentence 5?

(1) replace <u>customer's</u> with <u>customers</u>

(2) change <u>is</u> to <u>are</u>

(3) replace <u>with</u> with <u>between</u>

(4) change <u>end</u> to <u>ends</u>

(5) no correction required

47. Sentence 6: **About two years ago, *The Wall Street Journal* ran an article entitled, Poorly treated employees treat the customer just as poorly.**

Which addition should be made to sentence 6?

(1) place quotation marks before <u>Poorly</u> and after <u>poorly</u>

(2) remove the comma after <u>ago</u>

(3) remove the comma after <u>entitled</u>

(4) remove italics from *The Wall Street Journal*

(5) no correction required

48. Sentence 7: **We had dealt with a frightening percentage of managers who do not realize that their staffs are their internal customers.**

Which correction should be made with sentence 7?

(1) replace <u>frightening</u> with <u>frightened</u>

(2) change <u>staffs</u> to <u>staff</u>

(3) change <u>had dealt</u> to <u>have dealt</u>

(4) place an apostrophe after <u>managers</u>

(5) no correction required

49. Sentence 8: **That the quality of service that a company provides to its customers — we are convinced — is a direct reflection of how the staff of the company are treated by their managers.**

Which is the best way to begin sentence 8? If the original is best choose option (1).

(1) That the quality of service . . .

(2) We are convinced . . .

(3) How the staff of the company . . .

(4) That a company provides . . .

(5) A direct reflection of how . . .

50. Sentence 9: **View your staff members as some of your most important customers and <u>treat them accordingly</u>.**

Which is the best way to revise the underlined?

(1) accordingly treat them

(2) treat accordingly them

(3) them treat accordingly

(4) remove <u>them</u>

(5) no correction required

# Language Arts, Writing, Part II

### Essay Directions and Topic

Look at the box on the following page. In the box, you find your assigned topic and the letter of that topic.

You must write on the assigned topic **ONLY.**

Mark the letter of your assigned topic in the appropriate space on your answer sheet booklet.

You have 45 minutes to write on your assigned essay topic. If you have time remaining in this test period after you complete your essay, you may return to the multiple choice section. Do not return the Language Arts, Writing Test booklet until you finish both Parts I and II of the Language Arts, Writing Test.

Two evaluators will score your essay according to its overall effectiveness. Their evaluation will be based on the following features:

- ✔ Well-focused main points
- ✔ Clear organization
- ✔ Specific development of your ideas
- ✔ Control of sentence structure, punctuation, grammar, word choice, and spelling

**REMEMBER, YOU MUST COMPLETE BOTH THE MULTIPLE-CHOICE QUESTIONS (PART I) AND THE ESSAY (PART II) TO RECEIVE A SCORE ON THE LANGUAGE ARTS, WRITING TEST. To avoid having to repeat both parts of the test, be sure to observe the following rules:**

- ✔ Before you begin writing, jot notes or outline your essay on the sheets provided.
- ✔ For your final copy, write legibly <u>in ink</u> so that the evaluators will be able to read your writing.
- ✔ Write on the assigned topic. If you write on a topic other than the one assigned, you will not receive a score for the Language Arts, Writing Test.
- ✔ Write your essay on the lined pages of the separate answer sheet booklet. Only the writing on these pages will be scored.

Note that if you do not pass one portion of the test, you must take both parts over again.

*Go on to next page*

**Topic B**

Cellphones have certainly made a difference in our lives. You may own and use one or have put up with other people who use them while driving or at the movies. Cellphones have made our lives better, more difficult, or both.

Write an essay explaining the positive or negative effects — or both — of this innovation in communication. Use examples to support your point of view and be as specific as possible.

Part II is a test to determine how well you can use written language to explain your ideas.

In preparing for your essay, you should take the following steps:

- Read the DIRECTIONS and the TOPIC carefully.
- Plan your essay before you write. Use the scratch paper provided to make any notes. These notes will be collected but not scored.
- Before you turn in your essay, reread what you have written and make any changes that will improve your essay.

Your essay should be long enough to develop the topic adequately.

**END OF EXAMINATION**

**WRITING TEST: Part II**

Use a No. 2 pencil to write the letter of your essay topic in the box,
then fill in the corresponding circle.

TOPIC ⬜ Ⓐ Ⓑ Ⓒ Ⓓ Ⓔ Ⓕ Ⓖ Ⓗ Ⓘ Ⓙ Ⓚ Ⓛ Ⓜ Ⓝ Ⓞ Ⓟ Ⓠ Ⓡ Ⓢ Ⓣ Ⓤ Ⓥ Ⓦ Ⓧ Ⓨ Ⓩ

**USE A BALLPOINT PEN TO WRITE YOUR ESSAY**

Continue your essay on the next page

# Chapter 19

# Answers and Explanations for the Language Arts, Writing Tests

················································

## Answer Key (for Part 1)

After taking the Language Arts, Writing, Part I Test in Chapter 18, use this section to check your answers.

| | | |
|---|---|---|
| 1. 4 | 18. 2 | 35. 4 |
| 2. 1 | 19. 1 | 36. 1 |
| 3. 3 | 20. 5 | 37. 2 |
| 4. 3 | 21. 3 | 38. 5 |
| 5. 4 | 22. 2 | 39. 2 |
| 6. 1 | 23. 1 | 40. 3 |
| 7. 2 | 24. 3 | 41. 1 |
| 8. 4 | 25. 1 | 42. 1 |
| 9. 3 | 26. 3 | 43. 3 |
| 10. 2 | 27. 5 | 44. 1 |
| 11. 3 | 28. 4 | 45. 2 |
| 12. 1 | 29. 4 | 46. 4 |
| 13. 4 | 30. 1 | 47. 1 |
| 14. 1 | 31. 4 | 48. 3 |
| 15. 2 | 32. 2 | 49. 2 |
| 16. 3 | 33. 1 | 50. 5 |
| 17. 1 | 34. 1 | |

# Analysis of the Answers for Part 1

If you aren't sure why an answer was incorrect, use this section to get quick explanations of the answers.

1. **4.** The assessment belongs to each customer and requires a possessive form of customer: customer's. The other answers neither correct nor improve the sentence.

2. **1.** The meaning of this sentence is that the clerk should listen to the customer, so put the most important information first. The best way to start this sentence is with the words "When she explains the situation from her perspective . . . ."

3. **3.** "Waving" means to motion with the hand, while "waive" means to dismiss. It may be interesting to wave at a charge, but the proper meaning of the sentence is to dismiss (or not collect) the charge. These two words are *homonyms* (words that sound the same but have different spellings and meanings). You are expected to understand most homonyms.

4. **3.** The only place you can use a comma in this sentence is after the introductory clause, "At other times."

5. **4.** "Exceptable" may sound like a word, but it's not. The correct word to use is "acceptable."

The more reading you do as you prepare for the test, the better the chance you have of recognizing misspellings.

6. **1.** A gift for you; no correction is required.

If you chose number 5, keep in mind that this is a one-subject, two-verb sentence, and these types of sentences don't require a comma between the two verbs. Not sure about subjects and verbs? Here, the subject is "step" and two verbs are "begins" and "gives." If the sentence had a second subject before the second verb, it would need a comma.

7. **2.** If you live anywhere near Amish country, you know that the horse comes before the cart. Or you may have heard the idiomatic expression, "Don't put the cart before the horse." In either case, the proper correction is to reverse the order of horses and carts.

8. **4.** "Its" is possessive (meaning that it shows that something belongs to "it"), while "it's" stands for "it is." Here, the sentence clearly means "it is."

This is a common error that's usually tested in some way. Master the difference between "its" and "it's."

9. **3.** "Farther" always refers to distance. "Further" is a matter of degree.

If you didn't know the answer, this question is a good example of one that can be answered by intelligent guessing. Answer 1 isn't correct because "looses" isn't a word. Answer 2 doesn't make sense in the context of the sentence, Answer 4 isn't right because the person losing ground is you, and because you don't own the ground, you wouldn't want to use a possessive.

10. **2.** Commas used in moderation help sentences. Extra commas hurt sentences. A comma is never used to separate a subject from a verb.

11. **3.** "The York Square Employment Resource Center" is a title; as such, all words (except prepositions and articles) are capitalized.

12. **1.** Moving "since April 2002" is the only good answer here. The current sentence sounds as though the training programs have been in existence since April 2002 when, in fact, the partnership has been in existence since that time.

13. **4.** Most (although not all) lists begin with a colon. You don't need semi-colons after the items in the list (the bullets serve as separators). You need a comma after the introductory clause (answer 1), and you wouldn't separate a direct object from an indirect object with a comma (answer 5).

14. **1.** No correction is required.

15. **2.** The subject of the sentence is "fact," which is singular, but the verb is "are," which is plural. Verbs must agree with their subjects.

16. **3.** In its current form, this sentence forces the reader to pause too long and remember too much. Rewriting it to "She has pursued her responsibilities with a high degree of professional competence and efficiency" is far more straightforward.

17. **1.** This is a run-on sentence. In addition, the word "but" in the middle distorts the meaning. Break into two sentences.

18. **2.** "Shoppe" is quaint but is not in common usage. If you were living in Williamsburg two hundred years ago, the answer would be different. Today, people use the shorter and more common, "shop."

19. **1.** Before the change, the first sentence was missing a verb, making it an incomplete sentence. "State-of-the-art" is correct because the four words are acting as a single adjective to "copiers," and multi-word adjectives are nearly always hyphenated. Answer 4 is incorrect because the first sentence is clearly describing the store, not the copiers.

20. **5.** No change is required in this sentence. The copy shop may want to consider changing the way it hires and trains its staff, but that's another matter altogether.

21. **3.** Lists have to be parallel. In this case, you have apologizing, explaining, and care, which isn't parallel (all three are verbs, but the first two are gerunds, the second is an infinitive). Changing "care" to "caring" makes the list parallel.

22. **2.** This is a classic run-on sentence. A good change is as follows: "Okay, I thought, fair enough. They're new and getting their act together. No big deal." (Note that the third sentence does not appear to have a verb, but the implied subject and verb are "it is," as in "It is no big deal.")

23. **1.** The correct answer is to add a comma after "later." Most of the time, you want to set off an introductory clause with a comma; however, be aware that when the introductory clause is very short, the convention isn't always clear: some people use the comma and others don't. However, on this test, you're always better off putting a comma after any introductory clause.

24. **3.** Change "apologised" to "apologized," which is the correct spelling. The other answers do nothing to improve the sentence.

25. **1.** Add a comma after the introductory clause. See the answer to Question 23 for further explanation.

26. **3.** Whenever a sentence has two clauses, each with a subject and a verb, a comma has to separate them. In this sentence, "Two weeks later" is an introductory clause that requires a comma after "later." "I went back" is a clause that has both a subject ("I") and a verb ("went"). "And the same thing happened again" is another clause that has a subject ("thing") and verb ("happened").

27. **5.** This is a gift. The sentence is correct.

A point of interest with this sentence is that it uses one of the dreaded two/to/too words. Each of these words is a homonym: words that sound the same but have different spellings and meanings. Here, it's correct, but be sure you put these three words on your list of homonyms to study.

28. **4.** "My opinion" is a singular subject that needs a singular verb. "Were" is a plural verb and must be changed to the singular form "was." Don't let that prepositions phrase "of their services" throw you off. Just act as if that part of the sentence weren't there.

If you have trouble with singular and plural verbs and subject-verb agreement, try changing the subject into a pronoun. This sentence would become "It were" which sounds wrong. Changing it to "It was" sounds right. Trust your ears.

One exception to this "sounds right" rule is the subjunctive. Whenever something is contrary to fact, you use "were" with singular subjects. For example, "If I were taller" is correct. Look for terms like "If," "I wish," and "If only": These are usually followed by the subjunctive form of the verb.

29. **4.** This is a good example of getting the right answer by elimination. Option 1 introduces the wrong verb tense. Option 2 introduces a punctuation error, because the comma is needed. Answer 3 introduces another punctuation error: This comma is also needed. When you plug in answer 4, the sentence reads more smoothly, so you know you have a winner.

30. **1.** Answer (1) is the best option of those presented that doesn't change the meaning. The others, except option 4, are all errors in verb form; option 4 changes the sentence to present tense, which then changes the meaning.

31. **4.** The words, "this knowledge" are out of place, but they are necessary because they add to the meaning of the sentence. The sentence can be improved by moving "This knowledge" to the front of the sentence and changing "Combined" to "combined". Another way to change the sentence is to simply remove the comma after "knowledge" (because subjects and verbs are never separated by a comma), but that's not given as an option.

32. **2.** This sentence contains a spelling mistake. Change "merchandize" to "merchandise."

33. **1.** This sentence is badly in need of a comma transfusion. It should read "This concept, combined with speedy service, helped the industry grow every year." These two little commas help the sentence by separating the phrase "combined with speedy service."

34. **1.** This sentence is fairly long and rambly, but none of the options offers a way to split it into two. However, the sentence does have an error: Schools have "principals," people and businesses (you hope!) have "principles." These two word are homonyms, meaning that they sound alike but have different meanings and spellings.

35. **4.** The phrase should be changed to "located." The other answers introduce new errors.

36. **1.** From the context of the passage, Concord is a town or city and deserves a capital letter at the beginning of the word.

37. **2.** The sentence is supposed to say that he had established the validity of the concept before (1991) and then (later) he wanted to establish a corporate store. Rewriting the sentence in this way says this correctly. "Having established the validity of the concept in Wellesley, in 1991, he then opened the corporate store." The other answers don't keep this meaning.

Option 4 may look good, but it changes the meaning of the sentence. He didn't open the corporate store in 1991; he established the validity of the concept in 1991.

38. **5.** Okay, it's a really long sentence, but technically, nothing is wrong with it. If you had an option of splitting it into two sentences, you'd want to take it. Because you're not given that option and all other options are incorrect, leave it as is.

39. **2.** Here, "start up" is acting as an adjective for "costs." Most multi-word adjectives are hyphenated.

If you chose answer 3, you must have thought that the second half of the sentence had a second subject in it. If so, reread that part of the sentence to try to find the subject. It's not there. This is a sentence with one subject ("cost") and two verbs ("will require" and "will be regained"). A sentence like this, with only one subject and two verbs, doesn't require a comma. If it had a second subject before the second verb, it would need a comma.

40. **3.** Changing the phrase to "in more depth" improves the sentence structure. The other answers don't really make much sense when plugged into the sentence.

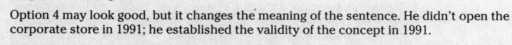

41. **1.** Moving "on the customer" to the end of the sentence improves the sentence organization by placing the direct object ("the impact") closer to the second indirect object ("the customer"). (What's the first indirect object? "This new concept.")

If you chose answer 5, you essentially said that the customer would have a wide selection of accessories added to him or her.

42. **1.** "Among" is used when comparing three or more entities; between is used to compare only two things. Here, you have two types of customers, so "between" is correct.

43. **3.** "Where you rarely see the light of day" is an improved word order because you want an adverb (in this case, "rarely") to be as close as possible to the verb it's modifying (here, "see").

44. **1.** The needs belong to the customers, so you make it possessive by making it "customers."

45. **2.** "Providing somebody for something," does not make sense. It is most unusual to provide people for things; instead, you provide things for people.

46. **4.** Examine "that always end up." What is it referring to? "Important link," right? Yes, but "link" is singular," so you don't say, "link . . . end." Instead, you say "link . . . ends."

47. **1.** "Poorly treated employees treat the customer just as poorly" is the title of an article and must be in quotation marks. Names of newspapers are in italics, while the stories that are run in them are placed in quotes.

This idea of the entire thing (newspaper) being in italics, while the inner workings (the articles) are in quotes extends to other situations. A book name is in italics, while the name of each chapter is in quotes. A TV series is in italics, while the name of each episode is in quotes.

48. **3.** This sentence has two related problems. First, the past tense of "deal" is "dealt," not "dealed." Second, by the context, you know that this action began in the past and continues in the present. That timeline is indicated by "have." To use "had" means that the action began in the past and also stopped in the past — it is not continuing today.

49. **2.** Putting "we are convinced" in the middle of the sentence interrupts the main point of the sentence — to point out a specific cause and effect relationship.

50. **5.** A final gift for you. No correction is needed and all the other options make the sentence worse.

# Sample Essays (for Part II)

The topic for the practice test in Chapter 18 is as follows:

> Cellphones have certainly made a difference in our lives. You may own and use one or have put up with other people who use them while driving or at the movies. Cellphones have made our lives better, more difficult, or both. Write an essay explaining the positive or negative effects — or both — of this innovation in communication. Use examples to support your point of view and be as specific as possible.

Although every essay will be unique, we provide a sample here to give you an idea of what the test graders will expect. Compare the structure of this essay to yours.

> My children and I recently signed up for family-rate calling plan — complete with four separate phones and phone numbers — so that we could communicate more easily. Although I put off the purchase for several years, thinking that having a cellphone would make me so accessible to others that I would never get any time to myself, the truth is, the phones have made all of our lives easier.

My three children attend three different schools. The youngest, Doug, is in 4th grade and takes a free acting class year-round at the local playhouse. His lessons run from 4:00 to 5:00 three days per week, but he can sometimes catch rides home with other children in the class. Because I work until 5:30, my oldest daughter, Sydney, who is a junior in high school, waits for him to call to tell her whether he needs a ride. Before we had cellphones, Doug always had to find a working pay phone, and Sydney had to wait by the phone at home.

The middle child, Maggie, is in 8th grade and plays three sports: soccer, basketball, and track. I can usually pick her up from practice on my way home from school, but her practices end at different times every day. While she, too, used to have to hunt down a pay phone and call me at work, now she just calls and lets me know where she'll be waiting. I can run errands while I wait for her call instead of waiting at work or by the curb at her school.

The best part of the phones, though, is that whenever people want to reach any of the four of us, they call the number for the individual, not the entire family. I no longer answer the phone for all of Doug's, Maggie's, and Sydney's friends, and people trying to reach me no longer get a busy signal.

For us, cellphones are the ultimate convenience. In fact, we like our cellphones so much that we no longer have regular phone service in our home.

# Tips and Ideas for Mastering Part II

Keep the following tips and ground rules in mind about writing an essay for Part II of the Language Arts, Writing test:

- You must write an essay in 45 minutes of about 250 words based on a single topic.

- The topic is always a brief one about an issue or situation that's familiar to you.

- The essay tests your ability to write about an issue that has positive or negative implications but about which you have some general knowledge.

- The essay doesn't test how much you know; instead, it tests your ability to express yourself in writing.

- An essay usually consists of a number of paragraphs, each of which contain a topic sentence stating a main idea or thought. Be sure each paragraph relates to the overall topic of the essay.

- A topic sentence is usually (but not always) placed at the beginning of the paragraph and focuses on the main point you want the readers to understand.

- Effective paragraphs use a variety of sentence types: statements, questions, commands, exclamations, even quotations.

- Some sentences may be short, others long to catch the readers' attention. Vary your sentence structure and choice of words to spark the reader's interest.

- Paragraphs create interest in several ways: by developing details, by using illustrations and examples, by presenting events in a time or space sequence, by providing definitions, by classifying persons or objects, by comparing and contrasting, or by demonstrating reasons and proof. Organize your paragraphs and sentences in a sequence that expresses your ideas.

- Specific examples and details support your point of view, so use them liberally.

- The readers are checking whether you can express your ideas clearly and logically.

# Chapter 20

# The Social Studies Test

· · · · · · · · · · · · · · · · · · · · · · · · · · · · · · · · · · · · · · · · · ·

### Directions

The Social Studies Test consists of multiple-choice questions that measure general social studies concepts. The questions are based on short readings that often include a map, graph, chart, political cartoon, or figure. Study the information given and then answer the question(s) following it. Refer to the information as often as necessary in answering the questions.

You have 70 minutes to answer the 50 questions in this test. Work carefully, but do not spend too much time on any one question. Be sure you answer every question.

Do not mark in this test booklet. Record your answers on the separate answer sheet provided. Be sure that all requested information is properly recorded on the answer sheet.

To record your answers, fill in the numbered circle on the answer sheet that corresponds to the answer you select for each question in the test booklet.

---

**EXAMPLE:**

Early colonists of North America looked for settlement sites with adequate water supplies and access by ship. For this reason, many early towns were built near

(1)   mountains

(2)   prairies

(3)   rivers

(4)   glaciers

(5)   plateaus

(On Answer Sheet)

① ② ● ④ ⑤

The correct answer is "rivers"; therefore, answer space 3 would be marked on the answer sheet.

---

Do not rest the point of your pencil on the answer sheet while you are considering your answer. Make no stray or unnecessary marks. If you change an answer, erase your first mark completely. Mark only one answer space for each question; multiple answers will be scored as incorrect. Do not fold or crease your answer sheet. All test materials must be returned to the test administrator.

**DO NOT BEGIN TAKING THIS TEST UNTIL TOLD TO DO SO**

## SOCIAL STUDIES TEST

1 ① ② ③ ④ ⑤    26 ① ② ③ ④ ⑤

2 ① ② ③ ④ ⑤    27 ① ② ③ ④ ⑤

3 ① ② ③ ④ ⑤    28 ① ② ③ ④ ⑤

4 ① ② ③ ④ ⑤    29 ① ② ③ ④ ⑤

5 ① ② ③ ④ ⑤    30 ① ② ③ ④ ⑤

6 ① ② ③ ④ ⑤    31 ① ② ③ ④ ⑤

7 ① ② ③ ④ ⑤    32 ① ② ③ ④ ⑤

8 ① ② ③ ④ ⑤    33 ① ② ③ ④ ⑤

9 ① ② ③ ④ ⑤    34 ① ② ③ ④ ⑤

10 ① ② ③ ④ ⑤    35 ① ② ③ ④ ⑤

11 ① ② ③ ④ ⑤    36 ① ② ③ ④ ⑤

12 ① ② ③ ④ ⑤    37 ① ② ③ ④ ⑤

13 ① ② ③ ④ ⑤    38 ① ② ③ ④ ⑤

14 ① ② ③ ④ ⑤    39 ① ② ③ ④ ⑤

15 ① ② ③ ④ ⑤    40 ① ② ③ ④ ⑤

16 ① ② ③ ④ ⑤    41 ① ② ③ ④ ⑤

17 ① ② ③ ④ ⑤    42 ① ② ③ ④ ⑤

18 ① ② ③ ④ ⑤    43 ① ② ③ ④ ⑤

19 ① ② ③ ④ ⑤    44 ① ② ③ ④ ⑤

20 ① ② ③ ④ ⑤    45 ① ② ③ ④ ⑤

21 ① ② ③ ④ ⑤    46 ① ② ③ ④ ⑤

22 ① ② ③ ④ ⑤    47 ① ② ③ ④ ⑤

23 ① ② ③ ④ ⑤    48 ① ② ③ ④ ⑤

24 ① ② ③ ④ ⑤    49 ① ② ③ ④ ⑤

25 ① ② ③ ④ ⑤    50 ① ② ③ ④ ⑤

**Directions:** Choose the one best answer to each question.

Questions 1 through 5 refer to the following passage.

### Industry and Trade in the Thirteen Colonies

The colonies were part of an Atlantic trading network that linked them with England, Africa, and the West Indies. The pattern of commerce, not too accurately called the Triangular Trade, involved the exchange of products from colonial farms, plantations, fisheries, and forests with England for manufactured goods and the West Indies for slaves, molasses, and sugar. In New England, molasses and sugar were distilled into rum, which was used to buy African slaves. Southern Europe was also a valuable market for colonial foodstuffs.

Colonial industry was closely associated with trade. A significant percentage of Atlantic shipping was on vessels built in the colonies, and shipbuilding stimulated other crafts, such as the sewing of sails, milling of lumber, and manufacturing of naval stores. Mercantile theory encouraged the colonies to provide raw materials for England's industrializing economy; pig iron and coal became important exports. Concurrently, restrictions were placed on finished goods. For example, Parliament, concerned about possible competition from colonial hatters, prohibited the export of hats from one colony to another and limited the number of apprentices in each hatmaker's shop.

*P. Soifer and A. Hoffman,* CliffsQuickReivew U. S. History I *(Wiley Publishing, Inc.)*

1. What did England, Africa, and the West Indies have in common?
   (1) they all had fisheries
   (2) they all bought slaves
   (3) they all distilled rum
   (4) they all had forests
   (5) they all exchanged products

2. What was rum used for?
   (1) colonial farms
   (2) milling of lumber
   (3) purchase of slaves
   (4) molasses and sugar
   (5) manufactured goods

3. Why were the colonies important to Atlantic trade?
   (1) they built the ships
   (2) they sewed sails
   (3) they had naval stores
   (4) they milled lumber
   (5) they stimulated other crafts

4. How did the colonies support British industry?
   (1) sewing
   (2) finished goods
   (3) mercantile theory
   (4) raw materials
   (5) restrictions

5. What product was threatened by colonial competition?
   (1) coal
   (2) pig iron
   (3) hats
   (4) lumber
   (5) cotton

*Go on to next page*

Questions 6 through 11 refer to the following passage.

## Charges Against the King

He has forbidden his governors to pass laws of immediate and pressing importance, unless suspended in their operation till his assent should be obtained; and when so suspended, he has utterly neglected to attend to them.

He has refused to pass other laws for the accommodation of large districts of people, unless those people would relinquish the right of representation in the legislature — a right inestimable to them, and formidable to tyrants only.

He has called together legislative bodies at places unusual, uncomfortable, and distant from the depository of their public records, for the sole purpose of fatiguing them into compliance with his measures.

He has dissolved representative houses repeatedly, for opposing, with manly firmness, his invasions on the rights of the people.

He has refused, for a long time after such dissolutions, to cause others to be elected; whereby the legislative powers, incapable of annihilation, have returned to the people at large, for their exercise, the state remaining in the meantime exposed to all the dangers of invasion from without, and convulsions within.

He has endeavored to prevent the population of these states; for that purpose obstructing the laws for naturalization of foreigners; refusing to pass others to encourage their migration hither, and raising the conditions of new appropriations of lands.

He has obstructed the administration of justice, by refusing his assent to laws for establishing judiciary powers.

He has made judges dependent on his will alone, for the tenure of their offices, and the amount and payment of their salaries.

He has erected a multitude of new offices, and sent hither swarms of officers, to harass our people, and eat out their substance.

He has kept among us, in times of peace, standing armies, without the consent of our legislature.

He has affected to render the military independent of, and superior to, the civil power.

*from The Declaration of Independence*

*Go on to next page*

6.  What is one way that the king neglected the colonies?

    (1) lack of money

    (2) failure to pass laws

    (3) remove their right of condemnation

    (4) given power to his governors

    (5) does not visit the Colonies

7.  How did the king treat the legislative bodies?

    (1) he never called them together

    (2) he made them comfortable

    (3) he made sure they were well rested

    (4) he made them comply with his wishes

    (5) he deposited their records

8.  How did the king threaten the rights of the people?

    (1) dissolved representative houses

    (2) abdicated the throne

    (3) annihilated them

    (4) returned them to the people

    (5) he was ambitious

9.  How did the king feel about adding to the population of the Colonies?

    (1) gave away free land to people willing to settle

    (2) encouraged people to settle

    (3) settled there himself

    (4) sent his son over to settle

    (5) discouraged people from settling

10. How did the king obstruct the judicial system?

    (1) made it independent of his authority

    (2) erected new offices

    (3) controlled its operation

    (4) harassed the people

    (5) paid for houses

11. What was one of the ways freedom of the people was threatened?

    (1) a dependent military

    (2) an independent military

    (3) civil authority

    (4) a tea party

    (5) friendly officers

*Go on to next page* ⟶

Questions 12 through 17 refer to the following passage.

### The War of 1812

For the United States, the most obvious British target was Canada. Its population was small, many Canadians were actually Americans by birth, and a quick victory there would stop British plans to ruin American trade. The military facts painted a different picture, however. Thousands of Native Americans in the northwestern territories sided with the British when the war began, bolstering their strength, while the small U. S. army was composed of poorly trained state militiamen led by elderly and incompetent generals.

In July 1812, an American army led by General William Hull moved from Detroit into Canada. Almost immediately the Shawnee cut his supply lines, forcing him back to Detroit. Although Hull commanded two thousand men, he surrendered to a considerably smaller British and Native American force. Other embarrassments followed as the United States suffered defeat at Queenston Heights in western New York and the militia under General Henry Dearborn refused to march to Montreal from northeastern New York.

The United States fared better on Lake Erie in 1813. The Royal Navy could not reach the lake from the St. Lawrence River, so both the British and Americans raced to build ships on opposite sides of the lake. On September 10, 1813, the small American fleet under Oliver Hazard Perry defeated the British in the Battle of Lake Erie. "We have met the enemy, and they are ours," he reported, a victory statement that became legendary.

Less than three weeks later, on October 5, William Henry Harrison (a general by then) defeated a combined British and Native American force at the Battle of the Thames. Tecumseh was killed in this battle, ending Native Americans' hopes for a coalition that could stand against the advance of U. S. settlement. Despite these victories, U. S. efforts to capture Canada ended in a stalemate.

*P. Soifer and A. Hoffman,* CliffsQuickReview U. S. History I *(Wiley Publishing, Inc.)*

12. Why was Canada a target for the United States?

    (1) citizens were American by birth

    (2) it had a large population

    (3) it was a British possession

    (4) they had visited many times

    (5) it would protect American trade

13. Whom did Native Americans support in the conflict?

    (1) the British

    (2) the Canadians

    (3) the Americans

    (4) the U. S. army

    (5) the French

14. Why did General Hull surrender?

    (1) forced to Detroit

    (2) two thousand men

    (3) the Thames

    (4) British force

    (5) supply lines cut

15. What did Queenston Heights represent for the U. S.?

    (1) a victory

    (2) an embarrassment

    (3) a proposal

    (4) a refusal to march

    (5) a lot of suffering

*Go on to next page*

16. What kept the Royal Navy fleet from Lake Erie?

    (1) St. Lawrence River

    (2) Detroit River

    (3) Lake Ontario

    (4) Lake St. Clair

    (5) not enough information given

17. What was the result of the War of 1812?

    (1) Americans won

    (2) British won

    (3) ended in a stalemate

    (4) Native Americans won

    (5) Tecumseh was killed

*Go on to next page*

Questions 18 through 23 refer to the following passage.

### Gettysburg Address

"Four score and seven years ago our fathers brought forth upon this continent a new nation, conceived in liberty and dedicated to the proposition that all men are created equal. Now we are engaged in a great civil war, testing whether that nation or any nation so conceived and so dedicated can long endure. We are met on a great battlefield of that war. We have come to dedicate a portion of that field as a final resting place for those who here gave their lives that that nation might live. It is altogether fitting and proper that we should do this. But, in a larger sense, we cannot dedicate, we cannot consecrate, we cannot hallow this ground. The brave men, living and dead, who struggled here have consecrated it far above our poor power to add or detract. The world will little note nor long remember what we say here, but it can never forget what they did here . . . ."

*Lincoln's Gettysburg Address, November 19, 1863.*

18. What issues were of primary importance in a great civil war?

    (1) happiness and friendship
    (2) safety and security
    (3) liberty and equality
    (4) wealth and greed
    (5) peace and prosperity

19. Where was President Lincoln's speech delivered?

    (1) on a train
    (2) at the White House
    (3) in a playground
    (4) on a battlefield
    (5) on the radio

20. What does "little note nor long remember" mean?

    (1) the audience is not taking notes
    (2) the TV crews are getting in the way
    (3) Lincoln has a bad memory
    (4) the soldiers are not there to hear the speech
    (5) people around the world will not remember the speech

21. What will a portion of the battlefield be used for?

    (1) burial ground
    (2) athletic field
    (3) cow pasture
    (4) shopping area
    (5) farming

22. Who has "hallow[ed] this ground"?

    (1) President Lincoln
    (2) the U. S. government
    (3) the Confederate government
    (4) the Union government
    (5) those who fought there

23. What does "four score and seven" probably refer to?

    (1) soldiers
    (2) consecration
    (3) time
    (4) the war
    (5) speeches

*Go on to next page* ⟶

Questions 24 through 29 refer to the following passage.

**Causes of World War I**

On June 28, 1914, a Serbian nationalist assassinated the Archduke Franz Ferdinand, the heir to the throne of Austria-Hungary. Austria demanded indemnities from Serbia for the assassination. The Serbian government denied any involvement with the murder and, when Austria issued an ultimatum, turned to its ally, Russia, for help. When Russia began to mobilize its army, Europe's alliance system, ironically intended to maintain the balance of power on the continent, drew one country after another into war. Austria's ally, Germany, declared war on Russia on August 1 and on France (which was allied with Russia) two days later. Great Britain entered the war on August 4, following Germany's invasion of neutral Belgium. By the end of August 1914, most of Europe had chosen sides: the Central Powers — Germany, Austria-Hungary, Bulgaria, and the Ottoman Empire (Turkey) — were up against the Allied Powers — principally Great Britain, France, Russia, and Serbia. Japan joined the Allied cause in August 1914, in hopes of seizing German possessions in the Pacific and expanding Japanese influence in China. This action threatened the Open Door Policy and led to increased tensions with the United States. Originally an ally of Germany and Austria-Hungary, Italy entered the war in 1915 on the side of Britain and France because they had agreed to Italian territorial demands in a secret treaty (the Treaty of London).

*P. Soifer and A. Hoffman,* CliffsQuickReview U. S. History II *(Wiley Publishing, Inc.)*

24. Where did the assassin of Archduke Ferdinand originate?

    (1) Great Britain

    (2) France

    (3) Russia

    (4) Serbia

    (5) Germany

25. How did Austria initially react to the assassination?

    (1) denied any involvement

    (2) demanded indemnities

    (3) turned to its ally

    (4) declared war

    (5) mobilized its army

26. Which countries were not allies?

    (1) Serbia and Russia

    (2) Austria and Hungary

    (3) Germany and France

    (4) France and Great Britain

    (5) Germany and Austria

27. What caused Great Britain to enter the war?

    (1) Germany invaded Belgium

    (2) Russia attacked Serbia

    (3) France invaded Russia

    (4) Austria invaded Hungary

    (5) Germany attacked Russia

28. Which country was not an Allied Power?

    (1) Great Britain

    (2) France

    (3) Germany

    (4) Russia

    (5) Serbia

29. Why did Italy join the Allies?

    (1) Open Door Policy

    (2) increased tensions

    (3) business demands

    (4) expanding Japanese influence

    (5) Treaty of London

*Go on to next page*

Questions 30 through 33 refer to the following political cartoon.

30. How would you describe the wishes of the young student?

    (1) excessive

    (2) somewhat realistic

    (3) minimal

    (4) rather dreamlike

    (5) technical

31. Why is President Bush portrayed as Santa?

    (1) the President gives children gifts

    (2) the President has a long beard

    (3) some politicians like to dress up

    (4) the President provides computers to children

    (5) some education funds come from federal government

32. What is the main message the cartoonist wishes to convey?

    (1) tests don't improve learning

    (2) poor children are at risk

    (3) schools are falling apart

    (4) playgrounds are fun

    (5) harder textbooks make better students

33. How can education be improved for students?

    (1) fewer teachers

    (2) fewer demands on school administrators

    (3) more sports

    (4) fewer learning materials

    (5) less testing

*Go on to next page*

Questions 34 through 37 refer to the following passage.

**Farm Production and Declining Prices**

Bringing new lands under cultivation and the widespread use of machinery led to a tremendous increase in farm production. The wheat crop, which became an export staple, grew from 170 million bushels at the end of the Civil War to more than 700 million bushels by the close of the century. Overproduction in the United States and expanded crop production in Argentina, Australia, Canada, and Russia drove agricultural prices down during the same period. Unfortunately, American farmers did not seem to understand how the market operated. When prices fell, the inclination was to plant more, which added to the worldwide surplus and pushed prices still lower.

The promise of wealth through agriculture failed to materialize for most settlers in the West. They had borrowed heavily to buy their land and equipment and, as prices continued to fall, were unable to pay their debts. Foreclosures and the number of tenant farmers steadily increased in the late nineteenth century, particularly on the Great Plains. Farmers typically blamed their plight on others: the railroads for charging exorbitant shipping rates; the federal government for keeping the supply of money tight by adhering to the gold standard; and middlemen, such as grain elevator operators, for not paying the full value for their crops. Although organizations such as the Patrons of Husbandry, or the Grange, (which was founded in 1867 and grew quickly to more than a million members) brought redress of some grievances, discontent among the farmers continued to grow at the end of the nineteenth century.

*P. Soifer and A. Hoffman,* CliffsQuickReview U. S. History I *(Wiley Publishing, Inc.)*

34. What have new land and the use of machinery done to farm production?

    (1) curtailed

    (2) expanded

    (3) encouraged

    (4) discouraged

    (5) destroyed

35. What impact did these changes have on the market?

    (1) drove prices up

    (2) caused underproduction

    (3) led to less protection

    (4) drove prices down

    (5) created a deficit

36. How did American farmers initially respond to falling prices?

    (1) planted more grain

    (2) sold their land

    (3) had larger families

    (4) went deeper in debt

    (5) lost their farms

37. What was the purpose of the Grange?

    (1) invent new machinery

    (2) plant more crops

    (3) buy and sell farm land

    (4) charge exorbitant shipping rates

    (5) help farmers settle their disputes with others

*Go on to next page*

Questions 38 through 42 refer to the following timeline.

### Timeline of Major Events in U.S. History

1900: Gold standard for currency adopted by United States

1914: World War I begins

1918: World War I ends

1929: Stock market crashes

1933: Gold exports banned; daily price established; U.S. citizens ordered to turn in all gold

1934: Price of gold fixed at $35 per troy ounce

1939: World War II begins

1945: World War II ends

1950: Korean Conflict begins

1953: Korean Conflict ends

1965: Vietnam War begins

1973: Vietnam War ends; gold prices allowed to float; U.S. currency removed from gold standard

1974: U.S. citizens allowed to own gold again

1979: Soviet Union invades Afghanistan

1979: U.S. hostages seized in Iran

1980: Historic high prices for gold

1987: Stock market crashes

1990: Gulf War begins

1991: Gulf War ends

*Go on to next page*

38. On what did the U. S. base the value of its currency in 1900?

    (1) stock market

    (2) value of gold

    (3) value of silver

    (4) trade surplus

    (5) interest rates

39. What caused the Great Depression in 1929?

    (1) price of gold

    (2) weak currency

    (3) stock market crash

    (4) World War I

    (5) President Roosevelt

40. What does "U.S. citizens ordered to turn in all gold" mean?

    (1) citizens turned into gold

    (2) citizens got to keep their gold

    (3) citizens had to tell the government about their gold

    (4) citizens could buy gold from each other, for profit

    (5) citizens had to take all their gold to government offices

41. When was U. S. currency removed from the gold standard?

    (1) 1934

    (2) 1945

    (3) 1969

    (4) 1973

    (5) 1974

42. Based on what you see in the timeline, what likely caused the price of gold to reach a historic high?

    (1) citizens allowed to hold bullion

    (2) sale of gold stocks

    (3) Soviet Union invaded Afghanistan

    (4) stock market crashed

    (5) Gulf War began

*Go on to next page*

Questions 43 through 46 refer to the following newscast.

### World Environmental News

Good evening and welcome to world environmental news.

Our stories this evening: cyclones in Korea, flooding in Europe and India, volcanic eruptions in New Guinea, draught in Australia, tornadoes in the United States, hailstorms in Italy, earthquakes in Iran, and locusts in Denmark.

Now, let's look at our top stories.

**Drought in Australia:** The wheat fields west of Canberra, New South Wales, are in great danger today because of the ongoing drought. In the next week, farmers may have to write off this year's crop, and this will likely lead to financial ruin for many of them. To add to the misery, hundreds of thousands of sheep had to be sold because there was not enough water for them to drink.

**Locusts in Denmark:** The unseasonably warm weather in Denmark is proving to be inviting to the lowly locust. Normally found along the Mediterranean coast, the locust has been found far from its normal habitat. These discoveries in southwest Denmark are causing concern because locusts have not been seen in Denmark for over 50 years.

**Hurricane near Mexico:** Hurricane Herman is losing force off the Pacific coast of Mexico. The country is giving a sigh of relief as the hurricane winds down.

**For wine drinkers:** And a last note for you wine drinkers. The recent violent hailstorms in Italy are expected to cause a poor grape harvest. This means lower wine production and, consequently, higher prices.

There's more as nature lashes out. Tune in again for world environmental news.

43. In which ocean is the tropical storm called hurricane Herman located?

    (1) Pacific

    (2) Arctic

    (3) Atlantic

    (4) Indian

    (5) Antarctic

44. According to the newscast, where is the extreme draught causing major loss of wheat crops?

    (1) India

    (2) China

    (3) Saudi Arabia

    (4) Death Valley

    (5) Australia

45. Why have locusts been found in Denmark?

    (1) unseasonably warm weather

    (2) prevailing winds

    (3) foreign ships

    (4) wild birds

    (5) Mediterranean climate

46. What will be the impact of hailstorms in Italy?

    (1) lower olive oil prices

    (2) devastating floods

    (3) damaged cars

    (4) higher wine prices

    (5) more insurance coverage

*Go on to next page* →

Questions 47 through 50 refer to the following political cartoon.

47. What happens if oil prices rise?
    (1) SUV sales decrease
    (2) people stop traveling
    (3) oil companies make less profit
    (4) gas stations close
    (5) gasoline prices rise

48. How does a rise in oil prices affect the cost of living?
    (1) has no impact
    (2) controls oil prices
    (3) doesn't really matter
    (4) rich nations pay more
    (5) protects the oil companies

49. What adjective best describes the characters in the cartoon?
    (1) smug
    (2) arrogant
    (3) wasteful
    (4) thoughtful
    (5) angry

50. What phrase does not describe the SUV or its occupants?
    (1) pollution-creator
    (2) road-warrior
    (3) energy-saver
    (4) gas-guzzler
    (5) monster-truck

**END OF EXAMINATION**

# Chapter 21

# Answers and Explanations for the Social Studies Test

• • • • • • • • • • • • • • • • • • • • • • • • • • • • • • • • • • • • • • • • • • • • • • •

## Answer Key

After taking the Social Studies Test in Chapter 20, use this section to check your answers.

| | | |
|---|---|---|
| 1. 5 | 18. 3 | 35. 4 |
| 2. 3 | 19. 4 | 36. 1 |
| 3. 1 | 20. 5 | 37. 5 |
| 4. 4 | 21. 1 | 38. 2 |
| 5. 3 | 22. 5 | 39. 3 |
| 6. 2 | 23. 3 | 40. 5 |
| 7. 4 | 24. 4 | 41. 4 |
| 8. 1 | 25. 2 | 42. 3 |
| 9. 5 | 26. 3 | 43. 1 |
| 10. 3 | 27. 1 | 44. 5 |
| 11. 2 | 28. 3 | 45. 1 |
| 12. 3 | 29. 5 | 46. 4 |
| 13. 1 | 30. 2 | 47. 5 |
| 14. 5 | 31. 5 | 48. 2 |
| 15. 3 | 32. 1 | 49. 3 |
| 16. 5 | 33. 5 | 50. 3 |
| 17. 3 | 34. 2 | |

# Analysis of the Answers

If you aren't sure why an answer was incorrect, use this section to get quick explanations of the answers.

1. **5.** England, Africa, and the West Indies all traded products: The West Indies traded molasses, sugar, and slaves with England for food and wood. England (via the New England colonies) then made the molasses and sugar into rum and traded it with Africa for more slaves.

2. **3.** Rum was used to purchase slaves for use in the colonies. Other choices — colonial farms, milling of lumber, molasses and sugar, and manufactured goods — were all patterns of commerce but were not uses of rum.

3. **1.** Ships were built in the colonies to increase Atlantic trade. Sewing sails, naval stores, milled lumber, and other crafts were products of the colonies that shipbuilding stimulated, but ships were primary, while the others were secondary.

4. **4.** The colonies provided raw materials for British manufacturing industries. According to the passage, "Mercantile theory encouraged the colonies to provide raw materials for England's industrializing economy . . . ."

5. **3.** The export of hats — a finished good — from the colonies was prohibited because it threatened British manufacturing. Coal, pig iron, lumber, and cotton are raw materials, which were not threats to English manufacturing.

6. **2.** According to the first paragraph of the passage, the king has neglected the Colonies in a number of ways. Of those listed here, only failing to pass laws (ones that would alleviate grievances) is correct.

7. **4.** According to the third paragraph of the passage, the legislative bodies were forced to comply to the king's rule.

8. **1.** According to the fourth paragraph of the passage, when the king dissolved the representative houses, he threatened the rights of the people.

9. **5.** The sixth paragraph of the passage says that "He has endeavored to prevent the population of these states." That means he discourages newcomers from settling.

10. **3.** The king obstructed the judicial system by controlling its operation. In the seventh paragraph, the passage states that the king did not give his okay to laws that would have created a local judicial system.

11. **2.** The king made sure that the military was independent from the Colonists (last paragraph). This means that the Colonists didn't have any authority over hiring or firing soldiers, how large the military was, or who the officers were. Only the king made those kinds of decisions.

12. **3.** Canada was a target for the U.S. because it was a British possession (see the first sentence of the passage).

13. **1.** The first paragraph states that Native Americans were loyal to the British in the war.

14. **5.** Hull surrendered because his supply lines were cut. The second paragraph of the passage discusses this.

15. **3.** The battle of Queenston Heights was a defeat for the U.S. — not a victory but an embarrassment. Refusal to march and suffering are also incorrect answers. A battle is not likely ever to be considered a "proposal."

16. **5.** Although you may know that the Royal Navy was stopped from sailing from the St. Lawrence River into Lake Erie by the Niagara Falls, the passage does not say this. "Not enough information given" is the best answer here.

17. **3.** The last sentence of the passage states that the War of 1812 ended in a stalemate, with neither side claiming victory.

18. **3.** As stated in the first two sentences of the passage, the issues of prime importance in the Civil War were liberty and equality. Happiness and friendship, safety and security, wealth and greed, and peace and prosperity are not better answers.

19. **4.** You know from the passage that President Lincoln is delivering his speech on a battlefield at Gettysburg. That rules out every other answer except "on the radio" (he could have recorded his speech, and it could have been broadcast by radio at the battlefield). However, because this speech was given in 1863, radios hadn't yet been invented.

20. **5.** Lincoln was saying that the world would remember the soldiers who died but would not remember his speech. (He was wrong, given that the Gettysburg address is one of the most famous speeches in American history.)

21. **1.** Some of the battlefield was to become a burial ground for the fallen. Athletic field, cow pasture, shopping area, and farming are not relevant answers.

22. **5.** The ground was hallowed by those who fought there. Lincoln believes that the people involved in the dedication of the battlefield cannot make the place holy or important; instead, only the people who fought on the battlefield can do that.

23. **3.** The word "years" follows "four score and seven," so you can assume that term relates to time. (By the way, a *score* is 20 years, so four score and seven is 87 years.)

24. **4.** Archduke Ferdinand was assassinated by a Serbian nationalist.

25. **2.** Austria demanded indemnities in response to the assassination. This is taken directly from the passage.

26. **3.** Germany and France were not allies in the war. Although the list of allies is rather confusing, the paragraph does sum up who was on which side.

27. **1.** You know that Great Britain entered the War when Germany invaded Belgium from the sentence that states, "Great Britain entered the war on August 4, following Germany's invasion of neutral Belgium."

28. **3.** Germany was not an Allied power. About halfway through the passage is a list of the Central powers (on one side of the war) and the Allied powers (on the other side).

29. **5.** Italy joined the Allies because of the Treaty of London. Open Door Policy, increased tensions, territorial demands, and Japanese influence may have played a part, but according to the passage, they are not the best answers.

30. **2.** The wishes of the student were somewhat realistic. They were not excessive or too minimal, nor were they dreamlike. "Technical" does not make sense in this context.

31. **5.** The U.S. federal government provides some funding for education, and President Bush is the leader of the United States.

32. **1.** The cartoonist believes that tests do not improve learning.

33. **5.** While the other answers (especially the one about sports) may be your opinion, the cartoon is saying that fewer tests will improve education.

34. **2.** New land and use of machinery have expanded farm production. The first sentence tells you this.

35. **4.** Improved production drove prices down. Prices up, underproduction, and deficit are the opposite of what the passage said. "Led to less protection" is nonsense — it doesn't have anything to do with the passage.

36. **1.** Farmers responded to falling prices by planting more grain. Although this may go against your instinct, which may be to say that they sold their land, went deeper into debt, or lost their farms, the passage clearly states that they planted more grain. The word "initially" in the question is important.

37. **5.** The term "redress of some grievances" is used to describe the Grange. "Redress" means "to set right," and "grievances" means "complaints" or "disputes."

38. **2.** The timeline shows that, in 1900, the gold standard was adopted for U.S. currency.

39. **3.** The Great Depression was caused by the crash of the stock market. The other answers — gold prices, weak currency, World War I, and President Roosevelt — may or may not have had some influence on the crash, but they were not the cause.

40. **5.** U.S. citizens had to take all their gold to U.S. offices and not keep any in their own homes. The timeline and graph don't tell you why this happened, just that it did. "Turn in" is the key phrase.

41. **4.** The U.S. currency was removed from the gold standard in 1973, not the other dates listed.

42. **3.** Gold reached a historic high when the Soviets invaded Afghanistan. You have to read both the timeline and graph together to answer this question.

43. **1.** According to the newscast, hurricane Herman is located off Mexico's Pacific coast.

44. **5.** The highest temperature is in Australia.

45. **1.** Because of unseasonably warm weather, locusts were found in Denmark. Locusts are drawn to warm weather, so they're leaving the warm Mediterranean for usually chilly Denmark.

46. **4.** The hailstorms will ruin many of the grapes that are on the vines when the storm hits. This will result in a reduced grape harvest and higher wine prices in Italy. One principal of economics is *supply and demand:* The less supply of something you have, the greater the demand, so the more you can charge for it. When something is in low supply, the price usually goes up.

47. **5.** If oil prices rise, gasoline prices will rise — this we know to be true. While you can guess that SUV sales may decrease and people may travel less, you don't have evidence of this in the passage.

48. **2.** OPEC controls oil prices, and because oil is used to fuel cars and some homes, if oil prices rise, the cost of living (the cost to live, which includes paying for gas and home heating) will rise.

49. **3.** The characters in the cartoon are willing to waste gasoline in order to drive their car. When you waste gasoline, you not only waste money, but you waste all of the natural resources and manpower that went into getting the oil out of the ground and turning it into gasoline.

50. **3.** The SUV is *not* an energy saver: That's the point of the cartoon.

# Chapter 22

# The Science Test

∙ ∙ ∙ ∙ ∙ ∙ ∙ ∙ ∙ ∙ ∙ ∙ ∙ ∙ ∙ ∙ ∙ ∙ ∙ ∙ ∙ ∙ ∙ ∙ ∙ ∙ ∙ ∙ ∙ ∙ ∙ ∙ ∙ ∙ ∙ ∙ ∙ ∙ ∙ ∙ ∙ ∙ ∙ ∙ ∙ ∙ ∙ ∙

### Directions

The Science Test consists of multiple-choice questions intended to measure general concepts in science. The questions are based on short readings that may include a graph, chart, or figure. Study the information given and then answer the question(s) following it. Refer to the information as often as necessary in answering the questions.

You have 80 minutes to answer the 50 questions in this test. Work carefully, but do not spend too much time on any one question. Be sure you answer every question.

Do not mark in this test booklet. Record your answers on the separate answer sheet provided. Be sure that all requested information is properly recorded on the answer sheet.

To record your answers, fill in the numbered circle on the answer sheet that corresponds to the answer you select for each question in the test booklet.

---

**EXAMPLE:**

Which of the following is the smallest unit in a living thing?

(1)   tissue

(2)   organ

(3)   cell

(4)   muscle            (On Answer Sheet)

(5)   capillary         ① ② ● ④ ⑤

The correct answer is "cell"; therefore, answer space 3 would be marked on the answer sheet.

---

Do not rest the point of your pencil on the answer sheet while you are considering your answer. Make no stray or unnecessary marks. If you change an answer, erase your first mark completely. Mark only one answer space for each question; multiple answers will be scored as incorrect. Do not fold or crease your answer sheet. All test materials must be returned to the test administrator.

**DO NOT BEGIN TAKING THIS TEST UNTIL TOLD TO DO SO**

**SCIENCE TEST**

| | | | | | | | | | | | | |
|---|---|---|---|---|---|---|---|---|---|---|---|---|
| 1 | ① | ② | ③ | ④ | ⑤ | | 26 | ① | ② | ③ | ④ | ⑤ |
| 2 | ① | ② | ③ | ④ | ⑤ | | 27 | ① | ② | ③ | ④ | ⑤ |
| 3 | ① | ② | ③ | ④ | ⑤ | | 28 | ① | ② | ③ | ④ | ⑤ |
| 4 | ① | ② | ③ | ④ | ⑤ | | 29 | ① | ② | ③ | ④ | ⑤ |
| 5 | ① | ② | ③ | ④ | ⑤ | | 30 | ① | ② | ③ | ④ | ⑤ |
| 6 | ① | ② | ③ | ④ | ⑤ | | 31 | ① | ② | ③ | ④ | ⑤ |
| 7 | ① | ② | ③ | ④ | ⑤ | | 32 | ① | ② | ③ | ④ | ⑤ |
| 8 | ① | ② | ③ | ④ | ⑤ | | 33 | ① | ② | ③ | ④ | ⑤ |
| 9 | ① | ② | ③ | ④ | ⑤ | | 34 | ① | ② | ③ | ④ | ⑤ |
| 10 | ① | ② | ③ | ④ | ⑤ | | 35 | ① | ② | ③ | ④ | ⑤ |
| 11 | ① | ② | ③ | ④ | ⑤ | | 36 | ① | ② | ③ | ④ | ⑤ |
| 12 | ① | ② | ③ | ④ | ⑤ | | 37 | ① | ② | ③ | ④ | ⑤ |
| 13 | ① | ② | ③ | ④ | ⑤ | | 38 | ① | ② | ③ | ④ | ⑤ |
| 14 | ① | ② | ③ | ④ | ⑤ | | 39 | ① | ② | ③ | ④ | ⑤ |
| 15 | ① | ② | ③ | ④ | ⑤ | | 40 | ① | ② | ③ | ④ | ⑤ |
| 16 | ① | ② | ③ | ④ | ⑤ | | 41 | ① | ② | ③ | ④ | ⑤ |
| 17 | ① | ② | ③ | ④ | ⑤ | | 42 | ① | ② | ③ | ④ | ⑤ |
| 18 | ① | ② | ③ | ④ | ⑤ | | 43 | ① | ② | ③ | ④ | ⑤ |
| 19 | ① | ② | ③ | ④ | ⑤ | | 44 | ① | ② | ③ | ④ | ⑤ |
| 20 | ① | ② | ③ | ④ | ⑤ | | 45 | ① | ② | ③ | ④ | ⑤ |
| 21 | ① | ② | ③ | ④ | ⑤ | | 46 | ① | ② | ③ | ④ | ⑤ |
| 22 | ① | ② | ③ | ④ | ⑤ | | 47 | ① | ② | ③ | ④ | ⑤ |
| 23 | ① | ② | ③ | ④ | ⑤ | | 48 | ① | ② | ③ | ④ | ⑤ |
| 24 | ① | ② | ③ | ④ | ⑤ | | 49 | ① | ② | ③ | ④ | ⑤ |
| 25 | ① | ② | ③ | ④ | ⑤ | | 50 | ① | ② | ③ | ④ | ⑤ |

Questions 1 through 3 refer to the following passage.

### Hibernating Plants

Tulips are beautiful flowers that come up early every spring. They are fragile in appearance but manage to survive the uncertain weather of spring, blooming for a while, and then sleeping for the rest of the year. The next year, they are ready to peek out of the earth and brighten your spring again.

Tulips survive because they grow from bulbs. Each bulb stores moisture and food during good weather. When the weather turns, the plant hibernates: The roots and leaves dry out and fall off, but the bulb develops a tough outer skin to protect itself. The bulb becomes dormant until the following spring, when the whole cycle begins again.

1. Which part of the tulip allows it to survive a rough winter?

   (1) the leaves

   (2) the buds

   (3) the bulb

   (4) the roots

   (5) the stem

2. If you wanted an early-blooming plant to give your garden color in spring, which of the following would you plant?

   (1) rose

   (2) petunia

   (3) tulip

   (4) begonia

   (5) impatience

3. When you are enjoying you garden in spring or summer, the flowers that look so pretty are composed of cells. These cells are the basic unit of all living things in the universe. In addition to flowers, weeds, trees, and even you are composed of cells. Although garden plants are composed of cells, the cells are different from plant to plant. That is why some plants produce roses and others produce dandelions.

   Which of the following is not composed of cells?

   (1) dogs

   (2) clouds

   (3) gravity

   (4) rocks

   (5) the forest

*Go on to next page*

Questions 4 and 5 refer to the following passage.

### Gunpowder

As you watch a western on television, have you ever wondered how the bullet is propelled out of the gun when the trigger is pulled?

Bullets are made of two parts, the jacket and the projectile. The jacket is filled with gunpowder and an ignition device, and when the ignition device is hit, the gunpowder explodes, hurling the projectile out of the barrel of the gun.

4.  In the movies, guns with blank cartridges are used for effect. What part of the cartridge would be different from a cartridge used for target practice?

    (1) bullet

    (2) casing

    (3) barrel

    (4) gunpowder

    (5) projectile

5.  If you wanted to reduce the force with which a projectile was hurled out of the barrel, what would you change?

    (1) use a smaller jacket

    (2) use a smaller projectile

    (3) use a smaller gun

    (4) use less gunpowder in the jacket

    (5) use more gunpowder

*Go on to next page*

Questions 6 and 7 refer to the following passage.

### Rocket Propulsion

Have you ever wondered how a rocket ship moves? Perhaps you have seen science-fiction movies in which a captain uses a blast of the rocket engines to save the ship and its crew from crashing onto the surface of a distant planet.

Usually, a fuel, such as the gas in a car, needs an oxidizer, like air, to create combustion, which powers the engine. In space, there is no air and thus no oxidizer. The rocket ship, being a clever design, carries its own oxidizer. The fuel used may be a liquid or a solid, but the rocket ship always has fuel and an oxidizer to mix together. When the two are mixed and combustion takes place, a rapid expansion is directed out the back of the engine. The force pushing backward moves the rocket ship forward. In space, with no air, the rocket ship experiences no resistance to the movement. The rocket ship moves forward, avoids the crash, or does whatever the crew wants it to do.

6. Why is the rocket engine the perfect propulsion method for space travel?

   (1) it's very powerful

   (2) it can operate without an external oxidizer

   (3) it carries a lot of fuel

   (4) you can't hear the noise it makes

   (5) it accelerated quickly

7. Fuel on a rocket ship may be

   (1) an oxidizer

   (2) a gas

   (3) an air

   (4) an expansion

   (5) a liquid

*Go on to next page*

Questions 8 through 16 refer to the following figure and passage.

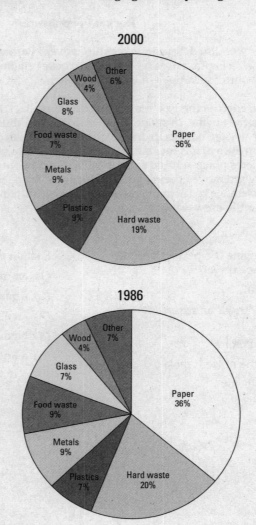

From James Trefil and Robert M. Hazen, The Sciences: An Integrated Approach, 3rd Edition (Wiley Publishing, Inc.)

## The Problem of Urban Landfills

The fact that nothing is ever really thrown away has become a concern in urban America. The problem is that American cities generate garbage (so-called *solid waste*) at an ever-increasing rate. New York City alone adds 17,000 tons of solid waste to its landfill on Staten Island every day. Environmental engineers estimate that, at current rates, every individual American will generate solid waste equivalent in volume to the Statue of Liberty in only about five years. (See the nearly identical graphs above for the make-up of this waste in 1986 and in 2000, in spite of recent efforts to encourage recycling.)

To make matters worse, the nature of modern landfills is such that the normal process of breakdown and decay in the carbon and nitrogen cycles has slowed considerably. In a landfill, solid waste is dumped on the ground and compacted to reduce the space it occupies, covered with a layer of dirt, covered with another layer of compacted waste, covered with another layer of dirt, and so on. Material in such a landfill is cut off from air and water, and

*Go on to next page*

the bacteria that normally operate to decompose the waste cannot thrive. Archeologists digging into landfills have discovered, for example, that newspapers from the 1950s are still readable after having been buried for 40 years! This means that, unlike an ordinary garden compost pile in which materials are quickly broken down by the action of bacteria, a landfill is really more like a burial site than a location for recycling.

Recycling has become important in the United States as part of the general growth in environmental awareness. Most people are willing to support an effort like the recycling of newspapers whether they can make money at it or not, based on the general notion that it is worthwhile because it saves energy and lessens the environmental impact of paper use. Something as simple as recycling newspapers may not be a business proposition, for example, but most municipalities realize that they can save money in the long run by paying whatever is needed to recycle newspapers instead of finding a new waste disposal site in which to dump them.

*Adapted from James Trefil and Robert M. Hazen,* The Sciences: An Integrated Approach, 3rd Edition *(Wiley Publishing, Inc.)*

8. Why are modern landfills as much a part of the problem as a part of the solution?

   (1) they look very ugly

   (2) they take up a lot of valuable land

   (3) the bacteria that aid decomposition do not thrive

   (4) newspapers are readable after 50 years

   (5) archeologists have no place to dig

9. Why is recycling of paper important?

   (1) it looks neater

   (2) it reduces the need for new landfill sites

   (3) newspaper is not biodegradable

   (4) it saves money

   (5) newspapers do not fit into compost heaps

10. Why is solid waste compacted in a modern landfill?

    (1) to reduce the odor

    (2) to help the bacteria decompose the waste

    (3) to make the landfill look better

    (4) to reduce the amount of space it occupies

    (5) to speed up the nitrogen cycle

11. What is the modern landfill compared to?

    (1) an efficient way of ridding cities of solid waste

    (2) a burial site for solid waste

    (3) a place for bacteria to decompose solid waste

    (4) a site for archeologists to explore

    (5) a huge compost bin

12. Why is it important for cities to establish recycling programs?

    (1) it makes people feel good about their garbage

    (2) it is cheaper to recycle

    (3) recycling lets someone else look after your problem

    (4) you are running out of bacteria to decompose waste

    (5) it is cheaper than the cost of new landfill sites

13. What can individual Americans do to reduce the amount of waste that is going into the landfills?

    (1) eat less

    (2) reuse and recycle as much as possible

    (3) stop using paper

    (4) import more nitrogen

    (5) grow more bacteria

*Go on to next page*

14. Bacteria provide what helpful purpose in composting?

    (1) they help get rid of illness

    (2) they make rodents sick

    (3) they are part of the inorganic cycle

    (4) they help decompose composting waste

    (5) they make yogurt taste distinctive

15. If municipalities lose money recycling paper, why do they continue?

    (1) the politicians don't know they are losing money

    (2) municipalities don't have to make money

    (3) the public likes to recycle paper

    (4) the cost is less than acquiring more landfill sites

    (5) recycling paper has become part of urban life

16. How does recycling paper save money for the city?

    (1) recycling trucks run on diesel fuel

    (2) new landfill sites cost money to buy

    (3) municipalities don't have to burn the paper

    (4) in a landfill site the heavy machinery uses a lot of fuel

    (5) newspapers have to be delivered

*Go on to next page*

Questions 17 and 18 refer to the following passage.

**Air Bags**

Most new cars are equipped with air bags. In a crash, the air bags quickly deploy, protecting the driver and front-seat passenger by inflating to absorb the initial force of the crash The air bags deploy so quickly and with such force that they can injure a short adult sitting too close to the dashboard or a child in a car seat. This safety device has to be treated with respect. With the proper precautions, air bags save lives. In fact, a person in the front seat of a modern car equipped with air bags who also wears a seat belt stands a much better chance of surviving a crash than an unbelted person. The two safety devices work together to save lives.

17. In a front end collision what absorbs the force of the crash?

   (1) air bags

   (2) the car's frame

   (3) the seats

   (4) padded dashboards

   (5) the windshield

18. Where is the safest place for an infant in a car seat in a car equipped with air bags?

   (1) in the rear seat

   (2) in the front seat

   (3) on the right side of the car

   (4) on the left side of the car

   (5) where they can be tended by an adult

*Go on to next page*

Questions 19 through 22 refer to the following diagram.

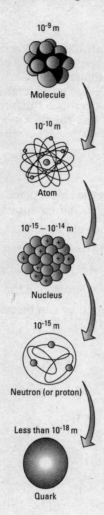

$10^{-9}$ m

Molecule

$10^{-10}$ m

Atom

$10^{-15} - 10^{-14}$ m

Nucleus

$10^{-15}$ m

Neutron (or proton)

Less than $10^{-18}$ m

Quark

From James Trefil and Robert M. Hazen,
The Sciences: An Integrated Approach, 3rd Edition
(Wiley Publishing, Inc.)

19. According to this diagram, what is the building block upon which the other particles are made?

(1) atom

(2) molecule

(3) neutron

(4) quark

(5) proton

20. According to this diagram, how many times larger is a molecule than a quark?

(1) 100

(2) 1,000

(3) 1,000,000

(4) 1,000,000,000

(5) 10,000,000,000

21. Scientists thought that the atom was the smallest particle that existed, but they were wrong. There are smaller particles than the atom, and the atom is not itself a solid. If people cannot see atoms, how can scientists know that there are smaller particles than atoms?

(1) guessing

(2) experimentation

(3) using powerful magnifying glasses

(4) using logic

(5) another scientist told them

22. The seat you are sitting on seems solid, but in reality, it is composed of atoms. Each of the atoms is composed of a nucleus, which is composed of neutrons and protons, but much of the space occupied by an atom is just empty space. This means that the chair you are sitting on is mostly empty space. It follows that when you stand on the floor of a building, you are ultimately being supported by:

(1) wood

(2) concrete

(3) girders

(4) atoms

(5) chemical reactions

*Go on to next page*

Questions 23 and 24 refer to the following passage.

**The Surface of the Moon**

The surface of the moon is a hostile, barren landscape. Astronauts have found boulders as large as houses in huge fields of dust and rock. They've had no maps to guide them but have survived, thanks to their training for the mission.

23. What is there about the lunar landscape that may make landing there dangerous?

    (1) possibility of hostile aliens

    (2) large, uncharted spaces with very large boulders

    (3) unlit landing fields with uncertain footings

    (4) not all maps of the moon are accurate

    (5) space craft has poor brakes for this type of terrain

24. What aspect of the moon makes the height of a boulder unimportant for the astronauts moving about?

    (1) astronauts have training in flying

    (2) there are special tools for flying over boulders

    (3) they can drive around an obstruction

    (4) low gravity makes climbing easier, if it's necessary

    (5) the boulder is not that big

*Go on to next page*

Questions 25 and 26 refer to the following passage.

### Pushing Aside the Water

If you fill a glass right to the brim with water, you have to drink it at its present temperature. If you decide that you want to add ice, the water spills over the brim. The ice has displaced an amount of water equal to the volume of the ice.

When you lower yourself into a luxurious bubble bath in your tub, the water rises in the tub. If you could measure that rise, you could figure out the volume of your body. Because you would displace a volume of water in the tub equal to the volume of your body, the new combined volume of you plus the water, minus the original volume of the water, equals the volume of your body. Next time you sink slowly into that hot bathwater, make sure that you leave room for the water to rise or that you are prepared to mop the floor.

25. When you sink into a tub of water, you displace

    (1) your weight in water

    (2) a lot of water

    (3) bubbles

    (4) a volume equal to the volume of your body

    (5) the soap

26. If you wanted to find the volume of an irregularly shaped object, how could you do it?

    (1) put it in a pre-measured volume of water and measure the increase

    (2) measure the object and calculate

    (3) weigh the object and calculate the volume

    (4) put the object in an oven and heat it

    (5) look it up

*Go on to next page*

Questions 27 through 29 refer to the following passage

### Newton's First Law of Motion

Isaac Newton proposed three laws of motion in 1687. The first law states that a body prefers its present state of motion; that is, body at rest prefers to remain at rest and a body at motion prefers to remain in motion. So, these states must be changed by an external force. If you want to move a box from one place to another, you have to apply an external force to do so. If you want to stop a ball rolling down a hill at you, you have to apply an external force to stop it.

The tendency of an object to remain in uniform motion is called *inertia*. A body at rest tends to remain at rest because of its inertia, while a moving body tends to keep moving because of its inertia. You often use this idea of inertia in everyday speech; for example, you may talk about the inertia in a company or government organization that is resistant to change.

*Adapted from James Trefil and Robert M. Hazen,* The Sciences: An Integrated Approach, 3rd Edition *(Wiley Publishing, Inc.)*

27. If your car becomes stuck in a snow bank, what must be done to free it?

    (1) apply a force downward to increase the traction of the wheels

    (2) leave it at rest until it wants to move

    (3) apply a force in the direction you want it to move

    (4) sit on the hood to increase the weight on the front tires

    (5) blame Newton

28. A company that refuses to change its ideas is said to suffer from

    (1) downturns

    (2) stability

    (3) manipulation

    (4) inertia

    (5) poor management

29. When you are driving at a steady speed on the highway, why does it take great effort to stop suddenly?

    (1) cars should have the right of way

    (2) it takes too much power to start driving again

    (3) pedestrians should stay in parks

    (4) your car tends to continue at the same rate

    (5) driving is difficult enough without distractions

*Go on to next page* ➡

Question 30 refers to the following passage.

**Newton's Second Law of Motion**

Newton's second law of motion states that when a body changes, its velocity because an external force is applied to it, that change in velocity is directly proportional to the force and inversely proportional to the mass of the body. That is, the faster you want to stop your car, the harder you must brake. The brakes apply an external force that reduces the velocity of the car. The faster you want to accelerate the car, the more force must be applied. Increasing the horsepower of an engine allows it to apply greater force in accelerating. That is why drag racer cars seem to be all engine.

30. If you want a car that accelerates quickly, which attributes give you the best acceleration?

   (1) lightweight and two doors

   (2) high horsepower and automatic transmission

   (3) automatic transmission

   (4) automatic transmission and two doors

   (5) lightweight and high horsepower

*Go on to next page*

Question 31 refers to the following passage.

**Newton's Third Law of Motion**

Newton's third law of motion states that for every action there is an equal and opposite reaction. If you stand on the floor, gravity pulls your body down with a certain force. The floor must exert an equal and opposite force upward on your feet, or you fall through the floor.

31. A boxer is punching a punching bag. What is the punching bag doing to the boxer?

    (1) bouncing away from the boxer

    (2) reacting with a force equal and opposite to the force of his punch

    (3) swinging with a velocity equal to that of the punch

    (4) swinging back with a force greater than that of the punch

    (5) remaining still

*Go on to next page*

Questions 32 through 34 refer to the following passage.

### Why Don't Polar Bears Freeze?

Watching a polar bear lumber through the frigid Arctic wilderness, you may wonder why it doesn't freeze. If you were there, you would likely freeze. In fact, you may feel cold just looking at photographs of polar bears.

Professor Stephan Steinlechner of Hanover Veterinary University in German set out to answer the question of why polar bears don't freeze. Polar bears have black skin. This means that, in effect, polar bears have a huge solar heat collector covering their body. Covering this black skin are white hollow hairs. These hairs act as insulation, keeping the heat inside the fur covering. This is like an insulated house. The heat stays in for a long period of time.

This is an interesting theory and does answer the question, except you may still wonder how they keep warm at night, when the sun isn't out!

32. The most important element in retaining the polar bear's body heat is its:

    (1) paws

    (2) scalp

    (3) skin

    (4) blood

    (5) hair

33. What is the polar bear's solar heat collector?

    (1) caves

    (2) ice

    (3) their furry coat

    (4) the snow

    (5) its skin

34. If you had to live in the arctic, what sort of clothing would be most appropriate?

    (1) insulated coats

    (2) silk underwear

    (3) black clothing with fur covering

    (4) white clothing with fur covering

    (5) heavy wool

*Go on to next page* ⟶

Questions 35 and 36 refer to the following diagram.

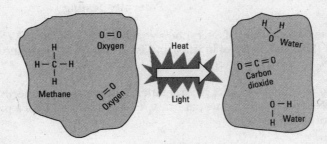

*From James Trefil and Robert M. Hazen,* The Sciences: An Integrated Approach, 3rd Edition *(Wiley Publishing, Inc.)*

35. When methane burns, it produces light, heat, carbon dioxide, and water. Why would natural gas be a good choice for keeping your house warm in winter?

    (1) the chemical reaction produces carbon dioxide

    (2) the chemical reaction produces light

    (3) the chemical reaction produces water

    (4) the chemical reaction uses oxygen

    (5) the chemical reaction produces heat

36. If firefighters were faced with a methane fire, what would they want to eliminate to put out the fire?

    (1) heat

    (2) light

    (3) water

    (4) carbon dioxide

    (5) oxygen

*Go on to next page*

Questions 37 and 38 refer to the following passage.

## Paternity Testing

DNA has become part of everyone's vocabulary. DNA has put criminals in jail and freed others. It is used as proof in trials and is an important dramatic tool on many television dramas.

Another use for DNA is not as dramatic. Because a child inherits the DNA of his or her parents, DNA testing can prove paternity. This is an example of a practical use for a scientific discovery.

37. Paternity testing compares the DNA of the child with the DNA of the:

    (1) mother
    (2) father
    (3) father's aunt
    (4) father and grandfather
    (5) both sides of the family

38. Why is there no need for maternity testing when a child is born?

    (1) a mother's DNA is always the same as her children's
    (2) fathers are liable for support
    (3) mothers give birth to their children
    (4) it makes a better drama
    (5) fathers may have more than one child

*Go on to next page*

Questions 39 through 44 refer to the following passage.

**Space Stuff**

Each space flight carries items authorized by NASA, but the quirky little items carried in astronauts' pockets are what catch the interest of collectors. Auction sales have been brisk for material carried aboard various space flights.

On the second manned Mercury flight, Gus Grissom carried two rolls of dimes. He was planning to give these to the children of his friends after he returned to earth. If you carried two rolls of dimes around the earth, they would be worth ten dollars. When Gus Grissom returned to earth, however, these dimes became space mementos, each worth many times their face value.

Although NASA does not permit the sale of items carried aboard space missions, many items have found their way to market. Eleven Apollo 16 stamps, autographed by the astronauts, sold for $27,000 at auction. A corned beef sandwich that John Young offered to Gus Grissom never returned to earth.

**39.** What did Gus Grissom plan to do with his rolls of dimes?

(1) sell them at auction

(2) use them in vending machines

(3) give them to children

(4) donate them to charity

(5) keep them, as souvenirs

**40.** What happened to John Young's corned beef sandwich?

(1) it is in storage

(2) it was sold

(3) it was left on the moon

(4) it was eaten

(5) not enough information given

**41.** What is so special about items carried in an astronaut's pocket?

(1) weightlessness changes their composition

(2) they have been in space

(3) lunar radiation affects them

(4) the pockets are made of a special material

(5) they are autographed

**42.** What would NASA authorize astronauts to carry into space?

(1) toys to bring home to their kids

(2) bulletproof vest

(3) extra cup of coffee for the flight

(4) government documents

(5) tools for experiments

**43.** Why would autographed stamps be worth so much money?

(1) they are rare when personally autographed

(2) stamps always become valuable

(3) people collect autographs

(4) astronauts don't give autographs

(5) auctions always get high prices

**44.** Why would the contents of an astronaut's pocket become so valuable after a space flight?

(1) NASA told them not to carry things in their pockets

(2) auctions increase the value of articles

(3) collectors value anything that exists in limited quantities

(4) space travel makes articles magical

(5) the astronauts held out for the highest price

*Go on to next page*

Questions 45 and 46 refer to the following passage.

### Work

Scientists say that work is done whenever a force is exerted over a distance. If you pick up this book and raise it up by one foot, your muscles apply a force equal to the weight of the book over a distance of one foot. You did work.

This definition of work differs considerably from everyday usage. From a physicist's point of view, if you accidentally drive into a tree and smash your fender, work has been done, because a force deformed the car's metal a measurable distance. On the other hand, a physicist would say that you haven't done any work if you spend an hour in a futile effort to move a large boulder, no matter how tired you get. Even though you have exerted a considerable force, the distance over which you exerted it is negligible.

*Adapted from James Trefil and Robert M. Hazen,* The Sciences: An Integrated Approach, 3rd Edition *(Wiley Publishing, Inc.)*

45. If the formula for work is Work = Force × Distance, how much more work would you do in lifting a 10 pound barbell 3 feet instead of 2 feet?

 (1) half as much

 (2) 3 times as much

 (3) ⅓ as much

 (4) 1½ times as much

 (5) 2⅓ times as much

46. While you may see that you do work in climbing a flight of stairs, why do you also do work when you descend a flight of stairs?

 (1) it is hard to climb down stairs

 (2) you have traveled a distance down the stairs

 (3) you feel tired after descending stairs

 (4) you have exerted a force over a distance

 (5) if you do it at work, it's work

*Go on to next page*

Questions 47 and 48 refer to the following figure and passages.

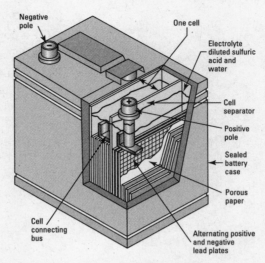

**Lead-Acid Storage Battery**

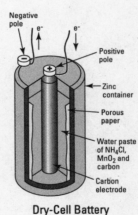

**Dry-Cell Battery**

*From C. Lon Enloe, Elizabeth Garnett, Jonathan Miles, and Stephen Swanson;*
*Physical Science: What the Technology Professional Needs to Know (Wiley Publishing, Inc.)*

### The Lead-Acid Storage Battery

One battery you rely on is the 12-volt lead-acid storage battery used in cars and trucks. This battery is composed of six separate cells, each developing about 2 volts. By connecting the six cells in series, the overall voltage becomes the sum, or 12 volts.

### The Dry-Cell Battery

The traditional dry-cell or flashlight battery is a zinc-carbon battery. It derives its name from the fact that the liquid portion has been replaced by a moist paste of ammonium chloride, manganese dioxide, and carbon. These components are the anode portion of the cell, and the zinc container serves as the cathode.

*Go on to next page*

47. If you wanted a 48-volt lead acid battery, how many cells would it need?

    (1) 24

    (2) 26

    (3) 28

    (4) 36

    (5) 48

48. What replaces the liquid acid portion of the lead acid battery in a dry-cell?

    (1) a moist paste

    (2) a powder

    (3) dry acid

    (4) carbon and zinc

    (5) a stick of acid

*Go on to next page*

Questions 49 and 50 refer to the following passage.

**The Cell and Heredity**

Each cell in a living organism consists of a membrane surrounding a cytoplasm. The cytoplasm is like jelly and has a nucleus in its center. Chromosomes are part of the nucleus. They are important, because they store DNA. DNA stores the genetic code that is the basis of heredity.

49. What determines what traits you inherited from your parents?

    (1) the cell

    (2) the atom

    (3) the nucleus

    (4) the neutron

    (5) DNA

50. What part of the chromosome carries the genetic code?

    (1) membrane

    (2) cytoplasm

    (3) nucleus

    (4) atom

    (5) DNA

**END OF EXAMINATION**

# Chapter 23

# Answers and Explanations for the Science Test

. . . . . . . . . . . . . . . . . . . . . . . . . . . . . . . . . . . . . . . . .

## Answer Key

After taking the Science Test in Chapter 22, use this section to check your answers.

| | | |
|---|---|---|
| 1. 3 | 18. 1 | 35. 5 |
| 2. 3 | 19. 4 | 36. 5 |
| 3. 3 | 20. 4 | 37. 2 |
| 4. 5 | 21. 2 | 38. 3 |
| 5. 4 | 22. 4 | 39. 3 |
| 6. 2 | 23. 2 | 40. 5 |
| 7. 5 | 24. 4 | 41. 2 |
| 8. 3 | 25. 4 | 42. 5 |
| 9. 2 | 26. 1 | 43. 1 |
| 10. 4 | 27. 3 | 44. 3 |
| 11. 2 | 28. 4 | 45. 4 |
| 12. 5 | 29. 4 | 46. 4 |
| 13. 2 | 30. 5 | 47. 1 |
| 14. 4 | 31. 2 | 48. 1 |
| 15. 4 | 32. 5 | 49. 5 |
| 16. 2 | 33. 5 | 50. 5 |
| 17. 1 | 34. 3 | |

# Analysis of the Answers

If you aren't sure why an answer was incorrect, use this section to get quick explanations of the answers.

1. **3.** The passage describes how the bulb changes to survive the winter.

2. **3.** The passage states that tulips bloom early and grow each year from the bulb. A *perennial plant* is one that grows each year without replanting.

3. **3.** All of the answers except gravity are substances that are made up of cells. Gravity is a force.

4. **5.** Because the projectile is the only part that leaves the gun, and because movie producers and directors don't want to hurt anyone, the guns are altered so that the projectile does no harm.

5. **4.** The force that propels the projectile out of the barrel is the explosion in the jacket. The force of the explosion is determined by the quantity of powder in the jacket. If there is less powder in the jacket, there is less force propelling the projectile out of the barrel.

6. **2.** In space, there is no oxidizer to take part in the chemical reaction needed for combustion. A rocket ship carries its own oxidizer and thus can travel through space.

7. **5.** The passage states that "fuel used may be a liquid or a solid."

8. **3.** The passage states that with the methodology used for burying solid waste in a modern landfill, the bacteria needed for decomposition cannot survive.

9. **2.** Recycling reduces the need for new landfill sites. In large cities, land is expensive and few people want to live next to a landfill site. Even if you remove the garbage on barges, it still has to be dumped somewhere. This information is stated in the passage and agrees with what you may have read in newspapers and seen on television.

Even though you may feel you know the answer, read the passage quickly to make sure.

10. **4.** The reason solid waste is compacted is to reduce the amount of space it occupies and make the landfill last longer.

11. **2.** A modern landfill is compared to a burial site for solid waste. The methods used prevent proper decomposition.

12. **5.** The passage states that recycling is cheaper than continuing to acquire new landfill sites. Answer 2 looks like a possible answer, but it is not complete.

Read the answers carefully. You do not want to choose an incomplete answer.

13. **2.** As long as you dispose of waste by taking it to the curb or the dump, there will be an excess amount disposed of. Every piece that you can reuse or recycle lives on to be useful again.

14. **4.** The passage states that bacteria decomposes waste.

15. **4.** Landfill sites are more expensive to acquire than the cost of recycling.

16. **2.** Recycling reduces the amount of space required in landfill sites. These sites are large and expensive for any city to buy. Needing fewer landfill sites (or smaller landfill sites) would save money.

17. **1.** The purpose of the airbag, according to the passage, is to absorb some of the forces in a front-end crash.

One or more of the other answers to a question may be correct from your memory, but if they are not mentioned in the passage, don't use them. A correct answer in a multiple-choice question is either mentioned or suggested in the passage.

18. **1.** An infant is safest in the rear seat because the air bag is powerful enough to injure a small person when deployed.

19. **4.** The diagram (going from bottom to top) indicates the process of building up a molecule. The quark is the smallest particle, and the molecule is the largest. Sometimes, you have to read a diagram in an unfamiliar way to answer the question.

20. **4.** According to the diagram, a quark is $10^{-18}$ m across and a molecule is $10^{-9}$ across. The molecule would be $10^{-9} \div 10^{-18} = 1 \div 10^{-9}$ or 1,000,000,000 times the size of a quark.

    A number with a negative exponent, like $10^{-9}$, equals $1 \div 10^9$.

21. **2.** Scientists often develop experiments to test theories about items that are invisible to the naked eye. Curiosity drives scientists to try to find answers; experimentation proves that smaller particles than atoms exist. The other answers do not directly answer the question.

22. **4.** The passage states that everything is composed of atoms. The floor then must be composed of atoms.

23. **2.** Landing a space ship on large boulders is impossible, and the lack of charts makes accidentally meeting a boulder a possibility.

24. **4.** The moon has less gravity than earth. Climbing requires lifting your weight against the force of gravity. It's easier to climb on the moon.

25. **4.** The passage tells you that you would displace a volume equal to your own volume. Answer 1 looks like it may be correct, but the passage is about volume, not weight.

26. **1.** The object would displace a volume of water equal to its volume.

27. **3.** According to Newton, a force must be applied to move the car at rest. According to Newton, who never drove a car, you have to apply an external force on the object at rest, namely the car, in the direction you wanted it to move. If you want it to move deeper into the snow, you push it down. If you have a crane or a helicopter, which the passage doesn't mention, you apply a force upward to lift it out of the snow. Answer 3 is the best answer.

28. **4.** The answer is a direct quote from the passage.

29. **4.** When driving at a uniform rate of speed, the car resists changes in speed. The car wants to continue to travel at the same speed. In order to change that speed suddenly, great effort is required by the brakes.

30. **5.** Newton's second law of motion states that when a body changes its velocity because an external force is applied to it, that change in velocity is directly proportional to the force and inversely proportional to the mass of the body. If you decrease the weight of the body and increase the size of the external force, the acceleration increases.

31. **2.** Newton's third law of motion states that for every action there is an equal and opposite reaction. If the boxer is exerting a force upon the bag, the bag is exerting an equal and opposite force upon the boxer.

32. **5.** The passage states that the hair acts as insulation, that it retains the polar bear's body heat.

33. **5.** The passage states that the polar bear's skin collects heat from the sun.

34. **3.** If you were in the Arctic, you would want to duplicate the experience of the polar bear. Black clothing with a fur covering is the closest answer.

35. **5.** In cold weather, you need a source of heat to warm your house, and methane produces heat in the chemical reaction.

36. **5.** Methane requires oxygen to produce light and heat. If there is no oxygen, the methane can't burn.

37. **2.** Paternity refers to the male half of the couple. If mothers were tested, it would be called maternity testing.

38. **3.** No one ever has any doubt on the day of the birth about who gave birth to a child. The mother is always obvious on that day. If the child were separated from the mother, maternity could be an issue. But the question specifically asks about the day the baby is born.

39. **3.** According to the passage, Gus Grissom planned to give the dimes to the children of his friends.

40. **5.** The passage tells you that it was not returned to earth, but nothing more. There is no information about what happened to it. Any of the other answers are speculation, which may be fun in real life, but on tests, stick to the information you're given or not given.

41. **2.** Because being in space is a rare occurrence, anything that has been there takes on a certain importance.

42. **5.** The purpose of the space flights is scientific research, so you're looking for an item associated with carrying out experiments or for one that's used in performing the daily routine of space travel. None of the other choices fills the bill.

43. **1.** Anything autographed by a famous person is valuable. When the object autographed is also available in limited quantities, it becomes more valuable still.

44. **3.** Collectors like to collect unique things. Few items are as unique as something that has flown in space.

45. **4.** The force is directly related to the distance moved. The number of feet is 1½ times 2 feet, so the force is 1½ times.

46. **4.** Walking down the stairs, you have to exert a force against the force of gravity for a distance. This is the definition of work in physics.

47. **1.** If you want a 48-volt lead acid battery, and each cell produces 2 volts, you need 24 cells ($48 \div 2 = 24$).

48. **1.** The moist paste replaces the acid in the battery.

49. **5.** DNA stores the genetic code, which determines heredity.

50. **5.** DNA stores the genetic code, which determines heredity. This is the same answer as Question 49, but the question is different. Read the questions carefully and don't spend your time looking for patterns or tricks.

# Chapter 24

# The Language Arts, Reading Test

## Directions

The Language Arts, Reading Test consists of excerpts from fiction and nonfiction. Each excerpt is followed by multiple-choice questions about the reading material.

Read each excerpt first and then answer the questions following it. Refer back to the reading material as often as necessary in answering the questions.

Each excerpt is preceded by a *purpose question*. The purpose question gives a reason for reading the material. Use these purpose questions to help focus your reading. You are not required to answer these purpose questions. They are given only to help you concentrate on the ideas presented in the reading material.

You have 65 minutes to answer the 40 questions in this test. Work carefully, but do not spend too much time on any one question. Be sure you answer every question.

Do not mark in this test booklet. Record your answers on the separate answer sheet provided. Be sure that all requested information is properly recorded on the answer sheet.

To record your answers, fill in the numbered circle on the answer sheet that corresponds to the answer you select for each question in the test booklet.

---

**EXAMPLE:**

It was Susan's dream machine. The metallic blue paint gleamed, and the sporty wheels were highly polished. Under the hood, the engine was no less carefully cleaned. Inside, flashy lights illuminated the instruments on the dashboard, and the seats were covered by rich leather upholstery.

The subject ("it") of this excerpt is most likely

(1) an airplane

(2) a stereo system

(3) an automobile

(4) a boat

(5) a motorcycle

(On Answer Sheet)
① ② ● ④ ⑤

The correct answer is "an automobile"; therefore, answer space 3 would be marked on the answer sheet.

---

Do not rest the point of your pencil on the answer sheet while you are considering your answer. Make no stray or unnecessary marks. If you change an answer, erase your first mark completely. Mark only one answer space for each question; multiple answers will be scored as incorrect. Do not fold or crease your answer sheet. All test materials must be returned to the test administrator.

**DO NOT BEGIN TAKING THIS TEST UNTIL TOLD TO DO SO**

**READING TEST**

1  ① ② ③ ④ ⑤         21  ① ② ③ ④ ⑤
2  ① ② ③ ④ ⑤         22  ① ② ③ ④ ⑤
3  ① ② ③ ④ ⑤         23  ① ② ③ ④ ⑤
4  ① ② ③ ④ ⑤         24  ① ② ③ ④ ⑤
5  ① ② ③ ④ ⑤         25  ① ② ③ ④ ⑤
6  ① ② ③ ④ ⑤         26  ① ② ③ ④ ⑤
7  ① ② ③ ④ ⑤         27  ① ② ③ ④ ⑤
8  ① ② ③ ④ ⑤         28  ① ② ③ ④ ⑤
9  ① ② ③ ④ ⑤         29  ① ② ③ ④ ⑤
10 ① ② ③ ④ ⑤         30  ① ② ③ ④ ⑤
11 ① ② ③ ④ ⑤         31  ① ② ③ ④ ⑤
12 ① ② ③ ④ ⑤         32  ① ② ③ ④ ⑤
13 ① ② ③ ④ ⑤         33  ① ② ③ ④ ⑤
14 ① ② ③ ④ ⑤         34  ① ② ③ ④ ⑤
15 ① ② ③ ④ ⑤         35  ① ② ③ ④ ⑤
16 ① ② ③ ④ ⑤         36  ① ② ③ ④ ⑤
17 ① ② ③ ④ ⑤         37  ① ② ③ ④ ⑤
18 ① ② ③ ④ ⑤         38  ① ② ③ ④ ⑤
19 ① ② ③ ④ ⑤         39  ① ② ③ ④ ⑤
20 ① ② ③ ④ ⑤         40  ① ② ③ ④ ⑤

**Directions:** Choose the one best answer to each question.

Questions 1 through 6 refer to the following poem.

### WHAT DOES EVENING SIGNIFY TO THE POET?

Let the light of late afternoon
shine through chinks in the barn, moving
up the bales as the sun moves down.

Let the cricket take up chafing
(05) as a woman takes up her needles
and her yarn. Let evening come.

Let dew collect on the hoe abandoned
in the long grass. Let the stars appear
and the moon disclose her silver horn.

(10) Let the fox go back to its sandy den.
Let the wind die down. Let the shed
go black inside. Let evening come.

To the bottle in the ditch, to the scoop
in the oats, to air in the lung
(15) let evening come.

Let it come, as it will, and don't
be afraid. God does not leave us
comfortless, so let evening come.

*Jane Kenyon, "Let Evening Come," 1996 (Graywolf Press). Reprinted with permission.*

1. What is the overall setting for the poem?
   (1) a barn
   (2) a shed
   (3) a farm
   (4) a den
   (5) a ditch

2. Why would the woman be taking up needles and yarn?
   (1) she is going to knit
   (2) she is going to sew
   (3) she is going to cook
   (4) she is going to harvest
   (5) she is going to cultivate crickets

3. What does silver horn refer to?
   (1) the brightness of the stars
   (2) dew drops
   (3) the shape of the moon
   (4) the fox's den
   (5) the dark shed

4. On what abandoned article do drops of water collect?
   (1) crickets
   (2) yarn
   (3) needles
   (4) chair
   (5) hoe

*Go on to next page*

5. Why shouldn't you be afraid?
   (1) because of God's comfort
   (2) you have air in your lungs
   (3) the sun moves down
   (4) the evening's coming
   (5) stars appear

6. What does "Let Evening Come" appear to signify to the poet?
   (1) day's end
   (2) death
   (3) life
   (4) contentment
   (5) happiness

*Go on to next page*

Questions 7 through 12 refer to the following excerpt.

**WHY IS UNDERSHAFT INTERESTED IN THE SALVATION ARMY?**

*Undershaft*: One moment, Mr. Lomax. I am rather interested in the Salvation Army. Its motto might be my own: Blood and Fire.

*Lomax (shocked):* But not your sort of blood and fire, you know.

*Undershaft:* My sort of blood cleanses: my sort of fire purifies.

(05) *Barbara:* So does ours. Come down tomorrow to my shelter — the West Ham Shelter — and see what we are doing. We're going to march to a great meeting in the Assembly at Mile End. Come and see the shelter and then march with us: It will do you a lot of good. Can you play anything?

*Undershaft:* In my youth I earned pennies, and even shillings occasionally, in the streets and (10) in public house parlors by my natural talent for stepdancing. Later on, I became a member of the Undershaft Orchestra Society, and performed passably on the tenor trombone.

*Lomax: (scandalized — putting down the concertina):* Oh I say!

*Barbara:* Many a sinner has played himself into heaven on the trombone, thanks to the Army.

*Lomax (to Barbara, still rather shocked):* Yes; but what about the cannon business, don't you (15) know? *(to Undershaft)* Getting into heaven is not exactly in your line, is it?

*Lady Britomart:* Charles!!!

*Lomax:* Well; but it stands to reason, don't it? The cannon business may be necessary and all that; we can't get along without cannons; but it isn't right, you know. On the other hand, there may be a certain amount of tosh about the Salvation Army — I belong to the (20) Established Church myself — but still you can't deny that it's religion; and you can't go against religion, can you? At least unless you're downright immoral, don't you know.

*Excerpted from George Bernard Shaw, "Major Barbara," 1905*

7. Why did Barbara invite Undershaft to the shelter?

   (1) to march in the band

   (2) to a great meeting

   (3) to earn pennies

   (4) for stepdancing

   (5) to be with them in the Assembly

8. What does stepdancing for pennies tell you about Undershaft?

   (1) he has natural talent

   (2) he frequented public houses

   (3) he had an impoverished youth

   (4) he performed passably

   (5) he was a skilled musician

9. What can Undershaft contribute to the march?

   (1) stepdancing

   (2) pennies

   (3) shillings

   (4) trombone playing

   (5) natural talent

10. How would you describe Lomax's treatment of Undershaft?

   (1) friendly

   (2) bitter

   (3) encouraging

   (4) philosophical

   (5) critical

*Go on to next page*

11. Why might Undershaft's motto be "Blood and Fire"?

    (1) he makes cannons
    (2) he plays the trombone
    (3) he is a sinner
    (4) he doesn't belong to the Established Church
    (5) he marches for the Salvation Army

12. How do you know Barbara is committed to doing good?

    (1) she is in the Salvation Army
    (2) she operates a shelter
    (3) she joins in marches
    (4) she plays the concertina
    (5) she recruits others to join

*Go on to next page*

Questions 13 through 18 refer to the following excerpt.

## WHAT CAN YOU LEARN FROM THE MOUNTAINS?

Whoever has made a voyage up the Hudson must remember the Kaatskill mountains. They are a dismembered branch of the great Appalachian family, and are seen away to the west of the river, swelling up to a noble height, and lording it over the surrounding country. Every change of season, every change of weather, indeed, every hour of the day, produces some
(05) change in the magical hues and shapes of these mountains, and they are regarded by all the good wives, far and near, as perfect barometers. When the weather is fair and settled, they are clothed in blue and purple, and print their bold outlines on the clear evening sky; but, sometimes, when the rest of the landscape is cloudless, they will gather a hood of gray vapors about their summits, which, in the last rays of the setting sun, will glow and light up
(10) like a crown of glory.

At the foot of these fairy mountains, the voyager may have descried the light smoke curling up from a village, whose shingle-roofs gleam among the trees, just where the blue tints of the upland melt away into the fresh green of the nearer landscape. It is a little village of great antiquity, having been founded by some of the Dutch colonists, in the early times of the
(15) province, just about the beginning of the government of the good Peter Stuyvesant, (may he rest in peace!) and there were some of the houses of the original settlers standing within a few years, built of small yellow bricks brought from Holland, having latticed windows and gablefronts, surmounted with weather-cocks.

*Excerpted from Washington Irving,* Rip Van Winkle, *1820*

13. How would you locate the Kaatskill Mountains?

    (1) ask directions

    (2) journey up the Hudson

    (3) look for a dismembered branch

    (4) notice fresh green

    (5) enjoy the surrounding country

14. According to line 5, how do the wives tell the weather?

    (1) with perfect barometers

    (2) by the clear evening sky

    (3) with the crown of glory

    (4) through gray vapors

    (5) with magical hues and shapes

15. What might you look for to find the village?

    (1) fairy mountains

    (2) shingle-roofs

    (3) light smoke curling

    (4) blue tints

    (5) great antiquity

16. Who originally founded the village?

    (1) Peter Stuyvesant

    (2) Appalachian family

    (3) the voyager

    (4) Dutch colonists

    (5) the government

17. Why is the phrase "may he rest in peace!" (lines 15 and 16) used after Peter Stuyvesant?

    (1) he has since died

    (2) he was an original settler

    (3) he was a voyager

    (4) he was a soldier

    (5) he was the governor

18. What materials came from Holland?

    (1) weather-cocks

    (2) yellow bricks

    (3) latticed windows

    (4) gable fronts

    (5) shingle-roofs

*Go on to next page*

Questions 19 through 24 refer to the following excerpt.

### WHAT DO YOU NEED TO BE A MAN?

Dave struck out across the fields, looking homeward through paling light . . . One of these days he was going to get a gun and practice shooting, then they couldn't talk to him as though he were a little boy. He slowed, looking at the ground. Shucks, Ah ain scareda them . . . even ef they are biggern me! Aw, Ah know whut Ahma do. Ahm going by ol Joe's sto n git that
(05)  Sears Roebuck catlog n look at them guns. Mebbe Ma will lemme buy one when she gits mah pay from ol man Hawkins. Ahma beg her t gimme some money. Ahm ol ernough to hava gun. Ahm seventeen. Almost a man. He strode, feeling his long loose-jointed limbs. Shucks, a man oughta hava little gun aftah he done worked hard all day.

He came in sight of Joe's store. A yellow lantern glowed on the front porch. He mounted
(10)  steps and went through the screen door, hearing it bang behind him. There was a strong smell of coal oil and mackerel fish. He felt very confident until he saw fat Joe walk in through the rear door, then his courage began to ooze.

"Howdy, Dave! Whutcha want?"

"How yuh, Mistah Joe? Aw, Ah don wanna buy nothing. Ah jus wanted t see ef yuhd lemme
(15)  look at tha catlog erwhile."

"Sure! You wanna see it here?"

"Nawsuh. Ah wants t take it home wid me. Ah'll bring it back termorrow when Ah come in from the fiels."

"You plannin on buying something?"

(20)  "Yessuh."

"Your ma lettin you have your own money now?"

"Shucks. Mistah Joe, Ahm gittin t be a man like anybody else!"

*Excerpted from Richard Wright, "The Man Who Was Almost a Man," from* Eight Men, *1958*

19. What was Dave's place of employment?

  (1) Joe's store
  (2) Sears Roebuck
  (3) Hawkins's fields
  (4) with his Ma
  (5) unemployed

20. Why did he want "to get a gun" in line 2?

  (1) to show he wasn't "scareda" the others
  (2) to prove he wasn't unemployed
  (3) to make his Ma proud
  (4) to impress Joe
  (5) to get a better job

*Go on to next page*

21. From where did Dave hope to get a gun?
    (1) "Joe's sto"
    (2) "ol man Hawkins"
    (3) from "Ma"
    (4) Sears Roebuck "catlog"
    (5) field-hands in the field

22. How would you find Joe's store at night?
    (1) the smell of mackerel
    (2) the banging screen door
    (3) the smell of coal oil
    (4) a yellow lantern glow
    (5) through the rear door

23. Why do you think Dave asked to take the catalog home?
    (1) he'd lost his nerve
    (2) it was too dark to read
    (3) he had to be home for supper
    (4) he makes his own money
    (5) he had to ask his mother's permission

24. What must Dave do to get the gun?
    (1) find it in the catalog
    (2) convince Ma to give him the money
    (3) persuade Joe to place the order
    (4) return the catalog to Joe
    (5) get ol man Hawkins' permission

*Go on to next page*

Questions 25 through 30 refer to the following excerpt.

## HOW DID IT ALL BEGIN?

It began like any other winter school day in Chicago — grimly ordinary. The temperature a few degrees above zero, botanical frost shapes on the windowpane, the snow swept up in heaps, the ice gritty and the streets, block after block, bound together by the iron of the sky. A breakfast of porridge, toast, and tea. Late as usual, I stopped for a moment to look into my
(05) mother's sickroom. I bent near and said, "It's Louie, going to school." She seemed to nod. Her eyelids were brown, her face was much lighter. I hurried off with my books on a strap over my shoulder.

When I came to the boulevard on the edge of the park, two small men rushed out of a doorway with rifles, wheeled around aiming upward, and fired at pigeons near the rooftop.
(10) Several birds fell straight down, and the men scooped up the soft bodies and ran indoors, dark little guys in fluttering white shirts. Depression hunters and their city game. Moments before, the police car had loafed by at ten miles an hour. The men had waited it out.

This had nothing to do with me. I mention it merely because it happened. I stepped around the blood spots and crossed into the park.

*Excerpted from Saul Bellow,* Something to Remember Me By, *1990*

25. What words best describe the appearance of a winter school day in Chicago?

    (1) botanical frost

    (2) swept in heaps

    (3) grim and gritty

    (4) iron sky

    (5) block after block

26. What do you find out about the state of Louie's home life in lines 5 and 6?

    (1) he ate porridge, toast, and tea

    (2) he was late, as usual

    (3) he carried books on a strap

    (4) his face was much lighter

    (5) his mother was sick

27. What were the men doing in the doorway?

    (1) hunting for game

    (2) having target practice

    (3) staying out of the weather

    (4) hiding from police

    (5) making their way to the park

28. How do you know the men were good shots?

    (1) they ran indoors

    (2) they were small men

    (3) they had rifles

    (4) several birds fell

    (5) pigeons were near the rooftop

29. What adjective best describes the hunters?

    (1) angry

    (2) hungry

    (3) happy

    (4) brave

    (5) careless

30. Why didn't Louie tell the police about what he saw?

    (1) he was in a hurry to get to school

    (2) his mother was sick

    (3) it had nothing to do with him

    (4) the guys were his friends

    (5) they were depression hunters

*Go on to next page*

Questions 31 through 35 refer to the following excerpt.

## WHAT'S THE SECRET TO LOADING BATTERIES?

If you've ever had to figure out where to stick batteries in your child's latest electronic acqui- sition, then loading batteries in your point-and-shoot shouldn't be a challenge. Turn off your camera when you install them; the camera may go crazy opening and closing its lens. (Some cameras turn themselves off after you install new batteries, so you have to turn them back (05) on to shoot.)

With big point-and-shoot models, you typically open a latched cover on the bottom to install batteries. More compact models have a battery compartment under a door or flap that is incorporated into the side or grip of the camera. You may have to pry open such doors with a coin.

(10) More annoying are covers on the bottom that you open by loosening a screw. (You need a coin for this type, too.) And most annoying are battery covers that aren't hinged and come off completely when you unscrew them. If you have one of these, don't change batteries while standing over a sewer grate, in a field of tall grass, or on a pier.

Whether loading four AAs or a single lithium, make sure that the batteries are correctly ori- (15) ented as you insert them. You'll find a diagram and/or plus and minus markings, usually within the compartment or on the inside of the door.

If your camera doesn't turn on and the batteries are correctly installed, the batteries may have lost their punch from sitting on a shelf too long. Which is where the battery icon comes in.

(20) If your camera has an LCD panel, an icon tells you when battery power is low.

*Excerpted from Russell Hart,* Photography For Dummies *(Wiley Publishing, Inc.)*

31. Where will you be installing the batteries?

    (1) an electronic acquisition
    (2) a children's toy
    (3) a big point and shoot
    (4) a camera
    (5) a flashlight

32. What is the easiest model in which to replace the batteries?

    (1) compact models
    (2) big point and shoot
    (3) screw bottoms
    (4) covers not hinged
    (5) covers that come off completely

33. Why should locations such as sewer grates and tall grass be avoided when changing batteries?

    (1) water can get in the camera
    (2) your lens may get dirty
    (3) the glare would ruin the picture

    (4) your film would get exposed
    (5) the battery cover may be lost

34. How do you ensure that the batteries are correctly oriented?

    (1) use four AAs
    (2) use a single lithium
    (3) empty the compartment
    (4) find a diagram
    (5) check the inside of the film box

35. What tells you whether the batteries are low?

    (1) the LCD panel
    (2) the battery icon
    (3) the battery compartment
    (4) a single lithium battery
    (5) markings on the diagram

*Go on to next page*

Questions 36 through 40 refer to the following excerpt.

### WHO WAS THE KING OF VIBES?

NEW YORK — There was more than musical magic on stage that day in 1936 when Lionel Hampton joined Benny Goodman in a Manhattan ballroom — it was a breakthrough in American race relations.

(05) Hampton, a vibraphone virtuoso who died yesterday, broke a barrier that had kept black and white musicians from performing together in public. Through a six-decade career, he continued to build a name for himself as one of the greats in jazz history.

"He was really a towering jazz figure," said saxophonist Sonny Rollins, who played with Hampton in the 1950s. "He really personified the spirit of jazz because he had so much joy about his playing."

(10) The 94 year old showman and bandleader died of heart failure at Mount Sinai Medical Center, said his manager, Phil Leshin. Hampton suffered two strokes in 1995 and had been in failing health in recent years.

Hampton played with a who's who of jazz, from Goodman to Louis Armstrong to Charlie Parker to Quincy Jones. His own band helped foster or showcase other jazz greats including (15) Charlie Mingus, Dexter Gordon, Fats Navarro, Joe Williams and Dinah Washington.

"With Hampton's death, we've drawn closer to losing part of the origins of the early jazz era," said Phil Schaap, a jazz historian.

During his career, Hampton performed at the White House for presidents Truman, Eisenhower, Johnson, Nixon, Carter, Reagan and Bush. When he played for Truman, his was (20) the first black band to ever entertain in the White House, Hampton once said.

In 1997, Hampton received the National Medal of Arts — while wearing a borrowed suit, socks and shoes, because all his clothes and much of his bands' arrangements and other memorabilia had been destroyed in a fire two days earlier.

*Larry McShane, Associated Press, September 1, 2002. Reprinted with permission of The Associated Press.*

**36.** What was the breakthrough in American race relations?

   (1) the musical magic on stage

   (2) white and black musicians performing together

   (3) Benny Goodman in a Manhattan ballroom

   (4) Lionel Hampton in a Manhattan ballroom

   (5) that Hampton died yesterday

**37.** Why was Hampton "one of the greats in jazz" (line 6)?

   (1) his career lasted 60 years

   (2) he played with Sonny Rollins

   (3) he played the vibraphone

   (4) he broke a barrier

   (5) he had so much joy

*Go on to next page*

38. Why was Hampton's band famous at the White House?

    (1) showcased jazz greats

    (2) played for President Kennedy

    (3) included Dinah Washington

    (4) was the first black band to perform there

    (5) personified the spirit of jazz

39. What do you suppose Benny Goodman did for a living?

    (1) ballroom dancer

    (2) jazz musician

    (3) magician

    (4) hotel manager

    (5) White House aide

40. What is Hampton's greatest contribution to jazz history?

    (1) he created the National Medal of Arts

    (2) he played for presidents

    (3) he pioneered the early origins of jazz

    (4) he was a showman and bandleader

    (5) he played with who's who

**END OF EXAMINATION**

# Chapter 25

# Answers and Explanations for the Language Arts, Reading Test

## Answer Key

After taking the Language Arts, Reading Test in Chapter 24, use this section to check your answers.

| | | |
|---|---|---|
| 1. 3 | 15. 3 | 29. 2 |
| 2. 1 | 16. 4 | 30. 3 |
| 3. 3 | 17. 1 | 31. 4 |
| 4. 5 | 18. 2 | 32. 2 |
| 5. 1 | 19. 3 | 33. 5 |
| 6. 2 | 20. 1 | 34. 4 |
| 7. 1 | 21. 4 | 35. 2 |
| 8. 3 | 22. 4 | 36. 2 |
| 9. 4 | 23. 1 | 37. 1 |
| 10. 5 | 24. 2 | 38. 4 |
| 11. 1 | 25. 3 | 39. 2 |
| 12. 2 | 26. 5 | 40. 3 |
| 13. 2 | 27. 1 | |
| 14. 5 | 28. 4 | |

# Analysis of the Answers

If you aren't sure why an answer was incorrect, use this section to get quick explanations of the answers.

1. **3.** The poem takes place on a farm. Other answers, such as a barn, shed, or ditch can all be found on a farm, but aren't the best answers. A den refers to the fox's home.

2. **1.** Needles and yarn in lines 5 and 6 refer to knitting, which should lead you to believe that the woman is going to knit.

3. **3.** The moon has a silver color and is shaped like a horn. Bright stars, dew drops, fox's den, and dark shed are inappropriate answers.

4. **5.** The abandoned article is a hoe, and the drops of water are dew. The other articles were neither abandoned nor covered with dew.

5. **1.** God provides the comfort to combat feelings of fear. The other answers — air supply, sunset, evening, and stars — aren't related to being afraid.

6. **2.** The coming of evening symbolizes the end of life or death. Day's end, life, contentment, and happiness have different meanings than death.

7. **1.** Barbara was recruiting players for her marching band and saw Undershaft as a candidate. The other answers (meeting, earning pennies, stepdancing, and being in the Assembly) don't express her interest in Undershaft.

8. **3.** You know Undershaft had an impoverished youth because he had to stepdance for pennies to survive. During this time, poor children danced as an entertainment for people who might throw them pennies. This was a bit above begging, in that some entertainment was provided for the money donated.

9. **4.** Undershaft was a trombone player who could contribute his musical talents to the marching band. Stepdancing, pennies, or shillings aren't contributions to the band. Natural musical talent could be an answer, but because a more specific one exists, rule this one out.

10. **5.** Lomax criticizes Undershaft's work as a cannon manufacturer, implying that Undershaft won't get to heaven because of his work with cannons. Lomax may be a bitter person and he may be waxing philosophic, but those words don't describe his treatment of Undershaft. "Friendly" and "encouraging" certainly don't describe Lomax's demeanor, either.

11. **1.** Undershaft's motto could be "blood and fire" because he manufactures cannons used to kill people in war. Playing the trombone, being a sinner, belonging to the Church, and marching are not related to blood and fire.

12. **2.** She doesn't just preach about good works but operates a shelter to help poor people. This is a stronger reason than the others given, such as being in the Salvation Army, joining in marches, playing the concertina, or recruiting others.

13. **2.** If you journey up the Hudson, you pass the Kaatskill mountains. A dismembered branch, fresh green, and surrounding country aren't locations that are better at helping locate the mountains. Although asking directions would work, this approach isn't mentioned in the passage.

14. **5.** The wives use the magical hues and shapes of the mountains to forecast the weather. Other factors, such as the evening sky, gray vapors, or crown of glory, are not as good as indicators. A *barometer* is an instrument to measure air pressure.

15. **3.** You would first see light smoke curling from chimneys to help locate the village. The other sign, shingle-roofs, would not be seen as soon. Mountains, tents, and great antiquity are not signs for locating villages.

16. **4.** The Dutch colonists were the newcomers who founded the village. Peter Stuyvesant established the government. Appalachian family refers to the mountains. The voyager discovered the village in his travels.

17. **1.** Peter Stuyvesant, who had headed the government, had long since died. The other answers describe Stuyvesant as an original settler, a voyager, a soldier, and a governor, but don't refer to his death.

18. **2.** Settlers brought yellow bricks from Holland to build the houses. Other materials, such as weather-cocks, windows, gablefronts, and shingle roofs, were locally acquired.

19. **3.** Dave worked as a field-hand on the Hawkins's farm. He says that he hopes his mother will let him buy a gun with his wages from Hawkins. He was not unemployed, nor did he work at Joe's store, Sears Roebuck, or with his Ma.

20. **1.** He wanted to show the other field-hands that he wasn't scared of them. Dave mentions that he isn't afraid of them just before he first discusses buying the gun.

21. **4.** Dave had to purchase the gun through the Sears Roebuck catalog. Joe didn't keep guns in his store. Mr. Hawkins, Ma, or the field-hands are also not a source of guns.

22. **4.** Joe kept a yellow lantern glowing on the porch. Other answers, such as the smell of mackerel, the banging screen door, the coal oil smell, and the rear door, may also help to find the store but aren't the best indicators.

23. **1.** Dave lost his nerve and was afraid to ask Joe to see guns in the catalog. Other possibilities — too dark, home for supper, no money, and his mother's permission — are not the best answers.

24. **2.** Dave would have to convince Ma to give him the money to buy the gun. The other reasons, including finding it in the catalog, persuading Joe, returning the catalog, or ol' man Hawkins's permission, either aren't relevant or are not as important as Ma giving him the money.

25. **3.** The winter sky was grim and the streets were gritty in Chicago. Botanical frost refers to the windowpane. Snow was swept in heaps for block after block. Iron sky is but one characteristic, not the most important.

26. **5.** Louie was living with his mother, who was very ill and confined to bed. Other answers describing Louie's breakfast, his punctuality, his books, and his complexion are not good descriptions of the focus of his home life.

27. **1.** The men were hunting pigeons (game) for food. Target practice, out of the weather, hiding, going to the park are inappropriate answers if you've read the passage thoroughly.

28. **4.** They were able to knock several birds from the sky. Other factors, such as running indoors, size, rifles, and rooftop, don't relate to the question.

29. **2.** The hunters and their families must have been hungry for food to hunt pigeons in the street. Other adjectives — angry, happy, brave, and careless — don't adequately describe why they were hunting.

30. **3.** What Louie saw had nothing to do with him, and he didn't want to get involved. Other possible answers — hurrying to school, sick mother, friendships, or depression hunters — don't relate to why Louie wouldn't tell the police.

31. **4.** The batteries are installed in a camera. Other answers, such as electronics, children's toy, or flashlight, have no meaning in this excerpt. Point-and-shoot, while another term for a camera, is not the best answer.

32. **2.** The easiest model in which to replace batteries is in the point-and-shoot camera. Other answers — compact models, screw bottoms, and covers — don't relate directly to the question.

33. **5.** Avoid all the locations mentioned if you drop the battery cover. Sewer grate and tall grass are places where the cover could easily be lost. The rest of the answers refer to issues other than battery covers or getting lost.

34. **4.** To ensure that the batteries are correctly oriented, you must find the diagram and use it. Other choices, such as using four AAs or a single lithium, emptying the compartment, or checking inside the film box, don't answer the question.

35. **2.** You must check the battery icon to see whether the batteries are low. The LCD panel, compartment, lithium battery, and diagram markings aren't, according to the passage, correct answers.

36. **2.** The breakthrough was that black and white musicians were allowed to play together on the same stage. Music magic, Benny Goodman, and Lionel Hampton, and Hampton's death don't refer to race relations.

37. **1.** Hampton was considered great because of his longevity over 60 years as a jazz player. Other factors, such as playing with Sonny Rollins, playing the vibraphone, breaking a barrier, and his joy, aren't as important as the more than 60 years he spent as a jazz player.

38. **4.** Hampton's band was famous at the White House because it was the first black band to perform there. Other choices, such as showcasing jazz greats, including Dinah Washington, and the spirit of jazz may all be true, but they aren't the reason the band was famous at the White House. The band did not play for President Kennedy at the White House.

39. **2.** When the first paragraph refers to Hampton as someone who "joined Benny Goodman in a Manhattan ballroom," you're being told that the two performed together in that ballroom. In the fifth paragraph, Goodman is part of a list of the "who's who of jazz."

40. **3.** Hampton's greatest contribution to jazz history was his role as one of the pioneers in the early origins of jazz. The National Medal of Arts, playing for presidents, being a showman, and playing with who's who are not as important.

# Chapter 26

# The Mathematics Test: Parts I and II

## The Mathematics Test, Part 1

### Directions

The Mathematics Test consists of multiple-choice questions intended to measure general mathematics skills or problem-solving ability. The questions are based on short readings that often include a graph, chart, or figure.

You have 45 minutes to complete the 25 questions in this part of the test. Work carefully, but do not spend too much time on any one question. Be sure to answer every question.

Formulas you may need are given on the page before the first test question. Only some of the questions will require you to use a formula. Not all the formulas given will be needed.

Some questions contain more information than you will need to solve the problem; other questions do not give enough information. If the question does not give enough information to solve the problem, the correct answer choice is "not enough information given."

**The use of calculators is allowed in Part I only.**

Do not write in this test booklet. The test administrator will give you a blank paper for your calculations. Record your answers on the separate answer sheet provided. Be sure all information is properly recorded on the answer sheet.

To record your answers, fill in the numbered circle on the answer sheet that corresponds to the answer you select for each question in the test booklet.

---

**EXAMPLE:**

If a grocery bill totaling $15.75 is paid with a $20.00 bill, how much change should be returned?

(1)  $5.25

(2)  $4.75

(3)  $4.25

(4)  $3.75

(5)  $3.25

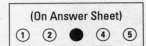

(On Answer Sheet)

① ② ● ④ ⑤

The correct answer is "$4.25"; therefore, answer space 3 would be marked on the answer sheet.

---

Do not rest the point of your pencil on the answer sheet while you are considering your answer. Make no stray or unnecessary marks. If you change an answer, erase your first mark completely. Mark only one answer space for each question; multiple answers will be scored as incorrect. Do not fold or crease your answer sheet. All test materials must be returned to the test administrator.

*Go on to next page*

**Calculator Directions**

To prepare the calculator for use the *first* time, press the ON (upper-rightmost) key. "DEG" will appear at the top-center of the screen and "0," at the right. This indicates the calculator is in the proper format for all your calculations.

To prepare the calculator for *another* question, press the ON or the red AC key. This clears any entries made previously.

To do any arithmetic, enter the expression as it is written. Press = (equals sign) when finished.

**EXAMPLE A:** 8 – 3 + 9

First press ON or AC

Enter the following: 8 , – , 3 , + , 9 , =

The correct answer is 14.

If the expression in parentheses is to be multiplied by a number, press × (multiplication sign) between the number and the parenthesis sign.

**EXAMPLE B:** 6(8 + 5)

First press ON or AC

Enter the following: 6 , × , ( , 8 , + , 5 , ) , =

The correct answer is 78.

To find the square root of a number

   ✔ Enter the number.
   ✔ Press the SHIFT (upper-leftmost) key ("SHIFT" appears at the top-left of the screen).
   ✔ Press $x^2$ (third from the left on top row) to access its second function: square root.

DO NOT press SHIFT and $x^2$ at the same time.

**EXAMPLE C:** $\sqrt{64}$

First press ON or AC

Enter the following: 6 , 4 , SHIFT , $x^2$ , =

The correct answer is 8.

To enter a negative number such as –8

   ✔ Enter the number without the negative sign (enter 8).
   ✔ Press the "change sign" ( +/– ) key, which is directly above the 7 key.

All arithmetic can be done with positive and/or negative numbers.

**EXAMPLE D:** –8 – (–5)

First press ON or AC

Enter the following: 8 , +/– , – , 5 , +/– , =

The correct answer is –3.

*Go on to next page*

**The Standard Grid**

Mixed numbers, such as 3½, cannot be entered in the standard grid. Instead, represent them as decimal numbers (in this case, 3.5) or fractions (in this case, ⁷⁄₂). No answer on a standard grid can be a negative number, such as –8.

To record your answer for a standard grid question

✔ Begin in any column that will allow your answer to be entered.

✔ Write your answers in the boxes on the top row.

✔ In the column beneath a fraction bar or decimal point (if any) and each number in your answer, fill in the bubble representing that character.

✔ Leave blank any unused column.

**EXAMPLE:**

The scale on a map indicates that ½ inch represents an actual distance of 120 miles. In inches, how far apart on the map will the two towns be if the actual distance between them is 180 miles?

The answer to the above example is ¾, or 0.75 inches. A few examples of how the answer could be gridded are shown below.

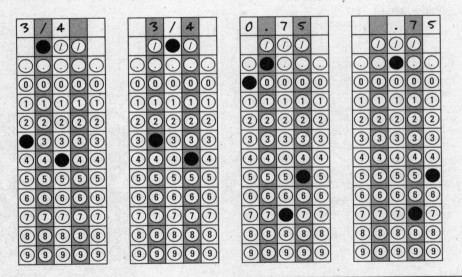

Points to remember:

✔ The answer sheet will be machine scored. **The circles must be filled in correctly.**

✔ Mark no more than one circle in any column.

✔ Grid only one answer even if there is more than one correct answer.

✔ Mixed numbers, such as 3½, must be gridded as 3.5 or ⁷⁄₂.

✔ No answer on a standard grid can be a negative number.

*Go on to next page*

**The Coordinate-Plane Grid**

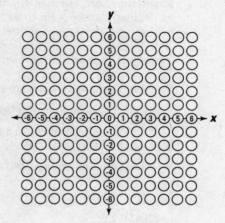

To record an answer on the coordinate-plane grid, you must have an *x*-value and a *y*-value. No answer for a coordinate-plane question will have a value that is a fraction or decimal.

**Mark only the <u>one</u> circle that represents your answer.**

**EXAMPLE:**

The coordinates of point A, shown on the graph below, are (2,–4).

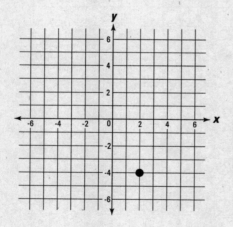

The coordinates of point B, not shown on the graph, are (–3,1). What is the location of point B?

DO NOT MARK YOUR ANSWER ON THE GRAPH ABOVE.

Mark your answer on the coordinate-plane grid on your answer sheet.

**CORRECT RESPONSE:**

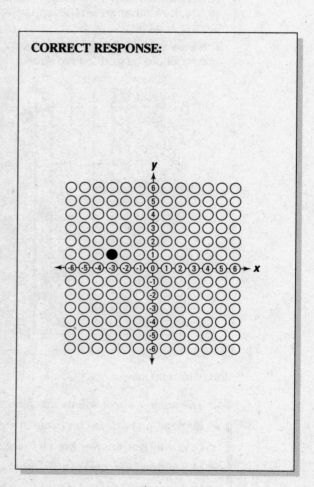

*Go on to next page*

**Formulas**

**AREA** of a:

| | |
|---|---|
| square | Area = side$^2$ |
| rectangle | Area = length × width |
| parallelogram | Area = base × height |
| triangle | Area = ½ × base × height |
| trapezoid | Area = ½ × (base$_1$ + base$_2$) × height |
| circle | Area = π × radius$^2$; π is approximately equal to 3.14 |

**PERIMETER** of a:

| | |
|---|---|
| square | Perimeter = 4 × side |
| rectangle | Perimeter = (2 × length) + (2 × width) |
| triangle | Perimeter = side$_1$ + side$_2$ + side$_3$ |

**CIRCUMFERENCE** of a circle — Circumference = π × diameter; π is approximately equal to 3.14

**VOLUME** of a:

| | |
|---|---|
| cube | Volume = side$^3$ |
| rectangular solid | Volume = length × width × height |
| square pyramid | Volume = ⅓ × (base edge)$^2$ × height |
| cylinder | Volume = π × radius$^2$ × height; π is approximately equal to 3.14 |
| cone | Volume = ⅓ × π × radius$^2$ × height; π is approximately equal to 3.14 |

**COORDINATE GEOMETRY**

distance between points = $\sqrt{(x_2 - x_1)^2 + (y_2 - y_1)^2}$; $(x_1, y_1)$ and $(x_2, y_2)$ are two points in a plane

slope of a line = $\frac{y_2 - y_1}{x_2 - x_1}$; $(x_1, y_1)$ and $(x_2, y_2)$ are two points on the line

**PYTHAGOREAN RELATIONSHIP**

$a^2 + b^2 = c^2$; $a$ and $b$ are legs, and $c$ is the hypotenuse of a right triangle

**MEASURES OF CENTRAL TENDENCY**

**mean** = $\frac{x_1 + x_2 + \cdots + x_n}{n}$; where the $x$'s are the values for which a mean is desired, and $n$ is the total number of values for $x$

**median** = the middle value of an odd number of *ordered* scores, and halfway between the two middle values of an even number of *ordered* scores.

**SIMPLE INTEREST** — interest = principal × rate × time

**DISTANCE** — distance = rate × time

**TOTAL COST** — total cost = (number of units) × (price per unit)

**DO NOT BEGIN TAKING THIS TEST UNTIL TOLD TO DO SO**

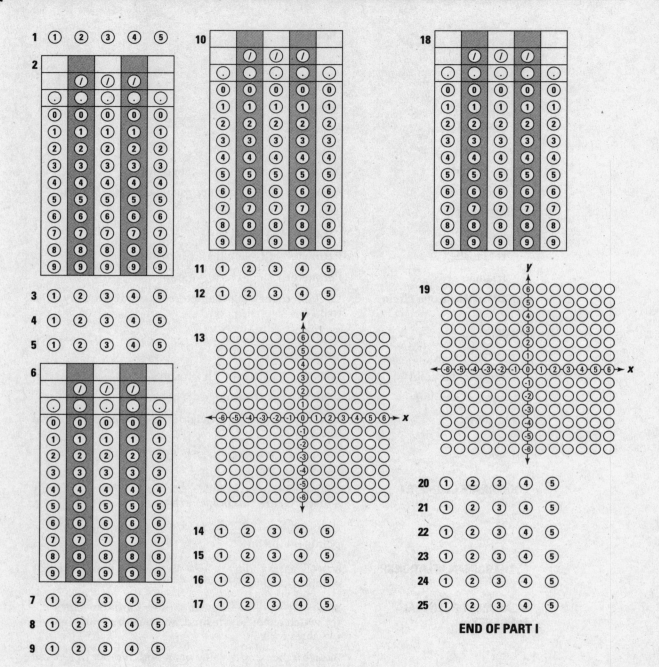

*Go on to next page*

**END OF PART I**

1. After measuring the area of his living room, Singh went shopping for a new carpet. What units should Singh use to tell the salesperson the size of the room?

   (1) cubic inches

   (2) gallons

   (3) feet

   (4) fathoms

   (5) miles

2. After asking instructions to a restaurant, Sarah was told it was 1,000 yards ahead, but her car's odometer reads distances in miles and tenths of miles. How many miles should she drive to find the restaurant to the nearest tenth? Write your answer on the standard grid on the answer sheet.

3. Arthur is making a circular carpet made up of small pieces of cloth glued to a backing. If he wants a carpet that is 7 feet across, how many square feet of backing does he need to cover?

   (1) 154

   (2) 46½

   (3) 83½

   (4) 24

   (5) 38½

4. The vertexes of a triangle are A(–6,4), B(–8,–6) and C(8,7). Which side is the longest?

   (1) AB

   (2) BC

   (3) CA

   (4) AC

   (5) not enough information given

Question 5 refers to the following graph.

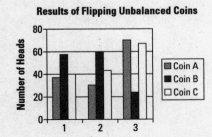

**Results of Flipping Unbalanced Coins**

5. As an experiment, a class flips three coins 100 times each and charted their results. The coins are not accurately balanced. From the chart, which coin during which series of tosses is closest to being balanced?

   (1) coin B, third set

   (2) coin C, third set

   (3) coin A, second set

   (4) coin B, first set

   (5) coin C, first set

6. Sam and Arnold were eating ice cream cones. Arnold wondered what volume of ice cream his cone would hold. Sam measured the cone and found it to be 2¼ inches across and 5½ inches high. How many cubic inches of ice cream would the cone hold? Record your answer on a standard grid on the answer sheet.

7. Donna was very involved with speed walking. In order to keep from getting too bored, she started counting how many breaths she takes for each of her steps. She figured that she takes 3 breaths for every 27-inch step. How many breaths does she take in a 1,000-yard walk?

   (1) 5332

   (2) 1280

   (3) 2126

   (4) 4767

   (5) 4000

8. Yvonne is studying a map. She is 47 miles due south of where she wants to go, but the road goes 17 miles due west to an intersection that then goes northeast to her destination. Approximately how much farther must she travel because of the way the road goes?

   (1) 3

   (2) 20

   (3) 16

   (4) 50

   (5) 45

*Go on to next page*

Questions 9 and 10 are based on the following information.

Carlos wants to buy a used car. He has been told that a car loses 4.3 cents from its book value for every mile over 100,000 that it has traveled. He sees just the car he wants, but it has 137,046 miles on the odometer. If the book value of the car is $13,500, what is the car actually worth?

9. Estimate the realistic value of the car to the nearest $10.

   (1) 10,907
   (2) 13,750
   (3) 87,046
   (4) 12,020
   (5) 12,000

10. Calculate the realistic value of the car to the nearest dollar. Record your answer on the standard grid on the answer sheet.

11. Elena wants to draw a mural on the wall of her house. The wall is 9 feet high and 17 feet long. In order to plan the mural, she draws a scale drawing of the area for the mural on a piece of paper 11.0 inches long. How high, in inches, should the drawing be to maintain scale?

   (1) 6.2
   (2) 5.8
   (3) 8.5
   (4) 9.0
   (5) 5.0

12. If the slope of a line is 0.75, and $y_2 = 36$, $y_1 = 24$, and $x_1 = 12$, what is the value of $x_2$?

   (1) 14
   (2) −28
   (3) 28
   (4) −14
   (5) 22

13. A line *DE* has a slope of 0 and a *y*-intercept (0,−4). Draw the *x*-intercept on the coordinate plane grid on the answer sheet. If there is no *x*-intercept, fill in the origin.

14. Valerie is planning her garden. She wants a circular flower bed that is 8 feet across with a row of petunias all around the edge. If petunias can be planted 1½ inches apart, how many petunias does she need?

   (1) 17
   (2) 220
   (3) 402
   (4) 137
   (5) 200

15. The probability of an event taking place, *P*, is equal to the number of ways a particular event can occur, divided by the total number of ways, *M*, or $P = N \div M$. To test this theory, a student removes all the picture cards from a deck. What is the probability that a card less than the number 6 will be drawn? (Aces are low in this case.)

   (1) 1 in 3
   (2) 1 in 5
   (3) 1 in 2
   (4) 1 in 4
   (5) 1 in 6

Questions 16 and 17 are based on the following information.

Peter's grades in his final year of high school classes are 81, 76, 92, 87, 79 and 83.

16. In order to get a scholarship, Peter's median grade must be above the median grade for the school, which was 82. By how many points is he above or below that standard?

   (1) 4
   (2) 2
   (3) 1
   (4) 0
   (5) 3

*Go on to next page* →

17. If Peter's goal is to graduate with a mean of 90%, by how many total points is he failing to achieve his goal?

    (1) 42

    (2) 43

    (3) 44

    (4) 45

    (5) 46

18. Olga has a propane-powered car. She was told it was safe to fill her cylindrical propane tank at a rate of 1¾ cubic feet per minute. If the propane tank measures 4.8 feet long and 2.1 feet in diameter and is empty, how long in minutes will it take to fill it? Record your answer on the standard grid on the answer sheet, rounded to one decimal.

19. A right triangle has its base drawn from (–4,–4) to (3,–4), and its perpendicular leg drawn parallel to the *y*-axis. If the perpendicular side is 9 units long, on the coordinate-plane grid, fill in the point where the hypotenuse intersects the perpendicular leg.

20. Consider the equation $E = mc^2$. If the value of *m* triples and the value of *c* remains constant, what is the effect on *E*?

    (1) 36 times larger

    (2) 9 times larger

    (3) 27 times larger

    (4) 3 times larger

    (5) no effect

21. An accident investigator calculates a car's speed during a skid by multiplying the following: the square root of the radius of the curve that the center of mass, *r*, follows × a constant, *k* × the drag factor of the road, μ. If the speed calculated was 47 miles per hour and the drag factor was 0.65, what was the radius of the curve that the car's center of mass follows?

    (1) 11.6

    (2) 8.5

    (3) 5.8

    (4) 4.9

    (5) not enough information given

22. Vladimir is designing gas tanks for trucks. The length of the tanks is fixed, but the diameter can vary from 3 to 4 feet. How many more cubic feet of gas does the largest tank hold?

    (1) 8.50

    (2) 3.00

    (3) 2.75

    (4) 4.75

    (5) not enough information given

Questions 23 through 25 are based on the following table.

| **Summary of Winning Numbers in Seven Consecutive Lottery Draws** | |
| --- | --- |
| *Draw Number* | *Winning Numbers* |
| 1 | 8, 10, 12, 23, 25, 39 |
| 2 | 1, 29, 31, 34, 40, 44 |
| 3 | 1, 14, 26, 38, 40, 45 |
| 4 | 1, 6, 14, 39, 45, 46 |
| 5 | 10, 12, 22, 25, 37, 44 |
| 6 | 13, 16, 20, 35, 39, 45 |
| 7 | 10, 16, 17, 19, 37, 42 |

23. Based only on the results in the table and assuming that there are 49 possible numbers in the set to be drawn, what are your chances of drawing a 1 in your first draw?

    (1) 1 in 343

    (2) 3 in 343

    (3) 3 in 7

    (4) 1 in 49

    (5) not enough information given

*Go on to next page* ⟩

24. If you had to pick one number in this lottery, what would be the odds based on these results that a number greater than 25 would appear in the winning numbers?

    (1) 26 in 49

    (2) almost certain

    (3) 20 in 49

    (4) 17 in 49

    (5) 21 in 26

25. Louise had a theory that the median of the winning numbers in each draw in this lottery would be very close. Considering the winning numbers presented, is Louise's hypothesis accurate?

    (1) not at all

    (2) almost always

    (3) about half the time

    (4) occasionally

    (5) about a quarter of the time

*Go on to next page*

# The Mathematics Test, Part II

### Directions

The Mathematics Test consists of multiple-choice questions intended to measure general mathematics skills or problem-solving ability. The questions are based on short readings that often include a graph, chart, or figure.

You have 45 minutes to complete the 25 questions in this part of the test. Work carefully, but do not spend too much time on any one question. Be sure to answer every question. If you finish early, you may go back to Part I, but without a calculator.

Formulas you may need are given on the page before the first test question. Only some of the questions will require you to use a formula. Not all the formulas given will be needed.

Some questions contain more information than you will need to solve the problem; other questions do not give enough information. If the question does not give enough information to solve the problem, the correct answer choice is "Not enough information given."

**The use of calculators is not allowed in Part II.**

Do not write in this test booklet. The test administrator will give you a blank paper for your calculations. Record your answers on the separate answer sheet provided. Be sure all information is properly recorded on the answer sheet.

To record your answers, fill in the numbered circle on the answer sheet that corresponds to the answer you select for each question in the test booklet.

---

**EXAMPLE:**

If a grocery bill totaling $15.75 is paid with a $20.00 bill, how much change should be returned?

(1)  $5.25

(2)  $4.75    (On Answer Sheet)

(3)  $4.25    ① ② ● ④ ⑤

(4)  $3.75

(5)  $3.25

The correct answer is "$4.25"; therefore, answer space 3 would be marked on the answer sheet.

---

Do not rest the point of your pencil on the answer sheet while you are considering your answer. Make no stray or unnecessary marks. If you change an answer, erase your first mark completely. Mark only one answer space for each question; multiple answers will be scored as incorrect. Do not fold or crease your answer sheet. All test materials must be returned to the test administrator.

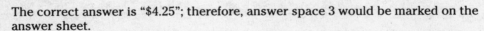

*Go on to next page*

### The Standard Grid

Mixed numbers, such as 3½, cannot be entered in the standard grid. Instead, represent them as decimal numbers (in this case, 3.5) or fractions (in this case, ⁷⁄₂). No answer on a standard grid can be a negative number, such as –8.

To record your answer for a standard grid question

- ✔ Begin in any column that will allow your answer to be entered.
- ✔ Write your answers in the boxes on the top row.
- ✔ In the column beneath a fraction bar or decimal point (if any) and each number in your answer, fill in the bubble representing that character.
- ✔ Leave blank any unused column.

---

**EXAMPLE:**

The scale on a map indicates that ½ inch represents an actual distance of 120 miles. In inches, how far apart on the map will the two towns be if the actual distance between them is 180 miles?

The answer to the above example is ¾, or 0.75 inches. A few examples of how the answer could be gridded are shown below.

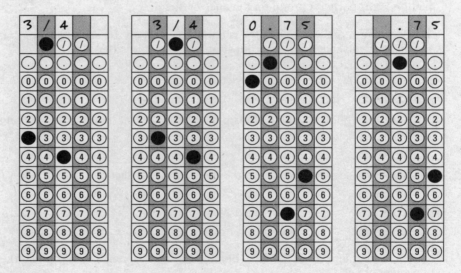

---

Points to remember:

- ✔ The answer sheet will be machine scored. **The circles must be filled in correctly.**
- ✔ Mark no more than one circle in any column.
- ✔ Grid only one answer even if there is more than one correct answer.
- ✔ Mixed numbers, such as 3½, must be gridded as 3.5 or ⁷⁄₂.
- ✔ No answer on a standard grid can be a negative number.

*Go on to next page* ⟶

**The Coordinate-Plane Grid**

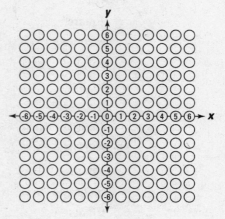

To record an answer on the coordinate-plane grid, you must have an *x*-value and a *y*-value. No answer for a coordinate-plane question will have a value that is a fraction or decimal.

**Mark only the <u>one</u> circle that represents your answer.**

**EXAMPLE:**

The coordinates of point A, shown on the graph below, are (2,–4).

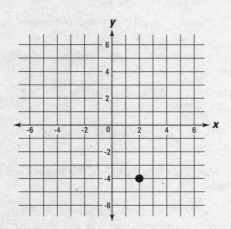

The coordinates of point B, not shown on the graph, are (–3,1). What is the location of point B?

DO NOT MARK YOUR ANSWER ON THE GRAPH ABOVE.

Mark your answer on the coordinate-plane grid on your answer sheet.

**CORRECT RESPONSE:**

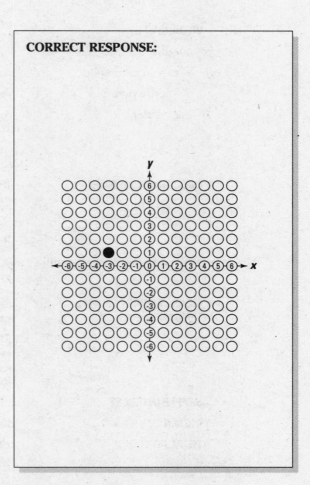

*Go on to next page*

## Formulas

**AREA** of a:

| | |
|---|---|
| square | Area = side$^2$ |
| rectangle | Area = length × width |
| parallelogram | Area = base × height |
| triangle | Area = ½ × base × height |
| trapezoid | Area = ½ × (base$_1$ + base$_2$) × height |
| circle | Area = π × radius$^2$; π is approximately equal to 3.14 |

**PERIMETER** of a:

| | |
|---|---|
| square | Perimeter = 4 × side |
| rectangle | Perimeter = (2 × length) + (2 × width) |
| triangle | Perimeter = side$_1$ + side$_2$ + side$_3$ |

**CIRCUMFERENCE** of a circle    Circumference = π × diameter; π is approximately equal to 3.14

**VOLUME** of a:

| | |
|---|---|
| cube | Volume = edge$^3$ |
| rectangular solid | Volume = length × width × height |
| square pyramid | Volume = ⅓ × (base)$^2$ × height |
| cylinder | Volume = π × radius$^2$ × height; π is approximately equal to 3.14 |
| cone | Volume = ⅓ × π × radius$^2$ × height; π is approximately equal to 3.14 |

**COORDINATE GEOMETRY**    distance between points = $\sqrt{(x_2 - x_1)^2 + (y_2 - y_1)^2}$; $(x_1, y_1)$ and $(x_2, y_2)$ are two points in a plane

slope of a line = $\frac{y_2 - y_1}{x_2 - x_1}$; $(x_1, y_1)$ and $(x_2, y_2)$ are two points on the line

**PYTHAGOREAN RELATIONSHIP**    $a^2 + b^2 = c^2$; $a$ and $b$ are legs, and $c$ is the hypotenuse of a right triangle

**MEASURES OF CENTRAL TENDENCY**    **mean** = $\frac{x_1 + x_2 + \cdots + x_n}{n}$; where the $x$'s are the values for which a mean is desired, and $n$ is the total number of values for $x$

**median** = the middle value of an odd number of *ordered* scores, and halfway between the two middle values of an even number of *ordered* scores.

**SIMPLE INTEREST**    interest = principal × rate × time

**DISTANCE**    distance = rate × time

**TOTAL COST**    total cost = (number of units) × (price per unit)

**DO NOT BEGIN TAKING THIS TEST UNTIL TOLD TO DO SO**

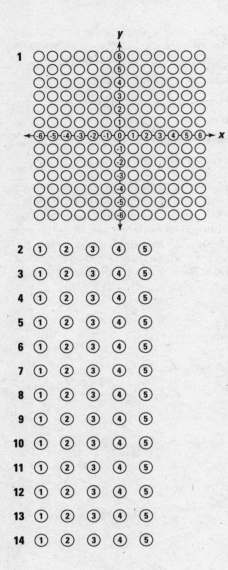

**1** (grid with x-y coordinate plane)

**2** ① ② ③ ④ ⑤

**3** ① ② ③ ④ ⑤

**4** ① ② ③ ④ ⑤

**5** ① ② ③ ④ ⑤

**6** ① ② ③ ④ ⑤

**7** ① ② ③ ④ ⑤

**8** ① ② ③ ④ ⑤

**9** ① ② ③ ④ ⑤

**10** ① ② ③ ④ ⑤

**11** ① ② ③ ④ ⑤

**12** ① ② ③ ④ ⑤

**13** ① ② ③ ④ ⑤

**14** ① ② ③ ④ ⑤

**15** (grid-in answer box)

| | / | / | / | |
|---|---|---|---|---|
| . | . | . | . | . |
| 0 | 0 | 0 | 0 | 0 |
| 1 | 1 | 1 | 1 | 1 |
| 2 | 2 | 2 | 2 | 2 |
| 3 | 3 | 3 | 3 | 3 |
| 4 | 4 | 4 | 4 | 4 |
| 5 | 5 | 5 | 5 | 5 |
| 6 | 6 | 6 | 6 | 6 |
| 7 | 7 | 7 | 7 | 7 |
| 8 | 8 | 8 | 8 | 8 |
| 9 | 9 | 9 | 9 | 9 |

**16** ① ② ③ ④ ⑤

**17** ① ② ③ ④ ⑤

**18** ① ② ③ ④ ⑤

**19** ① ② ③ ④ ⑤

**20** (grid-in answer box)

| | / | / | / | |
|---|---|---|---|---|
| . | . | . | . | . |
| 0 | 0 | 0 | 0 | 0 |
| 1 | 1 | 1 | 1 | 1 |
| 2 | 2 | 2 | 2 | 2 |
| 3 | 3 | 3 | 3 | 3 |
| 4 | 4 | 4 | 4 | 4 |
| 5 | 5 | 5 | 5 | 5 |
| 6 | 6 | 6 | 6 | 6 |
| 7 | 7 | 7 | 7 | 7 |
| 8 | 8 | 8 | 8 | 8 |
| 9 | 9 | 9 | 9 | 9 |

**21** ① ② ③ ④ ⑤

**22** ① ② ③ ④ ⑤

**23** (grid with x-y coordinate plane)

**24** ① ② ③ ④ ⑤

**25** ① ② ③ ④ ⑤

**END OF PART II**

*Go on to next page* ⟹

1. Jerri has a theory that she can increase her grades by 3 points for every hour she studies. She keeps track of her success on a graph by first drawing a goal point where her theory says her increase should be, and then graphing her actual increase in another color. If she uses the y-axis for the hours of study and the x-axis for her increase in points, where should she place her goal point after 2 hours of study? Place your answer on a coordinate plane grid on the answer sheet.

2. Sandra wants to paint the side of her staircase. The stairs are 9 feet tall and have a 10-foot base. How many square yards of wall must she paint?

    (1) 3
    (2) 4
    (3) 5
    (4) 6
    (5) 7

Question 3 refers to the following chart.

### Installed Geothermal-Electric Capacity in 2004

| Country | Installed Capacity (Megawatts) |
| --- | --- |
| China | 6 |
| El Salvador | 75 |
| Iceland | 86 |
| Italy | 502 |
| Japan | 275 |
| Mexico | 208 |
| New Zealand | 248 |
| Philippines | 64 |
| Russia | 26 |
| United States | 1,850 |
| Total for the world | 3,340 |

3. If the United States doubled its production of geothermal-electric capacity, how would this affect the total world capacity?

    (1) increase it to 6190 megawatts
    (2) increase it to 5190 megawatts
    (3) no change
    (4) decrease it to 6190 megawatts
    (5) decrease it to 5190 megawatts

4. Vivienne wants to clean out her rain gutters. She knows that her rain gutters are 29 feet above the ground. To be safe, the foot of her ladder should be set 6 feet out from the wall of the house. What is the height, in feet, of the shortest ladder she can use, if the tip of the ladder must reach 1 foot above the rain gutters?

    (1) 29
    (2) 29.7
    (3) 32.1
    (4) 30.6
    (5) 34.9

*Go on to next page*

Question 5 refers to the following table.

## Interest Rate Offered by Different Car Dealerships

| Dealer | Interest Rate Offered |
|--------|----------------------|
| A | Prime + 2% |
| B | 7.5% |
| C | ½ of prime + 5% |
| D | Prime + 20% of prime for administrative costs |

5. Donald is confused. He is looking for a new car, but each dealership offers him a different interest rate. If the prime lending rate is 6%, which dealer is offering Donald the best terms to finance his car?

   (1) Dealer D

   (2) Dealer C

   (3) Dealer B

   (4) Dealer A

   (5) not enough information given

6. The formula for average deviation in statistics is as follows:

   Average deviation = $\frac{|x|}{n}$, where $x$ is the deviation, $|x|$ is the absolute value of $x$, and $n$ is the number of values.

   If the values for the deviation are: $-7, +6, +2, -13, -9$ and $+17$, what is the average deviation?

   (1) 5

   (2) 6

   (3) 7

   (4) 8

   (5) 9

7. Henry wanted to find out how many people watched *Four's a Mob,* the newest sitcom. He did a survey of 12 of his favorite friends and found that 10 of them had seen the last episode. Knowing that the population of the United States is over 288,000,000, Henry calculated that 240,000,000 people watched his new favorite sitcom. What is wrong with Henry's conclusion?

   (1) there are more people than that in the United States

   (2) his sample is too small

   (3) some people may have gone out that evening

   (4) his calculation is wrong

   (5) nothing

Questions 8 and 9 are based on the following information.

In September, Ken and Ben wanted to lose some weight to be ready by the following July. They figured that by supporting each other, eating a balanced diet with reduced calories and exercising, they could lose 0.5 pound per week.

8. What Mathematical operations would you use to calculate the amount of weight they could lose between the beginning of September and the end of June?

   (1) division

   (2) counting and adding

   (3) division and counting

   (4) counting and multiplication

   (5) subtraction

*Go on to next page*

9. If they stuck to their plans, approximately how much could they each lose between the beginning of September and the end of June?

   (1) 20 pounds

   (2) 50 pounds

   (3) 30 pounds

   (4) 36 pounds

   (5) 48 pounds

10. Mary and Samantha are planning a 900-mile trip. Mary says that she can drive at an average speed of 45 miles per hour. Samantha says that she will fly, but it takes her 45 minutes to get to the airport and an hour and 15 minutes to get from the airport to her destination after she lands. If she has to be at the airport 3 hours before take-off and the airplane travels an average of 300 mph, how many hours will Samantha have to wait for Mary?

    (1) 2

    (2) 8

    (3) 9

    (4) 12

    (5) 16

Question 11 refers to the following information.

The Queenly Hat Company of Lansing, Michigan produces designer hats for women who feel that a hat completes an outfit. Their sales vary from quarter to quarter and factory to factory. The chart below reflects their sales for one year.

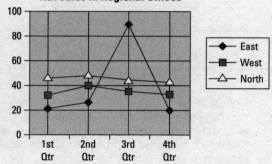

**Hat Sales in Regional Offices**

11. Of the three factories, which factories and in which quarters are sales figures approximately in the ratio of 2:1?

    (1) east and west in 2nd quarter

    (2) west and north in 3rd quarter

    (3) east and north in 3rd quarter

    (4) west and east in 1st quarter

    (5) east and west in 1st quarter

*Go on to next page*

Questions 12 and 13 are based on the following table.

### Life Expectancy for Urban Dwellers

| Age (in Years) | Males | Females |
|---|---|---|
| 10 | 61.4 | 67.3 |
| 20 | 50.3 | 55.1 |
| 30 | 40.4 | 45.1 |
| 40 | 32.8 | 36.5 |
| 50 | 22.1 | 26.4 |
| 60 | 15.2 | 17.8 |
| 70 | 9.9 | 10.7 |

12. From the data presented in the table, what interpretation could be reached?

    (1) women age better than men

    (2) men live longer than women in all age categories

    (3) the number of years yet to live decreases with increasing age

    (4) urban dwellers live longer than rural dwellers in all age categories

    (5) not enough information given

13. From the data presented, hypothesize why women live longer than men in an urban environment?

    (1) women take better care of their health

    (2) a greater percentage of men work in an urban setting

    (3) men are involved in more auto accidents in an urban setting

    (4) rural populations live longer

    (5) not enough information given

14. The cost of a finished item is equal to 2 times the production cost, plus 120% of the overhead costs at the retail level, plus profit. If three stores, A, B, and C each sell the product, and store B has a 50% raise in rent, how will this affect the selling price for the item?

    (1) the selling price would go down

    (2) the selling price would remain the same

    (3) the selling price would go up

    (4) everybody would raise their prices

    (5) everybody would lower their prices

15. Sol wanted to write the population of the United States in scientific notation for a project he was working on. If the population of the United States is 288,257,352, what is the value for $x$, if he wrote the population out as $28.8 \times 10^x$? Mark your answer on the standard grid on the answer sheet.

16. Harry and Karry are preparing for the big race. They have been keeping track of their times in the following table.

### Comparative Times in Seconds

| Harry (seconds) | Karry (seconds) |
|---|---|
| 15.6 | 15.9 |
| 14.9 | 16.1 |
| 16.0 | 15.8 |
| 15.8 | 16.2 |
| 16.1 | 14.8 |

Compare their mean times.

(1) Karry is slightly faster

(2) Harry is slightly slower

(3) they are about even

(4) Karry has a higher mean time

(5) Harry has a higher mean time

*Go on to next page*

17. Maria bought an apartment. The total floor area is 1,400 square feet. If the ceilings are 9 feet high, and her air system withdraws and replaces 63 cubic feet of air each minute, how long in minutes does it take to withdraw and replace all the air in her apartment?

    (1) 180
    (2) 200
    (3) 220
    (4) 240
    (5) 260

18. Peter is emptying his swimming pool. He can pump 9 cubic feet of water per minute. If his pool measures 45 feet by 12 feet with an average depth of 4 feet, when will his pool be empty if he starts pumping at noon on Tuesday?

    (1) 9:00 a.m. on Wednesday
    (2) 4:00 a.m. on Wednesday
    (3) 6:00 p.m. on Tuesday
    (4) 2:00 p.m. on Tuesday
    (5) 4:00 p.m. on Tuesday

19. Mohammed works in sales. He compares his average paychecks for the last four weeks and finds that he has earned an average of $420.00 per week for the four-week month. If he earned $480.00 the first week, $400.00 the third week, and $550.00 the final week, how much did he earn the second week of the month?

    (1) $250.00
    (2) $280.00
    (3) $340.00
    (4) $190.00
    (5) $300.00

20. Georgia started shopping with $500.00 in her purse. When she returned home after shopping she had $126.00 in her purse and $83 in credit card receipts. How much did she spend shopping? Record your answer in dollars on the standard grid on the answer sheet.

21. If you open a can flat along the seam and cut almost all the way around each end, what shape would you end up with?

    (1) a circle
    (2) a rectangle with a circle on each end
    (3) a rectangle
    (4) a circle with two rectangles on each end
    (5) a cone

22. Sonya's car uses gasoline in direct proportion to her speed. If she increases her average speed by 10 miles per hour to save time, what is the economic consequence?

    (1) she would save time
    (2) she would save money
    (3) she would arrive at about the same time
    (4) she would spend more money on fuel
    (5) she would spend the same amount as before

23. A circle is drawn with its center at the origin and a diameter of 8 units. Where will the circumference intersect the negative y-axis. Mark this point on the coordinate plane grid on the answer sheet.

*Go on to next page* ➡

24. An accurate fuel gauge reads ⅛ full. If the fuel tank holds 24 gallons, how many gallons of fuel will fill it?

    (1) 18
    (2) 19
    (3) 20
    (4) 21
    (5) 22

25. As part of a mathematics test, Ying was given the following equations to solve:

    $4x + 2y = 20$

    $2x + 6y = 35$

    What is the value of $y$?

    (1) 4
    (2) 5
    (3) 6
    (4) 7
    (5) 8

**END OF EXAMINATION**

*Go on to next page*

# Chapter 27

# Answers and Explanations for the Mathematics Tests

· · · · · · · · · · · · · · · · · · · · · · · · · · · · · · · · · · · · · · · · · · · · · · · · ·

## Answer Key (for Part 1)

After taking the Mathematic Test, Part I in Chapter 26, use this section to check your answers.

1. 3

2. 0.6 (on standard grid)

3. 5

4. 2

5. 4

6. 7.29 (on standard grid)

7. 5

8. 2

9. 4

10. 11,907 (on standard grid)

11. 2

12. 3

13.

14. 5

15. 3

16. 4

17. 1

18. 9.5 (on standard grid)

19.

20. 4

21. 5

22. 5

23. 4

24. 3

25. 4

# Analysis of the Answers for Part 1

If you aren't sure why an answer was incorrect, use this section to get explanations of the answers.

1. **3.** This problem tests your ability to select appropriate units of measure. Carpets are usually measured in feet. A typical example is a $9 \times 12$ carpet, which measures 9 feet in one direction and 12 feet in the other.

2. **0.6 (on standard grid).** 1,000 yards is about 0.57 miles $(1,000 \div 1,760 = 0.568)$. Odometers usually read to one decimal point, so she should drive about 0.6 miles, which would be just past the restaurant.

3. **5.** This question tests your skills in algebra by asking you to solve an equation. Arthur needs a circle of backing 7 feet across; that is, the diameter is 7 feet. The area of a circle is $\pi r^2$. The radius is ½ of the diameter, and $\pi = 3.14$. The area equals $(3.14)(3.5)(3.5) = 38.465$. The closest answer is 5.

4. **2.** This question tests your skill in geometry by asking you to calculate the lengths of sides of a triangle when given the *vertexes* (corners of a triangle).

| Side | Calculation | Length |
|------|-------------|--------|
| AB | $\sqrt{(-8-[-6])^2 + (-6-4)^2} = 10.20$ | 10.20 |
| BC | $\sqrt{(-8-[-8])^2 + (7-[-6])^2} = 20.62$ | 20.62 |
| CA | $\sqrt{(-8-[-6])^2 + (-7-4)^2} = 14.32$ | 14.32 |

BC is the longest side.

If you want a general idea of which side is longest, sketch it out quickly. A sketch isn't necessary, because you can calculate the length of the sides and compare them.

5. **4.** This question asks you to draw an inference from a chart. Looking carefully at the table, coin B, first set, comes closest to 50%, which is the theoretical chance of a head or tail landing when the coin is balanced.

6. **7.29 (on standard grid).** This question tests your understanding of algebra by asking you to use the equation for the volume of a cone to answer a question. You also need to know that the distance across a circle is the *diameter,* which is twice the radius. You substitute numbers into the equation $V = \frac{1}{3}\pi \times \text{radius}^2 \times \text{height}$, which is $(\frac{1}{3})(3.14)(1\frac{1}{8})^2(5\frac{1}{2}) = 7.29$ (rounded).

7. **5.** This problem asks you to solve a problem using basic operations. If Donna takes 3 breaths for every 27-inch step, and 1,000 yards is 36,000 inches. She took $36,000 \div 27 = 1333.3$ steps. If she took 3 breaths per step, she took $3 \times 1333.3 = 3999.9$ or 4000 breaths during her 1,000-yard walk.

8. **2.** This problem is a test of your knowledge in how to use the Pythagorean Relationship. Sketch out a map for this problem: Due south and due west are at right angles. So, Yvonne's journey is a triangle, with the last part of Yvonne's journey as the hypotenuse. Pythagoras (the guy who, as you may expect, came up with the Pythagorean Relationship) said that the square of the hypotenuse of a right triangle is equal to the sum of the squares of the other two sides. Thus, the square of the last leg of the journey equals $47^2 + 17^2 = 2,498$. The $\sqrt{2,498} = 49.98$. Since none of the numbers in this problem has any numbers beyond the decimal point, you can round the answer to 50. However, the question asks how much *farther* she traveled: She ended up traveling $17 + 50 = 67$ miles and would have traveled 47 miles. $67 - 47 = 20$ miles farther.

9. **4.** If you want to use approximate values in this problem, you could say that the car depreciates about 4 cents a mile over 100,000 miles. This car is about 37,000 miles over that milestone, which means it has depreciated about $4 \times 37,000$ cents. You want to solve this in terms of dollars, though, and because each dollar has 100 cents. To change cents into dollars, you divide by 100: $4 \times 370 = 1,480$.

   You can then subtract this approximate value from the original price: $13,500 - $1,480 = $12,020.

10. **11,907 (on standard grid).** Using the same calculation as problem #9, but using exact values, you get $13,500 - (4.3 \times 37,046) \div 100 = 11,907.02$ or $11,907$, when rounded to the nearest dollar.

11. **2.** This problem tests your skills in geometry by asking you to solve a problem involving similarity of geometrical figures. In order to draw a scale drawing, the lengths and widths must be reduced in the same ratio. If the wall is 17 feet or ($17 \times 12 = 204$ inches), and the paper is 11 inches long, the ratio of paper length to real length is 11:204. The width of the drawing must stay in the same ratio. If the height of the drawing is $H$, then 11:204 = $H(9 \times 12)$ or 11:204 = $H(108)$. $\frac{11}{204} = \frac{H}{108}$. By cross multiplying, you get $H = (11 \times 108) \div 204 = 5.8$. Note that the answer is rounded.

12. **3.** This question tests your skills in algebra by asking you to evaluate a term in an equation. The equation for the slope of a line is $= \frac{y_2 - y_1}{x_2 - x_1}$.

   Substituting into the equation, you get $0.75 = \frac{36 - 24}{x_2 - 12}$.

   Then, because 0.75 is the same thing as ¾, you can say the following: $\frac{3}{4} = \frac{12}{x_2 - 12}$.

   Cross multiplying, you get $3(x_2 - 12) = 4 \times 12$

   $3x_2 - 36 = 48$

   $3x_2 = 48 + 36$

   $3x_2 = 84$

   $x_2 = \frac{84}{3} = 28$

13. **(0,0) on coordinate plane grid.** Geometry and measurement are tested in this question. You're asked to remember that any line with slope 0 is parallel to the $x$-axis. Because the question asks you to fill in the origin if the slope is parallel to the $x$-axis, you fill in (0,0).

14. **5.** This question tests your skills in geometry by solving a problem involving the circumference of a circle. Valerie is planting petunias around the circumference of a circle with diameter 8. The formula for circumference = $\pi \times$ diameter = $3.14 \times 8 = 25.12$ feet = $25.12 \times 12 = 301.44$ inches. She would plant a petunia every 1×1/2 inches (1.5 inches). The number of petunias she could plant is 200.96.

   Of course, you can't plant less than one petunia, so the answer has to be 200.

15. **3.** You're being tested on your skills in calculating a probability. Use the formula given ($P = N \div M$) to calculate the results. To draw a card less than 6, the possible cards to be drawn are 5 (less than 6) times 4 (the number of suits) = 20. The total possible number of cards is 52 (total cards in a deck) minus the picture cards (4 jacks, 4 queens, and 4 kings) is $52 - 12 = 40$. Now, using the equation, the probability is $20 \div 40 = ½$. This is another way of writing 1 in 2.

16. **4.** This question tests your skill in statistics by asking you to solve a problem involving the median of a group of numbers. Peter's median grade was 82, which is found by putting his marks in ascending order: 76, 79, 81, 83, 87, 92 and taking the grade that's right in the middle. If you had an odd amount of numbers, choosing the grade that's in the middle would be easy. Because there are an even number of numbers, the median is the mean (average) of the two middle numbers, or $\frac{81 + 83}{2} = 82$.

17. **1.** This question is a test of your skills in data analysis. Peter's average points was $(81 + 76 + 92 + 87 + 79 + 83) \div 6 = 83$. He failed to meet his goal by 7%. Each percent is equivalent to one point per subject, or $7 \times 6 = 42$ points.

18. **9.5 (on standard grid).** You're being tested on your skills in measurement involving uniform rates, such as miles per hour, gallons per minute, or, in this case, cubic feet per minute. The tank fills at a uniform rate, and this means you can do the question without getting involved in a series of calculations. The volume of a cylinder = $\pi \times radius^2 \times height = 3.14 \times (2.1/2 \times 2.1/2) \times 4.8 = 16.6$. The safe fill rate is 1¾ or 1.75 cubic feet per minute. It would take $16.6 \div 1.75 = 9.5$ (rounded) minutes to fill the tank.

19. **(3,5) on the coordinate plane grid.** One vertex of the triangle is (3,–4) — the point on the x-axis, 3, is the one you want to use. Therefore, a point 9 units long, parallel to the y-axis and 3 units to the right of it is at the point (3,5).

20. **4.** This question tests your knowledge of equations, by asking you analyze how a change in one quantity in a exponential equation, $E = mc^2$, results in a change in the other quantity. The variation between $E$ and $m$ in this function is *linear* and *direct;* which means that whatever happens to $m$ also happens to $E$. If $m$ is 3 times larger, so is $E$.

21. **5.** This question tests your ability to figure out when you don't have enough information to complete a problem. Without the value of the constant, the answer can be anything.

22. **5.** Without the length of the tank, you do not have enough information to answer the question.

23. **4.** This question tests your skill in probability. If there are 49 possible numbers in a set, the probability of drawing any one number is 1 in 49.

24. **3.** This problem tests your skills in data analysis by asking you to make inferences from data. If there are 49 numbers drawn in each draw, the odds of drawing a number greater than 25 is 20 in 49. If you count the numbers greater than 25 in the table, you find 20 of them.

Although there is a lot of data in the table, lottery draws are *discrete events* (not dependent one on another), and the results of one don't affect the results of another. Thus, you can consider only one draw for this question.

25. **4.** This is a test of your knowledge of statistics and measures of central tendency (in this case, the median). Consider the following adaptation of the table. (The median is always the middle number when numbers are lined up from smallest to largest; when you have an even amount of numbers, as you do here, take the two middle numbers, add them, and divide by 2.)

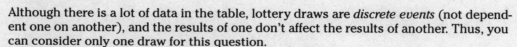

### Summary of Winning Numbers in Seven Consecutive Lottery Draws

| Draw Number | Winning Numbers | Median |
|---|---|---|
| 1 | 8, 10, 12, 23, 25, 39 | 17.5 |
| 2 | 1, 29, 31, 34, 40, 44 | 32.5 |
| 3 | 1, 14, 26, 38, 40, 45 | 32.0 |
| 4 | 1, 6, 14, 39, 45, 46 | 26.5 |
| 5 | 10, 12, 22, 25, 37, 44 | 23.5 |
| 6 | 13, 16, 20, 35, 39, 45 | 27.5 |
| 7 | 10, 16, 17, 19, 37, 42 | 18.0 |

Louise's theory is a curious one in that she seems to have no basis for it. When considering the numbers presented, two of the medians are close, so the best answer is "occasionally."

# Answer Key (for Part 11)

After taking the Mathematic Test, Part II in Chapter 26, use this section to check your answers.

1.

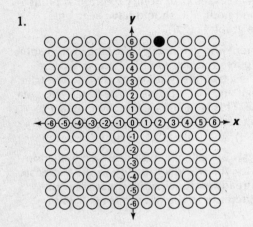

2. 3

3. 2

4. 4

5. 1

6. 5

7. 2

8. 4

9. 1

10. 4

11. 3

12. 3

13. 5

14. 3

15. 7 (on standard grid)

16. 4

17. 2

18. 5

19. 1

20. 457 (on standard grid)

21. 2

22. 4

23.

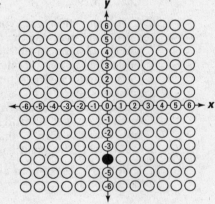

24. 4

25. 2

# Analysis of the Answers for Part II

If you aren't sure why an answer was incorrect, use this section to get explanations of the answers.

1. **(2,6) on coordinate plane grid.** This problem assesses your ability to graph a point based on information presented. On her second hour, she should have seen an increase of $2 \times 3$, or 6 marks. The point on the graph is (2,6).

2. **3.** This question tests your skills in measurement and geometry by asking you to solve a question involving congruence of figures (figures that are identical are said to be *congruent*). The wall at the side of a staircase is a triangle that's congruent to the triangle formed by the staircase, which is 9 feet high and 10 feet wide at the base. The area of a triangle is ½ base × height = ½($10 \times 9$) = 45. This is in square feet. To convert to square yards, you divide by 9, because 9 square feet equals one square yard. 45 ÷ 9 = 5 square yards.

3. **2.** This question tests your skills in data analysis by asking you to draw a conclusion from a table. If any country doubled its capacity, the world's capacity would increase. Because the capacity of the United States is already included at its present level, doubling the U.S. capacity means adding the increase to the world's total: 3,340 + 1,850 = 5,190.

4. **4.** This question tests your skills in geometry and measurement by asking you to solve a problem involving the Pythagorean Relationship. The ladder, the wall of the house, and the distance from the wall to the bottom of the ladder form a right triangle. If the ladder has to extend one foot above the rain gutters, the wall side of the triangle is 29 + 1 = 30 feet long. The other side of the triangle is 6 feet. Using the Pythagorean Relationship ($a^2 + b^2 = c^2$), hypotenuse$^2$ = $30^2 + 6^2$ = 936. The length of the hypotenuse is the square root of 936. You probably can't do square roots in your head, but you can square 30 to get 900 and square 31 to get 961, so you can get pretty close. You can estimate that the correct answer is close to 30 because this is the closest to the square root of 936. The exact answer, if you use a calculator, is 30.6.

5. **1.** This is a test of your ability to use number operations. If you adapt the table, it looks like this:

### Interest Rate Offered by Different Car Dealerships

| Dealer | Interest Rate Offered | Equivalent Rate |
|--------|----------------------|-----------------|
| A | Prime + 2% | 8% (6% + 2%) |
| B | 7.5% | 7.5% |
| C | ½ of prime + 5% | 8% ( 1/2 of 6% + 5% = 3% + 5%) |
| D | Prime + 20% of prime for administration | 7.2% (6% + [20% of 6%] = 6% + 1.2%) |

Dealer D is offering him the best terms for financing the car.

6. **5.** This is a test of your skill in algebra, because you're asked to use an equation to solve a problem.

The *absolute value* (what's inside the two vertical lines) of a number is its value without regard to its sign. So, the absolute value of a negative number is always a positive number.

This means that the average deviation is (7+6+2+13+9+17)/6 = 54/6 = 9. Because the absolute values are used, the numbers without the signs are used.

7. **2.** Two principles of statistics are that for the results to be valid, samples must be large and random. In this case, the sample is too small to tell anyone anything of statistical significance, and the entire sample consists of friends, not randomly selected people.

8. **4.** This question tests your skill in number operations by asking you to select the appropriate operations to solve this problem. To solve it, you count the number of weeks between September and the end of June and multiply by 0.5 (that is, 0.5 pound) to get the answer.

9. **1.** This question tests your skill in using estimation to solve a problem involving number operations. There are ten months between the beginning of September and the end of June. If you estimate that there are 4 weeks in each month (there are actually about 4.3 weeks per months), there are 40 weeks in this period of time. Each of them could lose about 20 pounds.

10. **4.** This question tests your skills in measurement to solve a problem involving uniform rates. If Mary can drive at an average speed of 45 miles per hour, it will take her $900 \div 45 = 20$ hours to drive the 900 miles. Samantha, on the other hand, will travel at 300 miles per hour on a plane for a time of $900 \div 300 = 3$ hours, but will add $45 + 75$ (1 hour and 15 minutes is 75 minutes) $+ 180$ (that's 3 hours in minutes) $= 300$ minutes. 300 minutes is 5 hours ($300 \div 60$). Her total trip would be 3 hours $+ 5$ hours $= 8$ hours in duration, or 12 hours shorter than Mary's trip.

11. **3.** Looking at the graph, in the 3rd quarter, the east seems to have produced twice as many hats as the north plant.

   This answer is considered an approximation because the graphs are not perfectly accurate.

12. **3.** This question tests your ability to interpret data presented in a table. The data presented is the number of years left to live at different age levels. The only interpretation that can be reached from this data is that the number of years yet to live decreases with increasing age.

   Read the answers as carefully as you read the questions. Women may have a greater life expectancy, but that doesn't necessarily mean they age better or worse than men. That is a topic for another question.

13. **5.** This question tests your skills in data analysis by asking you to evaluate arguments. You are also asked to discover whether you have enough information to decide on a cause for women living longer than men. In this case, you don't have enough information in the table to develop any hypothesis.

14. **3.** This question tests your skills in analysis by asking you to explain how a change in one quantity results in change in another quantity. The price of the article is set by a linear function involving the *overhead* (the costs of doing business that don't change with how many products you sell — things like rent, utility bills, salaries, and so on), the cost of acquiring the item, and the profit. If any of these go up, the selling price goes up.

15. **7 (on standard grid).** This question tests your skills in number operations by asking you to write a large number in scientific notation. To write 288,257,352 in scientific notation, you start with an approximation — 288,000,000 is close enough. The number of zeros defines the power of $x$. The population could be written as $288 \times 10^6$. Because Sol wants to write it more properly as $28.8 \times$ a power of ten, the power would have to be one higher, or 7.

16. **4.** This is a test of your skills in statistics, by asking you to compare measurements of central tendency (the *means* or *averages*). Harry's mean time is $(15.6 + 14.9 + 16.0 + 15.8 + 16.1) \div 5 = 15.68$. Karry's mean time is $(15.9 + 16.1 + 15.8 + 16.2 + 14.8) \div 5 = 15.76$. Karry has a higher mean time (which means that Harry is slightly faster).

17. **2.** This question tests your skill in measurement by asking you to solve a problem involving volume. If the total floor area is 1,400 square feet and the ceilings are 9 feet high, the volume of the apartment is $1,400 \times 9 = 12,600$ cubic feet. If the air system can replace 63 cubic feet per minute, it requires $12,600 \div 63 = 200$ minutes to replace all the air.

18. **5.** This is a test of your skills in measurement and geometry. You're being asked to solve a problem involving uniform rates. Peter's swimming pool holds $45 \times 12 \times 4 = 2160$ cubic feet of water. He can pump 9 cubic feet per minute. It would take him $2160 \div 9 = 240$ minutes. To get from hours to minutes, divide by 60 (because every hour has 60 minutes). $240 \div 60 = 4$ hours to empty his pool. Peter would finish at 4:00 p.m. on Tuesday.

An easy way to do this is to divide one number by 9 first. $45 \div 9 = 5$, then multiply: $5 \times 12 \times 4 = 240$. This is easier to do in your head than the long way.

19. **1.** This question tests your skill in algebra by asking you to analyze data used to calculate the mean of a set of numbers. If Mohammed earned an average of $420.00 for 4 weeks, he earned a total of $1,680.00. The other 3 weeks he earned $480.00 + $400.00 + $550.00 = $1,430.00. The other week he earned $1,680.00 – $1,430.00 = 250.00.

20. **457 (on standard grid).** This tests your skills in number operations. Georgia spent $500.00 – $126.00 = $374.00 plus $83.00 in credit card purchases. $374.00 + $83.00 = $457.00, or 457 in dollars on the standard grid.

21. **2.** This tests your skills in geometry and spatial visualization. If you opened a can flat along the seam, you would have a rectangle along with a circle on each end.

22. **4.** This question tests your skills by asking you to read carefully to answer a question. If Sonya's car uses gasoline in direct proportion to her speed, the faster she goes, the more gas she uses. The more gas she uses, the more it cost her to drive, and this is an economic consequence. Answer 1 is not an economic consequence, although it is true in fact.

Read the answers carefully. A right answer that doesn't answer the question is wrong.

23. **(0,–4) on coordinate plane grid.** If the center is at the origin, and the diameter (twice the radius) is 8 units, the circle it will intersect each of the axes (that's the plural of axis) at a distance of 4 units from it. Therefore, it intersects the negative $y$-axis at (0,–4).

24. **4.** If the gauge reads ⅛ full, it has $24 \div 8 = 3$ gallons of fuel left in it. Because it holds 24 gallons, it needs $24 – 3 = 21$ gallons to fill it.

25. **2.** This is a test of your skills in algebra. You are asked to solve a system of linear equations.

To solve this system, you have to eliminate $x$ by multiplying each equation by a number that allows you to subtract one from the other and end up with just $y$s. Here's how:

Multiply the second equation by 2 and leave the first equation as it is (or multiply by 1, which is the same thing).

$1(4x + 2y = 20) = 4x + 2y = 20$

$2(2x + 6y = 35) = 4x + 12y = 70$

Subtract, and you get $10y = 50$; $y = 5$.

(Note that you can also multiply the second equation by –2 and add the two equations together. Either way gets you the same answer.)

# Part V
# The Part of Tens

# In this part . . .

This part includes lists of tens to amaze, astonish, astound, amuse, clarify, edify, educate, elucidate, expound, and explain. (Note that we use *ten* verbs here.)

This part gives you tips for succeeding on the GED tests, plus ideas of what to avoid doing at all costs. We also dispel some common GED myths and give you some ideas on how you can use your diploma after you master the subject areas tested.

# Chapter 28

# Ten Ways to Improve Your GED Test Scores

• • • • • • • • • • • • • • • • • • • • • • • • • • • • • • • • • • • • • • • • • • • • • • • • • • • • •

### In This Chapter

▶ Finding ways to improve your skills for each test

▶ Giving yourself time to study and sleep

▶ Preparing yourself for the big day

• • • • • • • • • • • • • • • • • • • • • • • • • • • • • • • • • • • • • • • • • • • • • • • • • • • • •

**O**f course you want to do well on the GED — otherwise, you wouldn't be reading this book. But we also know that your time is limited, so this chapter gives you ten (er, eleven — we got carried away!) ideas and tips for doing well on your tests.

## Studying Subject-Matter Books

If you've taken one or both sets of practice tests in this book (see Parts III and IV), you may have identified key areas in which you're lacking skills. Although those practice tests can't predict your score, they do give you practice and a general idea of your strengths and weaknesses. If you didn't get 80% correct on any of the sample tests, you need to improve your skills in that area.

 We recommend that you visit your local bookstore or library for the many Dummies, CliffsNotes, and CliffsQuickReview books (all published by Wiley Publishing, Inc.) that are meant just for students. For example, consider the following Dummies books, which are fun, interesting, and easy to read, and can either improve your skills or simply make you more familiar with (and, therefore, more comfortable with) certain subjects.

- ✔ *Algebra For Dummies* by Mary Jane Sterling (mathematics)
- ✔ *Anatomy and Physiology For Dummies* by Donna Rae Siegfried (science)
- ✔ *Biology For Dummies* by Donna Rae Siegfried (science)
- ✔ *Astronomy For Dummies* by Stephen P. Maran (science)
- ✔ *Congress For Dummies* by David Silverberg, Dennis Hastert, and Tom Daschle (social studies)
- ✔ *English Grammar For Dummies* by Geraldine Woods (language arts)
- ✔ *Everyday Math For Dummies* by Charles Seiter, Ph.D. (mathematics)
- ✔ *Geography For Dummies* by Charles Heatwole (social studies, science)
- ✔ *Geometry For Dummies* by Wendy Arnone, Ph.D. (mathematics)
- ✔ *Poetry For Dummies* by The Poetry Center, John Timpane, and Maureen Watts (language arts)

- *Politics For Dummies,* 2nd Edition by Ann DeLaney (social studies)
- *Shakespeare For Dummies* by John Doyle and Ray Lischner (language arts)
- *Supreme Court For Dummies* by Lisa Paddock (social studies)
- *The Civil War For Dummies* by Keith D. Dickson (social studies)
- *U.S. History For Dummies* by Steve Wiegand (social studies)
- *Vocabulary For Dummies* by Laurie E. Rozakis, Ph.D. (language arts)
- *World History For Dummies* by Peter Haugen (social studies)
- *World War II For Dummies,* by Keith D. Dickson (social studies)

More Dummies books come out every month. To find out what books may have been published since this book was written, check out www.dummies.com.

In addition, consider browsing through the Dummies travel books to help with social studies. You may also want to review some of the Dummies workplace books on managing people and running a business to get acquainted with workplace reading material, which often appears on the Language Arts, Reading test.

The CliffsNotes Literature series helps you study specific books, plays, poems, and short stories. Although the Language Arts, Reading test doesn't test your knowledge of literature, reading literature is always a good idea to help you prepare for that test. Consider reading one or two of Shakespeare's plays and other drama, poetry from 1600 to present, novels from 1920 to present, and recent short stories. If you're unsure about anything you read, pick up the CliffsNotes book on that piece of literature and discover what you may have missed on your first reading. To find a CliffsNotes for the literature you're reading, surf to www.cliffs.com.

Books in the CliffsQuickReview and CliffsAP series may also be helpful. Note that the CliffsAP series is geared toward Advance Placement students, who are in high school but are trying to take tests that allow them to earn college credits. These books are pretty high-level! Cliffs and CliffsQuickReview books are geared specifically to high-school and college students who are struggling to understand a particular subject matter. Before buying, browse through each title you're considering to make sure it meets your needs.

Make full use of your library (including inter-library loan), so that you don't end up spending all your hard-earned money on books.

- *Cliffs Math Review for Standardized Tests* (mathematics)
- *Cliffs Memory Power for Exams* (general)
- *Cliffs Verbal Review for Standardized Tests* (language arts)
- *CliffsAP Biology* (science)
- *CliffsAP Chemistry* (science)
- *CliffsAP English Language and Composition* (language arts)
- *CliffsAP English Literature and Composition* (language arts)
- *CliffsAP United States History* (social studies)
- *CliffsQuickReview Algebra I* (mathematics)
- *CliffsQuickReview Algebra II* (mathematics)
- *CliffsQuickReview American Government* (social studies)
- *CliffsQuickReview Anatomy and Physiology* (science)
- *CliffsQuickReview Astronomy* (science)

- *CliffsQuickReview Basic Math and Pre-Algebra* (mathematics)
- *CliffsQuickReview Biology* (science)
- *CliffsQuickReview Chemistry* (science)
- *CliffsQuickReview Economics* (social studies)
- *CliffsQuickReview Geometry* (mathematics)
- *CliffsQuickReview Linear Algebra* (mathematics)
- *CliffsQuickReview Physical Geography* (social studies)
- *CliffsQuickReview Physics* (science)
- *CliffsQuickReview Psychology* (social studies)
- *CliffsQuickReview United States History I* (social studies)
- *CliffsQuickReview United States History II* (social studies)
- *CliffsQuickReview Writing, Grammar, Usage, and Style* (language arts)

Some *preparation books* (books like this one that prepare you to take the GED tests), also include tutoring in test-content areas. (Those books are usually from 800 to 1,000 pages long, which is far more pages than this book had room for.) Visit your bookstore or local library and look for an up-to-date test preparation book that gives you at least two additional sets of practice tests, is understandable, and includes some skill-building material in the areas you need help. You may also want to try taking an Official GED Practice Test. This test is available at testing centers and preparation classes. The official practice test can predict your score, which helps you focus your study.

You may also want to check out *The SAT For Dummies* and *The ACT For Dummies,* both by Suzee Vlk (Wiley Publishing, Inc.). Although they're aimed at juniors and seniors who are taking college-entrance exams, if you can master the review material and sample questions, you not only prepare yourself for the GED but for college-entrance exams after you receive your diploma.

# Enrolling in a GED Preparation Class

If you like to interact with other people and prefer a teacher to guide you through your preparation, choose a *GED preparation class:* a class designed to prepare you to take and pass the GED tests. These are generally offered free of charge.

To find your class, ask around: Referrals can be a good source of information. If you don't know anyone who has taken the GED, try your local high school or college. Your local GED testing center will also know of all preparation classes in the area. You may also be able to take *distance-learning courses* (which means you do your assignments on your own and contact your instructor via the Internet), which may be a good choice for you.

After deciding on a few potential classes, visit the class or instructor, if possible. Make sure that his or her teaching style is your learning style. The preparation class will be an investment of your time. Shop wisely.

After choosing a preparation class, ask about forming *study groups* — small groups of other GED test-takers who help each other with study questions. Be wary before committing to a group, though: If the other group members' idea of studying is to party for three hours to get ready for five minutes of study, and you want to study for three hours to get ready for five minutes of social activity, you won't be happy. Talk to the other members of the study group and listen to what they're looking for. If you can find a suitable group, make a commitment to it.

# Scheduling Time to Study

Whether you study on your own or with an instructor, set aside time each day to study. Stick to your schedule as if your grade depends on it (and, by the way, it does!). Work regularly by doing the following:

1. **Take practice tests to find out in which subject area you're weak.**

   Check each answer on the practice tests and read the answer explanations. Make sure you understand your mistakes.

2. **Focus your studies on the subject area(s) in which you're weak.**

3. **Take more practice tests.**

# Preparing for the Test in Your Mind

To make yourself less anxious about the GED tests, visualize yourself at the tests. In your mind, see yourself enter the room, sit down at the desk, hear the instructions, and pick up your pen or pencil. Go through this series in your mind until it begins to feel familiar. Then, see yourself opening the question booklet and skimming the questions. (Ones that are likely familiar to you because you've taken many practice tests.) See yourself noting the easy questions and begin answering them. By repeating this visual sequence over and over again in your mind, it becomes familiar. And remember that the familiar is not as stressful as the strange.

# Getting Good Rest the Week Before Your Test(s)

As part of your plan for preparation, include some social time, some down time, and plenty of time for rest, because everyone performs better on plenty of sleep. In fact, your memory and ability to solve problems improve remarkably when you're properly rested.

Whatever you do, don't panic about your upcoming tests and stay up all night (or every night for a week) right before your tests. Instead, plan your last week before the test so that you get plenty of sleep and are mentally and physically prepared for the test.

# Wearing Comfortable Clothes

Consider the following situation. You are about to sit for up to seven-and-a-half hours on what is probably an uncomfortable chair. The room may be too warm or too cold. So, choosing from the following answers, what is appropriate dress for the GED tests?

(1) formal dress, because this is an important occasion

(2) a parka over a bathing suit, because one can never predict the weather

(3) something very comfortable, so that you can concentrate on the tests

(4) your best clothes, because you need to impress others

(5) whatever is handiest in your closet

If you answered number 3, you have the idea. Dress comfortably and in layers. All of your concentration should be on the tests, not your clothes, not on the people around you, and not on the conditions in the room.

# Making Sure You Have the Proper Identification

To take the GED tests, you need acceptable picture identification. Because "acceptable" may vary from state to state, check with your state GED office or your local testing center (or check the information they send to you after you sign up) before the test.

You won't be asked to bring a photograph of you autographed by three Senators from different states. The picture I.D. required is usually a driver's license or passport; at any rate, it's usually something common and easy to obtain. Just check in advance what's required.

# Practicing Your Route from Home to the Test Site

On certain days, you just don't want to get lost. These days include your wedding day, an important interview, and the GED tests. Make sure you plan a route from your home to the testing site. Map it out and practice getting there.

Leave extra time for surprises. You never know when your street could be declared an elephant crossing and a pack of pachyderms decides to meander across your road. The crowd and elephants could make you late for the tests unless you allot extra time.

# Arriving Early

Consider two scenarios:

- ✔ Test Taker One arrives 15 seconds before the beginning of the tests and feels nothing but panic. Test Taker One barely arrives at the desk in time to lift a pencil and begin the test. Test Taker One is so distracted that he or she takes 15 minutes to calm down, and by then, the first test is well underway.

- ✔ Test Taker Two arrives 40 minutes early. Test Taker Two has time to drink some coffee and relax before the test. Sitting calmly at the desk, Test Taker Two relaxes, listens to the instructions, and begins to take the first test in a relaxed manner.

Which test taker would you rather be? Leave early for the test!

A couple of weeks before the tests, confirm the time your test is supposed to begin. You may receive a letter of confirmation before your testing date. If not, follow up with a phone call.

# Starting with Easy Questions

As you open each test, start with the easy questions — the ones you know you can do. As soon as you get the test, skim the questions, identify the easy ones, and do those problems first. Only then do you want to tackle the other questions in a relaxed, confident mood.

Whatever you do, don't mark in the test book! It could get you tossed out of the test.

# Using Relaxation Techniques

Feeling a bit of stress before taking the GED tests is normal. A little bit of stress can actually help you function better, but you don't want to become so stressed that you can't think.

You need to find some ways to relax. This section gives you some techniques that may work for you:

- **Think positively.** Instead of listing all the negative things that may happen, start listing the positive things. You can pass the GED tests. You can go on to college. You can get a great job. You can win the lottery — well, maybe that's going too far. Don't get greedy. Just be positive!

- **Breathe deeply.** The first thing to remember during a stressful situation is to breathe deeply.

  1. **Find your diaphragm.**

     Not a diagram, although you could use a diagram to find your diaphragm. Your *diaphragm* is that flat muscle under your ribcage that fills your lungs with air. It's above your navel.

  2. **Breathe in and make your diaphragm rise as much as you can.**

  3. **Exhale slowly.**

  4. **Repeat, making your diaphragm rise higher each time.**

  After you see how this relaxes you, try it before each test.

- **Count backward from ten (in your head).** You can do this before any test, not just mathematics. Start to count backward from ten with no thoughts in your mind. If a thought, even a teeny one, enters your mind, you have to start counting over. See how many times it takes to count from ten to one without a single thought entering your mind.

  Don't do this during one of the tests, only before. This exercise could eat up precious time if you tried it during one of the tests.

- **Clench and unclench your fists.** This simple relaxation technique involves your hands.

  1. **Sit with your hands in front of you.**

  2. **Inhale deeply as you slowly clench your fists.**

  3. **After they are clenched, slowly exhale as you unclench them.**

     You may have to repeat this several times, but within a couple of repetitions, you begin to feel relaxed.

- **Stare out a window.** Stare out the window, far into the distance. Try to see a point beyond the horizon. As you do, feel your eyes relax. Let your eyes relax until the feeling spreads to every part of your body. Enjoy the feeling long enough to let go of all the stress that has built up. When you are calm and full of energy, return to the test.

  If your testing room doesn't have a window, stare at a blank wall and envision your favorite relaxing scene. Don't be tempted, however, to close your eyes. If you're the least bit tired or stressed, you may fall asleep and not wake up until the test is over.

# Chapter 29

# Ten Ways to Avoid Messing Up Your GED Tests

- - - - - - - - - - - - - - - - - - - - - - - - - - - - - - - - - - - - - - - - - - - - - - - - - - - - - - - - - - - - - - - -

## In This Chapter

▶ Avoiding common mistakes

▶ Weeding out some bad habits so that you can succeed

- - - - - - - - - - - - - - - - - - - - - - - - - - - - - - - - - - - - - - - - - - - - - - - - - - - - - - - - - - - - - - - -

**I**n spite of your best intentions, you can mess up your GED experience with just a few common mistakes. This chapter points out ten (well really eight, but who's counting?) mistakes you really want to avoid.

## Selecting a Test Date During a Busy Time in Your Life

The worst time to plan to take your GED tests is when you have a million other things to do. You probably live a busy life. Find a period in that busy life when you can concentrate on preparing for and passing the tests. So choose the date wisely. If you don't have enough time to prepare, you won't do well. It's just that simple.

## Not Preparing

If you're thinking of just signing up for the test, waiting until the test day comes, and walking in to take it — without ever preparing or studying — you'll likely be disappointed at your test results. See Chapter 28 for quick ideas on preparing for the tests. Also spend some time reviewing the chapters in Part II, which give you specific tips and hints for preparing for each test.

Being confident is great. Being *over*confident can do you in. If you think you may be overestimating your knowledge, take as many practice tests as you can, and take them under the same conditions as the actual tests. If your confidence exceeds the results on the practice tests, don't knock the practice tests. Consider yourself lucky to know what areas you need to work on.

## Worrying about Everything and Anything

Make a list of all the things you could worry about. If you find it easier, make a series of lists: personal, family, community, state, country, region, world, ecological, environmental, financial, governmental, and so on. Make the list as long and complete as you can. Leave it for a day and try to add more items. When it's as complete as possible, read it, toss it, and promise not to worry about anything on the list until after you finish the GED tests. Worrying distracts you from the one and only thing that should be on your list: passing the GED tests.

# Being Late for the Tests

If you're late you probably won't be allowed to enter and will have to take the tests on another date. And you'll probably have to pay again to take the tests. Who needs all this grief?

# Talking to Strangers on Your Way into the Tests

A little bit of stress is normal walking into a test. The last thing you want, though, is to increase your stress levels. People hanging around the test center or walking into the tests who have a hundred hints to tell everybody are guaranteed to increase your stress level. If you have prepared, you're ready. Listen to the voice in your head that says you're ready. Don't listen to the sidewalk experts who are going into the tests with you.

# Letting Your Mind Wander

Letting your mind wander back to the greatest vacation you ever had can be very relaxing. Letting your mind wander during a test can be a disaster. You want your mind sharp and keen before and during the tests.

Be sure to get plenty of sleep in the nights and weeks before the test. If you're well rested, you'll have an easier time focusing on each question and answering it correctly.

# Looking at your Neighbor's Answer Sheet

If there is a Biggest Mistake Award for test takers, it will be awarded to someone who looks at his or her neighbor's paper. This is called *cheating* and is a serious matter. Not only will you be asked to leave the testing center, but you may have to wait from several months to a year before you're allowed to schedule another test.

Don't even give the slightest hint that you may, possibly, be looking at someone else's paper.

# Considering Yourself a Failure if You Don't Pass the Tests the First Time

Not everyone passes the tests the first time. Not passing the tests can be a learning experience, if you let it. Use your last test as motivation to discover your academic weaknesses. Sometimes, you can gain more from not succeeding than from succeeding.

You can retake the tests up to three times a year and over several years, if needed. Failing once is not a permanent condition.

# Chapter 30

# Ten Misguided Rumors about the GED

### In This Chapter

▶ Discovering the truth about who can take the GED tests

▶ Letting you in one some juicy facts about the GED tests

**R**umors have a life of their own. Somebody says something, and then word spreads. In the case of the GED, you may have heard one or two rumors that just aren't true — yet they keep spreading because people keep repeating them.

As a public service, in this chapter, we present ten (okay, only nine) untrue rumors and fill in the truth.

## Rumor #1: The GED Tests Are Only for Other People — Not for You

About a million people worldwide take the GED tests each year. That's a lot of people. Some are probably geniuses. Some can barely scrape by. Most are just like you. If you want to acquire a GED to improve your job opportunities and/or go to college, sign up for the tests. They're meant for you.

If you have a documented disability, the GED Testing Service may make special arrangements for you. Special editions of the test are offered in Braille, on audiocassettes, and in large type. It is possible to take an adapted test with a scribe, in a private room, or with frequent breaks. The testing service may grant candidates extended time or the use of a calculator for the entire Mathematics test. If you think you're eligible, document your case and apply (see the Appendix for the GED administrator in your area).

## Rumor #2: It's Expensive to Take the GED Tests

The state or local GED offices set the fees for your area, so check with your state GED administrator or your local testing center to see what the tests will cost you. (The Appendix gives you state contact information.) Generally, they aren't too expensive, ranging from $0 to $300. If you're on a limited budget, social service agencies may be able to help.

In addition to the fees for the tests, you may need to incur some other expenses. If you choose to take a preparation course, you may be charged a fee for that (although some areas also offer courses for free). If you buy subject-matter preparation books, that costs money, but your library may carry them or be able to get them for you through interlibrary loan. If your testing site isn't near your home, you have to get yourself there. When weighing the costs, however, think about what a difference a GED diploma can make in your life.

# Rumor #3: If You're Not Almost Finished with High School, You Shouldn't Try to Take the Tests

If you finished high school, you can't take the GED tests, because you already have a diploma. And if you've never been to high school (that is, you left in eighth grade or before), you probably can take the tests, although you must carefully plan your preparation program, because you may need to build additional skills that aren't taught at the elementary and middle-school levels.

If you attended from one semester to three years of high school, you can apply to take the tests and will likely do well. (Of course, the further you went, the easier the tests will likely be, but you can study to make up for the skills you lack.)

# Rumor #4: The GED Tests Measure Intelligence

According to the American Council on Education, the parent body of the GED tests, you need only the skills mastered by a high school graduate to pass the GED. Although your intelligence isn't tested, you must be disciplined enough to prepare before you take the tests.

The GED tests the skills that high-school graduates mastered in high school. The tests determine whether you understand and can answer questions about what you read, whether you can look at tables and graphs to answer questions, whether you can solve mathematics problems, and whether you can write an essay. They don't, however, test intelligence. That doesn't mean that you can't feel smart when you pass.

# Rumor #5: You Can't Study for the GED Tests

You really can't study for the GED tests the way you may have studied for some of your tests in school (by memorizing). That's because the GED tests don't ask you to recall information; instead, they require you to use skills that improve with practice. So, you can "study" for the GED by gaining and improving on your skills in reading, writing, problem-solving, analyzing information, and so on.

See Chapter 28 and the chapters in Part II for specific information on how you can prepare for the GED tests.

# Rumor #6: You Have to Answer All the Questions to Pass

No. Instead, you have to answer only enough questions correctly to get a passing score. The GED tests are marked and reported using a standard score. The minimum passing score is 410 in each test with an average standard score of 450 for the five tests. (Note that some states may set a higher standard score for passing.)

The simple answer is that you need to get about 60% of the questions correct to pass. However, why not try to get all the questions right? Study and practice as though you need to get 90% or 100% of the questions right, and you'll succeed for sure.

# Rumor #7: You Shouldn't Guess at Answers

On the GED tests, you get a point for each correct answer, but you don't lose points for wrong answers. If you aren't sure of an answer, always fill something in. If you can eliminate one, two, or more incorrect answers, your chances of choosing the correct answer are quite good. So always take a stab at answering all the questions.

# Rumor #8: You Can't Get Into College with a GED

In a recent survey, 60 percent of those taking the GED tests indicated that they were interested in post-secondary education (that's college). Fortunately, 95 percent of U.S. colleges and universities accept the GED as part of the admission application.

# Rumor #9: Nobody Important Ever Took the GED

If you choose to take the GED tests, at least one important person will be taking them — you. In the past, other names you may recognize have passed the tests: Bill Cosby, comedian and television star; singer Waylon Jennings; the late Dave Thomas, founder of Wendy's; Ruth Ann Minner, governor of Delaware; Ben Nighthorse Campbell, U.S. Senator from Colorado; and actor Christian Slater. After you pass the tests, your name joins this list!

# Chapter 31

# Ten Ways to Use Your GED After You Pass the Tests

*In This Chapter*
▶ Getting the most out of your diploma at work
▶ Using your diploma at home

**P**assing the GED tests makes life more rewarding, opening doors that you have not even known were there. You've probably already figured out why you want your GED; if not, this chapter shares ten (ahem — just eight, but that's close enough!) some great advantages the diploma can give you.

## A Diploma Helps You Get a Job

Many employers want to see a high school diploma or its equivalent in order to give you a job. A GED allows you to jump this hurdle. It shows potential employers that you've mastered skills equal to most of the graduates of high school. That is impressive.

The U.S. government, one of the country's largest employers, accepts a GED as an equivalent to high school graduation. Are you going to argue with Uncle Sam?

## A Diploma Helps You Get a Promotion

If you're already working, you want to show your supervisor that you're ready for promotion. The GED says, "I worked hard for this and achieved something special!" You show your employer that you're ready to do the same on the job. You have taken responsibility for your life and are ready to take on additional responsibility at work. You have a document that shows you have mastered skills and are ready to master still more. You have solved problems, have read charts and diagrams, and are ready to do the same at work.

## A Diploma Shows Former Teachers and Classmates That You Can Achieve

When you earn your GED, you show the world that you accomplished, on your own, what the rest of the high school students needed a building, teachers, counselors, principals, and at least four years to accomplish. Now is the time to visit old teachers and go to reunions.

## Building a portfolio

A portfolio is a way of gaining recognition for skills, knowledge, or competencies that you have learned as you grew. You may have learned these on the job, by taking training courses, through your own reading, by volunteering, or through hobbies.

No matter where or how you mastered these skills, knowledge, or competencies, if you can show people that you have them, you can ask for credit for them. Some colleges and universities give adult students credit for showing that they have mastered the skills and knowledge required to pass a particular course. Many employers are also interested in what you have learned both in and out of school.

# A Diploma Becomes an Important Part of Your College Portfolio

Your college portfolio is a binder that lists all of your skills and experiences in an organized manner. Many colleges have a particular format they would like you to use for your portfolio; employment counselors can suggest generic formats. You can also make up a format yourself. The important thing is to have a place that lists all your skills and experiences that you can take with you to college and job interviews.

Your GED is the centerpiece of your portfolio. The diploma is a stamp of approval on all your prior learning. It shows that you now officially know what high school graduates know.

# A Diploma Proves You're Ready for Further Education

After you master the skills equal to most high-school graduates, you're ready to go on to the next step: college. Most colleges accept a GED as proof of equivalency to high-school graduation. If your goal is further education, remind the registrar at the colleges you want to attend that you're also a mature student. Emphasize the real-world skills you've mastered by working in the real world.

# A Diploma Sets an Example for Your Kids

If you're like most people, you want your kids (or grandchildren) to be better educated and better off than you are. As soon as you pass the GED tests, you set the bar a little higher for them. Your accomplishment also reminds your kids that education is important — for you *and* them.

# A Diploma Looks Good on Your Wall

You may already have interesting mementos of your life hanging on your wall, but what could be more interesting than a GED with your name on it? A diploma looks great on your wall because it represents all the hard work you put in to pass the tests.

If you're going to have your diploma framed, before you do so, make a couple of copies for prospective employers and colleges. Make copies of the transcript of your test results, as well.

# A Diploma Makes You Part of a Select Group

When you get your GED, you have outperformed 40 percent of high school seniors. That in itself is impressive. Comedian Bill Cosby and Dave Thomas, the late founder of Wendy's, are GED graduates. No one can promise that passing the GED tests will make you a show-business star or help you start a fast-food chain, but it will make you feel very special. Who knows when you will become famous enough to be listed in this section of a future edition?

# Appendix

# GED Testing Centers

........................................................

**Y**ou can find GED testing centers around the United States and U.S. territories, offering testing material in English, Spanish, and French. You can also arrange to take the GED tests if you're currently serving in the military. You can even take the GED tests if you're serving a prison sentence. This appendix helps you find the proper person to contact.

Throughout this appendix, we include the names of the person in your area to contact. However, people retire, get promoted, or leave their jobs for other reasons. If the contact person listed here is no longer the GED administrator, ask for the person who has replaced him or her.

## GED State Testing Centers

You can locate state testing centers in the United States by calling 800-626-9433 (800-62-MY GED) or by calling the following state offices directly.

### Alabama

Mr. Nace J. Macaluso, GED Administrator
GED Testing Program
State Department of Postsecondary
Education
5343 Gordon Persons Building
P.O. Box 302101
Montgomery, AL 36130-2101
334-242-8181; 334-242-8182

### Alaska

Ms. Amy Iutzi-Mitchell, ABE/GED State
Director
Alaska Department of Labor and Workforce
Development
GED Testing Program
DOLWD — ES Division
1111 W. 8th Street
P.O. Box 25509
Juneau, AK 99802-5509
907-465-8714

### Arizona

Ms. Karen Liersch, State Director, Adult
Education
Arizona State Department of Education
1535 West Jefferson
Phoenix, AZ 85007
602-254-0265

### Arkansas

Ms. Janice Hanlon, GED Test Administrator
Arkansas Department of Workforce
Education
Luther S. Hardin Building
Three Capitol Mall
Room 304-D
Little Rock, AR 72201-2729
501-682-1980

## California

Dr. Mark Fetler, GED Administrator
State GED Office
California Department of Education
721 Capitol Mall, 6th Floor
P.O. Box 710273
Sacramento, CA 94244-0273
800-331-6316; 916-651-6623

## Colorado

Ms. Mary Willoughby, GED Administrator
Colorado Department of Education
201 East Colfax Avenue, Room 100
Denver, CO 80203
303-866-6611

## Connecticut

Mr. Carl Paternostro, GED Administrator
Bureau of Adult Education and Training
State Department of Education
25 Industrial Park Road
Middletown, CT 06457
860-807-2110

## Delaware

Dr. Fran Tracy-Mumford, State Supervisor
Adult and Community Education
Department of Public Instruction
J. G. Townsend Building
P.O. Box 1402
Dover, DE 19903
302-739-3743

## District of Columbia

K. Brisbane, GED Administrator
University of the District of Columbia
GED Office, Lower Level
4200 Connecticut Avenue NW
Washington, DC 20008
202-274-7173

## Florida

Ms. Nancy Cordill, GED Administrator
Bureau of Program Planning & Development
325 West Gaines Street
Turlington Building, Room 714
Tallahassee, FL 32399-0400
850-488-7153

## Georgia

Ms. Kimberly Lee, Director
Assessment, Evaluation and GED
Georgia Department of Technical and Adult
Education
1800 Century Place NE, Suite 555
Atlanta, GA 30345-4304
404-679-1621

## Hawaii

Dr. Glenn Honda, GED Administrator
Department of Education
School Improvement/Community Leadership
Branch
634 Pensacola Street, Room 222
Honolulu, HI 96814
808-594-0170

## Idaho

Dr. Shirley T. Spencer, Adult Education Coordinator
and GED Administrator
Department of Education
P.O. Box 83720
Boise, ID 83720-0027
208-332-6933

## Illinois

Ms. Brenda Carmody, State GED Administrator
New Learning Opportunities Division
Illinois State Board of Education
100 North First Street W-260
Springfield, IL 62777
217-782-0083

# Indiana

Ms. Paula Hill, GED Administrator
Division of Adult Education
Indiana Department of Education
State House, Room 229
Indianapolis, IN 46204
317-232-0522

# Iowa

Dr. John Hartwig, GED Administrator
Division of Community Colleges
Department of Education
Grimes State Office Building
Des Moines, IA 50319-0146
515-281-3636

# Kansas

Dr. Patricia M. Anderson, Associate Director,
Academic Affairs
Kansas Board of Regents
1000 SW Jackson Street, Suite 520
Topeka, KS 66612-1368
785-296-4917

# Kentucky

Dr. Brenda J. Helton, GED Administrator
Department for Adult Education and Literacy
500 Mero Street
3rd Floor CPT
Frankfort, KY 40601
502-564-5114, ext. 153

# Louisiana

Ms. Debi Faucette, Acting Director, Adult
Education and Training
Louisiana Department of Education
1201 North 3rd Street
Baton Rouge, LA 70802
225-342-0444

# Maine

Mr. J. Andrew McMahan, GED Administrator
State Department of Education
#23 State House Station
Augusta, ME 04333-0023
207-624-6754

# Maryland

Ms. Patricia Bennett, Acting GED Administrator
Maryland State Department of Education
200 West Baltimore Street
Baltimore, MD 21201
410-767-0538

# Massachusetts

Mr. Frank Shea, GED Administrator
Office of Certification
Massachusetts Department of Education
350 Main Street
P.O. Box 9120
Malden, MA 02148-9120
781-388-3300, ext. 651

# Michigan

Mr. Ben Williams, State GED Administrator
Adult Education Office
Michigan Department of Career Development
201 N. Washington Square
Victor Building, 1st Floor
P.O. Box 30714
Lansing, MI 48909
517-373-1692

# Minnesota

Mr. Patrick Rupp, GED Administrator
Minnesota Department of Children, Families, and
Learning
1500 Highway 36 West
Roseville, MN 55113-4266
651-582-8437

## Mississippi

Ms. Eloise Richardson, GED Administrator
State Board for Community and Junior Colleges
3825 Ridgewood Road
Jackson, MS 39211
601-432-6481

## Missouri

Mr. William Poteet, GED Administrator
State Department of Elementary and Secondary
Education
402 Dix Road
P.O. Box 480
Jefferson City, MO 65102
573-751-3504

## Montana

Mr. David Strong, GED Administrator
Office of Public Instruction
1300 11th Avenue
Box 202501
Helena, MT 59620-2501
406-444-4438

## Nebraska

Ms. Vicki L. Bauer, Director, Adult Education
Nebraska Department of Education
301 Centennial Mall South
P.O. Box 94987
Lincoln, NE 68509-4987
402-471-4807

## Nevada

Ms. Mary Katherine Moen, GED Administrator
Office of Career, Technical, and Adult Education
Nevada Department of Education
700 East Fifth Street
Carson City, NV 89701-5096
775-687-9167; or 775-687-9104

## New Hampshire

Ms. Deborah Tasker, GED Administrator
State Department of Education
State Office Park South
101 Pleasant Street
Concord, NH 03301
603-271-6698

## New Jersey

Marie Barry, Acting GED Administrator
Office of Vocational-Technical, Career, and Adult
Programs
100 River View Plaza
P.O. Box 500
Trenton, NJ 08625-0500
609-633-0665

## New Mexico

Lisa G. Salazar, State Director, GED Testing
State Department of Education
Education Building
300 Don Gaspar
Santa Fe, NM 87501-2786
505-827-6507

## New York

Dr. Patricia M. Mooney-Gonzalez, State GED Chief
Examiner
New York State Education Department
GED Testing
P.O. Box 7348
Albany, NY 12224-0348
518-486-5746; hotline: 518-474-5906

## North Carolina

Patrick Pittman, GED Administrator and
Coordinator of Adult High School
North Carolina Community College System
5024 Mail Service Center
Raleigh, NC 27699-5024
919-733-7051, ext. 465

## North Dakota

Mr. G. David Massey, Assistant Superintendent
Adult Education and Literacy
North Dakota Department of Public Instruction
600 East Boulevard Avenue
State Capitol Building
Bismarck, ND 58505-0440
701-328-2393

## Ohio

Ms. Joan Myers, GED Administrator
State Department of Education
25 South Front Street
Room 106, First Floor
Columbus, OH 43215-4183
614-466-1577

## Oklahoma

Ms. Linda Young, Director
State Department of Education
2500 North Lincoln Boulevard
Oklahoma City, OK 73105-4599
800-405-0355; 405-521-3321

## Oregon

Ms. Karen Madden Evans, Unit Leader
Adult Basic Skills & Family Literacy Unit
Oregon Department of Community Colleges &
Workforce Development
255 Capitol Street, NE
Salem, OR 97310-1341
503-378-8648, ext. 226

## Pennsylvania

Mr. James Shindledecker, GED Administrator
State Department of Education
333 Market Street, 12th Floor
Harrisburg, PA 17126-0333
717-787-6747

## Rhode Island

Mr. Robert Mason, GED Administrator
Department of Elementary and Secondary
Education
Office of Career and Technical Education
Shepard Building
255 Westminster Street
Providence, RI 02903-3414
401-222-4600, ext. 2180

Other contacts:

- Patricia Panzarella at 401-222-4600, ext. 2183
- Janet Gauslin 401-222-4600, ext. 2181

## South Carolina

Dr. David Stout, GED Administrator
State Department of Education
402 Rutledge Building
1429 Senate Street
Columbia, SC 29201
803-734-8347

## South Dakota

Ms. Marcia Hess, GED Administrator
Adult Education and Literacy/GED Literacy
Department of Labor
700 Governor's Drive
Pierre, SD 57501-2291
605-773-3101

## Tennessee

Ms. Phyllis Pardue, GED Administrator
Tennessee Department of Labor and Workforce
Development
11th Floor, Davy Crockett Tower
500 James Robertson Parkway
Nashville, TN 37245
800-531-1515; 615-741-7054

## Texas

Dr. Walter H. Tillman, Ph.D., Assistant
Commissioner
Educational Services
Texas Education Agency
William B. Travis Building
1701 North Congress Avenue
Austin, TX 78701-1494
512-463-5491

Other contact:

G. Paris-Ealy
Texas Education Agency
1701 North Congress Avenue
Austin, TX 78701-1494
512-463-8191

## Utah

For questions regarding Utah GED policies, eligibility for testing, requests for waivers, and other policies and procedures, contact:

Mr. Murray Meszaros
GED Administrator
Adult Education Services
Utah State Office of Education
250 East 500 South
P.O. Box 144200
Salt Lake City, UT 84114-4200
801-538-7870

For questions regarding GED score verification and testing records, contact:

Ms. Aleta Hansen
Utah State Office of Education
250 East 500 South
P.O. Box 144200
Salt Lake City, UT 84114-4200
801-538-7921

## Vermont

Ms. Bari Gladstone, GED Administrator
Career & Workforce Development
Vermont State Department of Education
120 State Street
Montpelier, VT 05620
802-828-3132

## Virginia

Mr. Robert W. MacGillivray, GED Administrator
Virginia Office of Adult Education
Department of Education
P.O. Box 2120
Richmond, VA 23218-2120
804-371-2333

## Washington

Ms. Alleyne Bruch, GED Administrator
State Board for Community and Technical Colleges
319 7th Avenue
P.O. Box 42495
Olympia, WA 98504-2495
360-704-4321

## West Virginia

Ms. Debra Dillon Kimbler, GED Administrator
West Virginia Department of Education
GED Office
1900 Kanawha Boulevard East
Building 6, Room 250
Charleston, WV 25305-0330
800-642-2670; 304-558-6315

## Wisconsin

Mr. Robert Enghagen, State GED Administrator
Wisconsin High School Equivalency Program
Department of Public Instruction
P.O. Box 7841
125 South Webster Street
Madison, WI 53707-7841
800-441-4563; 608-267-2402

## Wyoming

Ms. Karen Ross-Milmont, GED Administrator
Wyoming Department of Workforce Services
122 West 25th Street
Hershchler Building, 1st Floor East
Cheyenne, WY 82002
307-777-3545

Other contact:

Sandi L. Winters, GED Specialist
307-777-6911

# U.S. Territories and Other Jurisdictions

The GED tests are administered in places outside the United States. If you find yourself in one of these places, use contact information in this section.

## American Samoa

Mr. Mike Himphill, GED Administrator
Government of American Samoa
Pago Pago, AS 96799
011-684-633-5237

## Guam

Ms. Lolita C. Reyes, GED Administrator
Guam Community College
P.O. Box 23069
Main Postal Facility
Guam, GU 96921
011-671-735-6511

Other contact:

Evangeline Cruz, Test Examiner
011-671-735-5566

## Marshall Islands

Mr. John Tuthill, Interim President and
GED Administrator
College of The Marshall Islands
P.O. Box 1258
Republic of Marshall Islands
Majuro, MH 96960
011-692-625-3394; 011-692-625-3236

## Micronesia

Mr. Wehns Billen, GED Administrator
Federated States of Micronesia National
Government
Palikir, Pohnpei, FM 96941
011-691-320-2647

## Northern Mariana Islands

Ms. Fe Y. Calixterio, GED Administrator
Northern Marianas College
Adult Basic Education Program
P.O. Box 501250
Saipan, MP 96950
011-670-234-5498

## Palau

Mr. Paulino Eriich, GED Administrator
Ministry of Education
Bureau of Curriculum & Instruction
P.O. Box 189
Koror, Republic of Palau, PW 96940
011-680-488-5452

## Puerto Rico

Mrs. Myrna Gonzalez Vasquez, GED Administrator
Administration Adult Education Services
Department of Education
P.O. Box 190759
San Juan, PR 00919-0759
787-759-2000, ext. 4567, 4568, 2567, and 2570

## Virgin Islands

Ms. Anna L. Lewis, Director and GED Administrator
Division of Adult Education
Department of Education
44–46 Kongens Gade
Charlotte Amalie
St. Thomas, VI 00802
340-776-3484

# U.S. Military

If you're serving in the U.S. military, you also have the opportunity to take the GED tests, under a service called DANTES. If you're serving your country and wish to write the tests, contact your superior officer or the DANTES office for information.

Defense Activity for Non-Traditional Education Support (DANTES)
Mr. Steve Beckman
DANTES Administrator
Attn: Code 20B
6490 Saufley Field Road
Pensacola, FL 32509-5243
850-452-1089

# Correctional Facilities

If you're serving a prison sentence, you, too, can take the GED tests. Ask to contact the following person:

Ms. Huilan Larson, Education Specialist
Federal Bureau of Prisons
Department of Justice
320 First Street, NW
Washington, DC 20534
202-305-3808

# Index